An American Christian's World

(with exciting <u>proven hope</u> for your future!)

Dr. Neil Alan (Doc) Scott

ISBN: 1468148702

ISBN 13: 9781468148701

Library of Congress Copyright Card Number 2012900044

An American Christian's World

(with exciting <u>proven hope</u> for your future!)

TABLE OF CONTENTS

ACKNOWLEDGEMENT

Warm acknowledgments go to my younger sister Miriam, to our Friend "God-somebody," to our Family and other friends who pushed me to complete this little book – especially our daughter Sally – and to the "Great Tribulation" Church, which is promised Biblically in the mix of Revelation 7:9-14, 20:4 with 14:12-13, 13:10+17 and Daniel 8:13-14...courageous, faithful and loyal. Please check 'em out.

One goal here is to help this very brave assembly to be much smaller in number than it was expected to be, before *An American Christian's World* was written, published, distributed and digested.

FOREWORD

Throughout this Nation's history, in times of moral, political and spiritual crisis, America's Creator has provided loyal Citizens who show the way, and who help us to retain the course. This has required a high level of Citizenship and Self-Government, as was prayerfully set out by our Founding Fathers of chapter 21. We find evidences of these elements in our Nation's founding documents…the Constitution, Declaration of Independence, the supreme (see original Constitution) Court decisions that are in accord, and the Bible.

Dr. Scott is one of these loyal Citizens. This very rare **_Classic_** book, _An American Christian's World (with exciting proven hope for your future!),_ presents an inspired, skillful and proven solution to some filthy people now defrauding America's We the People, who undeniably have been brainwashed for decades toward helpless enslavement. Doc Scott has been referred to by his students around the world as "a master-teacher," with rare depths of knowledge, understanding, wisdom and faith. But we need to have patience with him, for with his English, Speech and Education college majors he has great fun with the language. He reminds us of one of his professors, Dr. Pooley, who stated "If it is understood, it is good English!" Meanwhile you can also enjoy this book's comprehensive _Index_, for looking up key topics.

Dr. Scott's writing goes far deeper than merely exposing America's deceivers, who work to take away your hard-earned freedom. This book lawfully provides ample documentation and serves to indict those in and out of government for the massive violations of our once-free America and great Law. Meanwhile, you who are *alert* to current world news know that World War III as in Revelation 6 may be just off the horizon, on target with ancient prophecy. Doc warns that bitter exchanges now between Middle East Israel's Prime Minister *Netanyahu* and Iran's President *Ahmadinejad* will begin it in late "springtime."

The author served as General Douglas MacArthur's youngest economics investigator in the Military Government of Japan. General MacArthur repeatedly expressed his concern about *"the insidious forces working from within"* Washington, DC and otherwise. After the three years of Doc's overseas duty ended, the General thoughtfully said to him, "If you want to do a service for our God and Country, *investigate thoroughly and prove who is knifing America in the back in Washington, and why...*" Scott returned to America at age 20. Fortunately you have the sizzling results of these investigations before you now to help save lives.

In some ways these investigations began way back in 1941. Now having completed them over a period of about 70 years, at great personal cost and sacrifice, Doc Scott has investigated and monitored these amazing activities at all levels of government. And with responsible Christian (Agape)-love, he has recorded these results for you. As an added bonus, the Bible's Jeremiah 23:20 promises *"In the last days you will clearly understand it."*

It is possible that you are holding in your hands the next-to-last chance for redemption of America (the subsequent one will be in Rev. 7:9-14's tribulation trap), and for your and your family's survival. From this point forward the responsibility will be yours. You can no longer remain a spectator in this silent war for mankind's minds, spirits, bodies and eternity.

After digesting the contents of this book, you will have the armor to defeat those enemy powers that would strip you of your rich heritage. You may want to keep this book close, and even enjoy an extra copy by your bedside for exciting reading and ready references. Enjoy. Thank you. Now I add my "good-bye," which in early-America 1776 meant "God be with Ye."

Jim Evans,* *natural born* free *private* American National and Article 3 State Citizen, without prejudice (reserving all of my rights), with Constitutional Articles 1:2:3, 2:1:5 and 3:2:1.

*_NOT_ a federal U.S. citizen, and *NOT* a Title 26 Code of Federal Regulations Ch. 1 [4-1-88 edition] §1.1-1(c): "Who is a [federal U.S.] citizen: Every person born or naturalized in the [federal] United States and subject to ITS jurisdiction is a [federal U.S.] citizen [and to IT for federal income-excise taxes]." (Thanks Doc!)

DEDICATION

An American Christian's World (with exciting <u>proven hope</u> for your future!) is dedicated to my younger sister Miriam and her offspring Sue, Mike, Kim and Tom; to our Mom and Dad; to our sister Helen and her Les, Jim, Alice, Jeanne, Larry, Pat, Jo and Barb; to our brother Jeff and his Faye, Jud and Joel; to my super-wife Fran (thank you!); to our Sally and her Brian, Steve and Becky; to our Mike and his Kerry, Jami, Steve, Brandon, Elly and Destan; to those who helped to proof read and edit our manuscript; to our extremely helpful computer geniuses, our super-son Mike Scott, and friends Jim Cary and Arvin Gonzalez; to countless other friends globally for their encouragement; and to all owners of this urgently-important book.

It is also dedicated to our ancestor and American Founding Father, Josiah Bartlett, signer of the Declaration of Independence, military officer, judge and governor of New Hampshire State Republic, who led the "Thanksgiving" idea.

Finally, this is dedicated to my unequalled military commander and third Dad, General Douglas MacArthur. With this book you can share many exciting, long-hidden now-proven secrets with your friends everywhere…and <u>help them choose</u> <u>their proven futures as in</u> <u>chapter 14</u>.

DISCLAIMER

The information in *An American Christian's World (with exciting proven hope for your future!)* is not legal advice, but rather is intended for educational purposes only. The writer reserves his entire natural born free unalienable Rights, as partially enumerated in our Constitution for the United States of America and the Declaration of Independence, using great substantive Law and the Bible without prejudice. These and related works were preserved for us American Citizens as "sovereign" Posterity by its brilliant and loyal Founding Fathers, thankfully.

PREFACE

In order to see this world's big picture, again you might wisely be keeping your eyes on the <u>boiling Middle East</u>, tuned to Bible prophecy. *No Biblical prophecy has ever missed its promised target in time and place*, making it a fun hobby to see what is coming up, with proof. You probably know that Israel is surrounded by enemy Muslim forces, which with Russia apparently plan to strike it in the "springtime." In history Russia has preferred springtime invasions. <u>We do not know the year</u> of this prophesied attack, but all of the "signs" for it have been interacting since June 1967's six-day war, as in our chapter 18.

Accordingly, we are promised that an *"approved"* group of mankind will "escape," just before this war begins, and Israel burns the weapons of war for Ezekiel 39:9's "seven years." During this time two-thirds of Israel's population will be killed, while in the last 3½ years the remaining third will escape to and be protected in Jordan's hidden rock city of Petra. Meanwhile we will also see prophecy promising that 1/3rd of this world's population will be killed from famine, pestilence and wild beasts, and another 1/4th dying within these seven years. You might want to verify these in your Bible's Revelation 6:8 and 9:15. Do share these insights when you can. And do not let friends say that they were not responsibly warned.

Reliable intelligence associates also report that the Muslim Brotherhood's Hezbollah forces in Lebanon can launch over 50,000 rockets aimed at Israel; while Israel's nuclear, neutron, bacterial and chemical missile arsenals are among the most advanced in the world. Fellow investigators and I find that these will devastate many of the Russian and Muslim enemies in WW III, including Iranian and Syrian, with no warning. Meanwhile Iran has horrible plans for America, exposed in chapter 14 etc. The U.S. Joint Chiefs of Staff may richly benefit from copies of this book, for the coming attack will be man's pivotal hour.

This explosive book, *An American Christian's World (with exciting proven hope for your* future!), is destined to be highly *controversial* – even *offensive* to the world's proven filthy liars. For them and you I *will try to repeat key insights*; will try to *keep these facts simple*; and will often provide *documentation with my statements*, rather than below in footnotes that we find few people look up. Also I accept any blame for human errors; and give all honors to our Friend "God-Somebody."

Again the **goal of this book** will be to help "**keep you from**" earth's coming "...*trap for...all those who dwell on the face of all the earth...*" as promised in your Bible's Luke 21:34b-35. This is seen with 21:36's "*escape*"-petitioning-prayer, for strength of faith to do so in the real Messiah/Creator Christ Jesus' Name. It is also promised this way with His Revelation 3:10b's "... that hour which is about *to come upon the whole world, to test those who dwell on the earth.*"

While enjoying the insights in this book, be sure to remember Isaiah 28:11–13's promise of Bible prophecy being given "...a *little here, a little there...*" – not necessarily in chronological order, but the above Revelation 6:8 and 9:15 are in the normal order. Another example of this reverse chronology is Revelation 20:4, which happens physically after 20:5b-6, the earlier escape. You understand this, don't you? Do not feel badly if you haven't grabbed such things immediately; it took me decades to sort out just Rev. 20:5b-6 and 20:4! Obviously the dedicated Roman priests at 1545+ A.D.'s Council of Trent did not know this reverse sequence, when they divided the Bible into chapters and verses for which we are thankful. Understanding knowledge and wisdom isn't really that difficult – something like touching your elbow with your hand, if you know how, by using the other hand. This overview gets a lot easier.

So is *anyone left out* of earth's coming "TRAP"? **Yes!** Today you have time to join those who are *alert,* as in Matthew 24:42, to come along with Matt. 7:14's relatively "few" (millions?) of people who will win this important next step. And for the sake of 7:13's "many" others, *you will be able to help them, too!* This book can assist the same "many" to understand (Matt. 24:39), and provide an easy-reading way to enjoy this huge win, as a valuable treasured member of chapter 7's *"approved."*

Meanwhile, people left on this burning earth will wish that they had been more alert to this book, as they awaken in Daniel 8:13-14's tribulation, with "2,300 evenings and mornings" (about 6.4 years) yet to go, well into Daniel 12:1-3, Matthew 24:21 and Revelation 7:9-14's *"great tribulation."* Prophecy shows that *it will begin in the "springtime,"* as in Isaiah 18:9, Matt. 24:34, Mark 13:23 and Luke 21:30, if my investigations are as accurate as I believe they are. Very important, with Amos 3:7 and Isaiah 42:9 in accord, Matt. 24:36 *should read "...no one has known..."* (mathematically correct, see chapter 17), instead of the *mistranslated "no one knows."* In accord, please enjoy Christ's Matt. 24:25's *"...I have told you in advance,"* with John 13:19 and 14:29, which is what the real Christ's prophecy is all about.

Many people keep themselves <u>too busy</u> to pay attention to what is really important. We all have just 24 hours in each day and night, don't we? In line with this, have you applauded or winced that sports stadiums are so jammed nowadays? I enjoy sports, but there is a limit. To entertain means to A-MUSE, which also means to "NO-THINK;" thus blocking people from really thinking for themselves. That's dumb! 2 Peter 3:3 prophesies of this "sporting...going their own way"...or doing their own thing, as in ancient Israel's Judges 17:6 and 21:25, while precious time ticks. And there are other dangerous mind-escapes such as too many newspapers, magazines, books, movies, television, sports and on and on....

We know from prophecy that *MANY WILL CHANGE THEIR MINDS*, meaning "repent" (Isaiah 18:1-7, Revelation 7:9-14, 14:12-13 with 20:4). We can also enjoy jewels such as Philippians 2:12's "work out your Salvation with fear and trembling," 2 Corinthians 6:2's "now is the day of Salvation," and Hebrews 9:28's "So Christ... will appear a second time for Salvation...to those who eagerly await Him."

Please remember that all additional emphasis here is mine. When you really want to help yourself, *silent prayers* ending in Jesus' Name can make it happen. With proofs, He is your Creator and can certainly hear your silent or loud voice! Thank you for considering this urgent, once-in-a-lifetime opportunity. Keep reading. You will find accurate and exciting answers to your precious life's questions.

Doc Scott, Author

CHAPTER

1

MIRACLES DO HAPPEN

It was in December of 1941, just days after the Japanese attacked Pearl Harbor, when my kid sister Miriam and I were left alone. That could have been terrifying if we had dwelled on it. We were ages 6 and 12, renting a tiny apartment above a Greek-American family in Oelwein, Iowa, which Mom had located for $12.50 a month. It might have only measured 7 by 40 feet, stretching it, but it was home.

We faced the prospect of growing up by ourselves, because of our parents' financial wreck from the 1929-1932 Great Depression, plus their divorce, followed by their being forced to leave us for distant paying jobs. I had won a good bike in our newspaper carriers' contest for getting new customers, making it easy to deliver papers on my *Oelwein Register* paper route up East Charles and along side streets. Also it was fun selling nightcrawler worms, fed with coffee grounds, to fishermen for 10¢ a dozen in season.

But we had no money that first Thursday evening. Miriam and I agreed to have water for dinner, since collecting from my paper route customers could not start for another day. Then it happened, as if a strong arm drew me to the back of our small wooden Zenith radio. There was a new shiny dime. Because Mom and we had often moved, there was no way that a dime could have stayed in there. Talk about excited!

With it we raced to the nearby grocery store for a can of Campbell's tomato soup. I don't ever remember enjoying a dinner more, and never was there a braver little sister. That evening also brought with it my new hunger for knowledge about our silent helper. What a feeling it was to live that miracle about 70 years ago, from this great Friend we called "God-somebody."

I still have a photo of Miriam when she was ready for church the following Sunday. She was a pretty girl, with blue eyes and flowing brown hair, wearing a lovely blouse and skirt covered by her warm blue jacket that matched her eyes.

At church we listened as the Methodist Episcopal minister led the congregation with, "We have done those things that we ought not to have done; we have not done those things that we ought to have done; and there is no health in us." I whispered to Miriam, "That's not us. Let's leave quietly." Mom and Dad had been leaders in the church for over 20 years, but now the busy minister had no time for us when we went to his house.

We had been taught the children's song "Jesus loves me, this I know, for the Bible tells me so. Little ones to Him belong; we are weak but He is strong." We did not know much about Jesus, and had little to unlearn about God-anybody; but we had been taught Matthew 19:19 and Exodus 20:12's "Honor your father and your mother," so we did.

Miriam was cheerful company in those months, with us providing a sense of security for each other. I honestly do not remember her crying or being afraid of anything, or us celebrating Christmas alone that December; probably because we had each other and we were kept very busy. Our favorite breakfast was hot oatmeal with a peanut butter and jelly sandwich, and sometimes we would split some canned fruit. When breakfast was ready, one of us would holler to the other, "Oatmeal's in the pan, milk is in the pot, come and get it now so you can get it hot!" Trying to fill in as an amateur cook of sorts, one weekend I baked a pie for us that was not as good as Mom's.

Financially those were tough years for most Americans, so it was then that I began to take an interest in economics. A kind neighbor gave me a new car tire, rationed at the time, for which a shrewd junk merchant paid this inexperienced kid a fat nickel – sensing my ignorance. We were as poor as church mice, but figured that most everyone else was, too.

Soon taking on a second paper route, delivering papers missed by other carriers, and selling the Sunday *Des Moines Register* and *Waterloo Courier* newspapers before church at Oelwein's main cross streets, our earnings grew to as much as many dads brought home.

Several months into that winter Miriam developed a bad cold, so with my permission she stayed home from school. Her teacher reported her absent, motivating the principal to walk the three blocks to our upstairs apartment, and to ask Miriam where our parents were. I've tried to imagine her reply as being something like "Mommy's in 'ington, Daddy's in 'aterloo, and they don't be comin' back."

Within a few hours Judge Woods' officers took us to an orphanage in Waverly, Iowa. But again we were helped by our silent Friend, who guided two of my customers, Laura Smith and Jean Sinclair, to hear about our predicament through their friends in Waverly. One telephone call from Laura got us out of the orphanage, from which we hitch-hiked and a friendly farm couple gave us a ride back to Oelwein.

Laura and Jean agreed to provide us with room and board in exchange for part of my Oelwein Register paper route money. I remember Laura as a loving motherly-type for me, and Jean's daughter Jeanie just happened to be in Miriam's 1st grade class. Meantime a wise old retired fireman allowed me to visit with him at the fire station most afternoons after school before I began my paper route, to listen to and absorb his wisdom. And Miriam earned superb grades. We were so blessed.

Although we were living far from our parents, the family's beliefs in different church denominations grew in importance to me as the years passed. I communicated by mail with Mom (an Episcopalian, died in 1974), who was working in Washington, D.C. for Naval Intelligence, earning $1,600 a year. Dad (a Methodist and Freemason, died in 1992), sold quality products and lived in Waterloo, about 35 miles southwest of us. He tried to keep in touch when he could.

Our older sister Helen (a Lutheran, died in 2010) also lived in Waterloo then, and later married Les. I remember them often laughing as they raised their big farm family consisting of Jim, Jeanne, Larry, Pat, Jo and Barb. Before that our older brother, Jeff, lived with Helen for a while and went on to serve in the U.S. Air Force. He later married Faye, had sons Jud and Joel, and he became senior economist for the Midwest Research Institute (Jeff was an atheist, who died in 1978). I wanted to know if any of their beliefs involved proven truth, in history, the sciences or otherwise (please see chapters 15, 16, 17 and 18).

That summer Miriam and I lived with our favorite Uncle Marvin and Aunt Libby, on their farm near Sumner, Iowa. We enjoyed helping milk the cows, plow the fields and bring in the crops. Miriam loved Libby and especially enjoyed tossing corn kernels to the chickens, ducks and geese, as well as reaching under the hens to get their eggs. Marvin was my special friend in those days, with his horse "Zeke."

This ended quickly, when my appendix heated up while he and I were out in the field shocking oats under the hot August sun. Same-day surgery was done for me in Oelwein's Mercy Hospital. Dad did a plus-quality job with that problem.

He invited Miriam to live with him in Waterloo the rest of that summer of 1942, while I again lived with Smiths. That fall, he gave me a 13th birthday football when I briefly lived with him, his second wife Gert, her son Jack, and Miriam. My 8th school year brought sensational grades (rare for me!), with our homeroom teacher assigning a boy, Frank, who was just released from juvenile reform school, to be "under my wing." He became my first real psychological study.

That same fall I worked part-time for Ticktock Grocery's friendly manager, Gil Hoeg, earning 5¢ an hour including Saturdays, which could total up to 30 hours a week besides school. His and his wife's financial goal was to save a big barrelful of U.S. silver dollars, which grew to be a fortune and sharpened my interest in wise investments. My first job at the grocery store was to eliminate the dozens or hundreds of rats that ran from basement to basement through holes above the ceilings' pipes. It was easy, by simply mixing crushed glass with plaster and cookie crumbs, and then stuffing that lunch into the holes.

CHAPTER

2

GROWING UP

Miriam grew up to be a beautiful lady (Roman Catholic), married Paul and produced Sue, Michael, Kim and Tom. We are good friends, even with the distance. I continued focusing on the world's conflicting religions and denominations that are described in related books, seeking to know more about our faithful Friend "God-somebody" – our Comforter, Helper, and Teacher. *I couldn't have cared less as to which religion proved to be the proven truth winner*. Gradually, simple proofs easily showed themselves by my *trying to examine and test everything* possible!

A fiasco happened in late 1942, when Dad sent Miriam and me by railroad train to stay with Mom, but without the $75 needed to salvage our shipped possessions. Mom met our train but had no extra money, nor did she have room to keep us for long in her small Washington D.C. apartment. We each had the clothes on our backs and a paper bag of stuff. However that year we did have a fun Christmas with Mom. The ground outside was white with snow, and we loved our 10-inch tree, for which I paid 7¢ to a new friend.

Miriam later told me that she was placed in a very loving Methodist orphanage in D.C. I moved in with Ed, a cooking school acquaintance of Mom, and his landlady, Dorothy, in Arlington, Virginia; and began commuting about 20 miles to Central High School in D.C. It was a sensational experience to explore that historic capital city, the White House, the Library of Congress, the National Archives, the Smithsonian Institution, the Naval Observatory etc. But changing schools and books took a toll on my grades...arghhh.

We didn't know beforehand that Ed was a practicing homosexual-sodomite, but he soon became my second informal psychological study. I wanted to find out why he was that way. The one time that he made a serious night-time advance in his and my bedroom, I just screamed loudly and he stopped.

Years later, after professionally analyzing other *homosexuals* psychologically, I found that many have had an overly dominant mother. Recent research at UCLA shows that about 4 million or 1.7% of American adults are homosexual, and a similar number are bisexual (source: San Diego Union-Tribune 4/8/11 p. A-7). This makes me wonder why such feminine-fussing goes on promoting these often spoiled, sometimes bright, sometimes nice and sometimes predatory fellow human beings. I was glad for his sake that Ed later freely chose to play it straight and happily married Dorothy.

To add insult to injury, with word-meaning changes since then, the 1970 Webster's Dictionary defined the word *"gay"* as "given to social life and pleasures, wanton, undisciplined, capricious, senseless, malicious, sexually loose behavior, *licentious*, homosexual." Changes in dictionary definitions have gradually aided changes in your society's attitudes about homosexuals – for example, toward sodomy. Such people are expected to repent, change the mind, *if they want to win real enduring happiness!*

While living at Ed and Dorothy's, early one Saturday morning as I was buying milk for our breakfast, another shrewd merchant asked

8

me to work that day for him. His Black deliveryman and store clerk was sick, and I could use the money from eight hours or so of work after doing my Washington Star paper route. He would not tell me what this work was worth to him, until closing time when he handed me a whole 15¢. It was interesting to later study his philosophy-filled *religion* (chapter 8), which honors such cheaters. I was learning economics the hard way, to always negotiate a *contract in advance, preferably* in writing.

Friends gave me a beautiful male German shepherd puppy, which we donated to the Army K-9 Corps so that he could have a stable home. Ed and Dorothy already had Shane, a wonderful Yorkshire terrier.

Miriam and I were moved back to Iowa in the mid-spring of 1943. She lived with Dad, Gert and Jack in Waterloo, and I moved in with Al and Winona Thody in Oelwein. It was delightful to work part-time with Al, a one-armed house painter and wallpaper hanger who could place a heavy 25-foot wooden ladder against a house with no strain. He never complained to me about being born with a tiny left arm.

That summer, my friend Xenia and I rode our bikes 20 miles east to Strawberry Point's Devil's Backbone State Park, and we camped out in a canvas tent. What a treat. But during the night, raccoons stole our bacon, eggs, butter, and bread from the saddlebags. On our way back to Oelwein we were followed by a friendly stray Dalmatian, but in no way could the Thodys let me keep a dog. After that trip I was hired by J.L. Butler Coal Company in Oelwein to keep the store clean, stock cans of paint on shelves, break up large chunks of coal that were stored in railroad coal cars, and shovel them down chutes to trucks.

When Winona Thody became pregnant, I moved to a cheap hotel on Oelwein's south side near the railroad tracks, and began 9th grade. My next part-time job was cleaning the Coliseum Ballroom's dance floor, men's and women's toilets, and beer and soft drink ice boxes, in exchange for meals at its bar. The lady owner, Bunny something, used to say that I was an 'adult before my time,' but she was very nice to me. You may have heard of the wonderful big bands that played the ballroom – Glen Miller, Tommy Dorsey, Lawrence Welk and others.

My good bike did its job as always when 10th grade school began, but then well-meaning authorities required me to move back to Dad and Gert's in Waterloo. Gert's son Jack was Miriam's age, a nice skinny little guy who we couldn't believe ate over a dozen pancakes at one Saturday breakfast!

Through 1944 my favorite East Waterloo High School English teacher was Mr. Zimmerman, just back from Europe as a World War II fighter pilot. He had shiny straight black hair, a warm smile, a good physique, and he was smart as a whip. Out of hero worship, I took every English course that he offered, including one on the library Dewey Decimal System, which would later prove helpful to my boss in the Military Government of Japan, General Douglas MacArthur.

Still living with Dad and Gert, my part-time summer job in 1945 was at the Riehl Street Grocery; keeping it clean, stocking the shelves and learning to cut up and sell various parts of meat. At age 15 after summer school with Dad's written permission, a good friend Clark Clayton and I rode our bikes – with wooden apple crates bolted on for our canned food – on a four-State tour. We spent the first night sleeping under the stars near Dubuque, about a 100 miles east of Waterloo. Our campsite was in high grass, but we soon noticed that we were surrounded by rattlesnakes. One of us had heard that if we circled a thick rope around our area, the snakes wouldn't cross over. Thankfully, they didn't.

A word to the wise, please: Don't ever pedal your bike up the steep Mississippi River hills with a heavy wooden crate of canned food! We slowly made it, and then pedaled eastward in Illinois, and then north into Wisconsin. One day we helped a dairy farmer process his 40 pound blocks of cheese for minimum pay. I learned not to get on a horse while it was eating grass, and slide down its neck to the ground.

The next day riding north, a loaded semi-truck roared past us with his brakes not working. He wisely drove the truck over a broad ditch to the left, on through barbed wire fencing and into a muddy corn field as he dove out of the cab. Later he told us that his two options were to either crash the truck, or do as he did while diving to safety. He was one smart trucker.

A day later Clark accidentally spilled his bike at the top of a high hill, as dozens of cans of fruit, vegetables, and meat rolled down the highway in wobbly rows like drunken troops. I broke out in hysterical laughter, but Clark obviously didn't think it was funny. We rode on into Madison, Wisconsin that evening. It was V-E Day (World War II's *"Victory in Europe"*), as happy crowds of people celebrated in the streets. After sleeping in a city park by a statue, we bicycled west into Minnesota, and finally headed south to Dad and Gert's home in Waterloo, Iowa.

Awaiting me there was a message from the former homosexual Ed, along with a round-trip railroad ticket to Syracuse, New York. He thought it might be a good idea for me to train to be a court reporter. I went to Syracuse but rejected that training, with respect. This was one of many fun summers, opening doors to far longer trips.

Those high school years involved wonderful friends and memories of playing football, swimming, wrestling, basketball, baseball, golf, track, Boy Scouts, Explorer Scouts, Sea Scouts, sailing and canoeing on Waterloo's Cedar River, church and YMCA programs. Every boy should have such blessings. Besides school, I found another part-time job, this time at Mr. Peterson's Waterloo Neckware, earning 50¢ an hour and working with pal Fay Lorenzon. We did most everything – accept supplies, stock shelves, fill orders, type invoices, and ship the boxes of products at the local Post Office to drug store owners throughout Iowa. Because Fay had worked there before me, I thought of him as my boss and friend.

The same left-handed Fay and with me being right-handed, we sometimes drove our football opponents up the wall. For instance, I would receive the ball and run toward the right side; then lateral it slightly backward across the field to Fay, who would be all alone and go for a touchdown. Our favorite kick-off player, big Barny Siedler, also demoralized competition by putting the football between the goalposts on the kickoff about every 5th time. Once in awhile Coach

Raffensberger let Fay and me play in the first team's scrimmage practice, in spite of our part-time jobs. With an undefeated four-year record, magnificent Raff went on to become head football coach at Iowa University, taking our punter Don Commack and his 55-yard average with him.

Summarizing homes, from 7th grade through high school graduation, I lived with 12 different families. The main ones were Mom and Miriam, the Smiths, Marvin and Libby, Dad and Gert, Ed and Dorothy, the Thodys, and the Mundts when lifelong friend Bill (Shirley later became his wife) joined the U.S. Navy and I was invited to move into his bed.

During those years Dad taught me to cut a "v" in my toenails to prevent them from getting ingrown, to launder shirts if there was any question about the collars, and Mom taught me to take long deep breaths for more oxygen when it was hard to sleep. Miriam and I learned to darn our holey stockings with needle and thread, and to put cardboard inside the soles of our shoes when we had worn holes in them, for protection when we didn't have the money to buy new ones.

The 12th family I lived with was Mom/Mary and Dad/Freeman Elliott (Lutherans, died in 1983 and 1996) with two fine children, Philip and Colleen, in farm country Evansdale, Iowa. My bed was in the basement near the furnace, with the family's beautiful dog, Lassie, snuggling in with me. Living there was wonderful, especially when it snowed. I often ran to or from the bus that took me to Waterloo for school and work, or back to Elliotts' memorable farm and family.

Those days were highlighted by precious visits with Mom Elliott, while this #2 Dad, Freeman, helped to expand my interest in knowledge, logic, understanding, wisdom, the FBI, our Friend "God-somebody," and we studied the Bible's Revelation of Jesus Christ. Dad Elliott, a heavy-equipment mechanic, was the only man I knew who could squeeze a steel can flat, end to end, with his bare fingers. I owe a depth of gratitude to a lot of these caring people and to our Friend "God-somebody," thankfully.

CHAPTER

3

THE FABULOUS MILITARY

Following a goal in high school, it was an honor after graduation to enlist in the U.S. Army's 11th Airborne Paratroops, beginning with basic training in Fort Jackson, South Carolina. We were issued winter uniforms the first day. Just after midnight of day two our 200-man company was awakened and ordered to dress quickly, eat hot "SOS" (ask any military person what that is), board big army "6-bi" trucks, and learn to fight out-of-control wildfires that were burning on three sides of us. While it was still dark, with combat boots on I stepped in an ice-covered foxhole, which made for an interesting night.

The fires lasted about two more days and nights, but battling them helped many of us to get acquainted. Then some mental giant ordered 198 of our troops shipped out to Kentucky, to be replaced by 198 deep-Southern rebels. Some of them blamed us two remaining Iowa Yankees for the Civil War (by Constitutional Law the South was allowed to secede). Even though the base heavyweight boxing champion Frankie Maudlin once offered to defend me, I preferred learning the martial arts of judo and karate for self defense, and accidentally broke an opponent's shoulder when he resisted.

The most memorable event at the base was General Dwight Eisenhower's inspection. One morning at the rifle range a jeep driver gave me written orders to report to our headquarters and escort a general prisoner (he had murdered somebody) seven miles west to Columbia's railroad station. In a hurry I ignorantly ran by the general and his large army, with my M-1 rifle positioned in a port arms salute. You are supposed to stop! He kindly saved my 17 year-old hide by answering our B Company's embarrassed Major Taber with, "At ease, Major. You can see that he's on a mission." General Eisenhower proved to be of great help to me indirectly, with the later essay contest win about him and the doctoral scholarships.

Unexpectedly, as basic training grew to a close our B Company's Captain McClosky presented me with the "Best Instructed Soldier Award," which didn't add joy to a few of the deep-Southern rebels. Later overriding a headquarters lieutenant's printed orders, personnel clerk and friend George Exacallus cut my orders to attend finance school in St. Louis, Missouri, in place of my being stuck in Fort Jackson as the lieutenant's adjutant.

While awaiting the start of finance school, my job was to clean and polish the countless brass door handles on the base. No sooner had school started than the roaring Mississippi River flooded – big time. All of us were ordered to assist where we could; so in an old borrowed row boat a fellow student and I plucked moms, dads, children, cats, dogs, chickens and a goat off the roofs of homes and sheds, and rowed them to safety. I still have a scar on my left thumb from a rusty nail that got in the way of my oar.

Finance school was more than superb. About this time, I had a strong urge to experience the world in order to better understand and empathize with those people globally who were suffering.

After a brief furlough home, next came a great train ride from Waterloo to the west coast's Camp Stoneman, near San Francisco, and then on a troopship to Hawaii, where I was ordered out of the Royal Hawaiian Hotel bar because of only being age 17. I went surfing near the hotel instead, and the next day our troopship set off for beautiful Guam, nicknamed "the rock."

On Guam I worked as a finance clerk, computing payrolls for the military. Workdays usually ranged from 7 A.M. until one o'clock in the afternoon. This was followed either by daily swims west of us at scenic Tumon Bay, or work at my part-time accounting job in the Post Exchange with friends. A girl there asked me to help her catch a baby octopus, so off we went. It was a cute little guy, with which we sat on a ledge about 10 feet above the roaring ocean, until a huge wave threw us back at least 60 feet. All the time she clung to that baby as though she was its mother.

Sometimes our captain asked me to fly payroll to our U.S. troops on Saipan, where its coastal waters of many blue colors are mind-boggling. In preparation for the paratroops, I often jogged at night on Guam's flat highways, then showered and slept like a rock. That lasted seven months, until at last my requested mal-assignment transfer came through, and I was off to the 11th Airborne Division at Camp Crawford, just west of Sapporo in Hokkaido, northern Japan. This new experience was a dream come true, but all too brief.

Several months into Jump School and Ranger training, during a vicious storm my parachute and I swung into a steel weapons carrier. I awoke 11 days later on a train headed south from Sapporo to Tokyo General Hospital. Sitting on my bunk was Gene Garrison, a high-level mess sergeant for General Douglas MacArthur, who thoughtfully asked if I needed anything. My reply was "Could I please have a toothbrush, sir?" Have you ever been in a coma for 11 days, unable to brush your teeth? For years afterward, this great friend and his family sent a toothbrush and love with their Christmas cards.

Gene and I visited for hours that first day. And the more we talked, the more he urged me to consider serving in the military government of Japan, especially since I had extra English and finance training.

Upon leaving the hospital in Tokyo, a pal and I went to the famous Ginza for souvenirs, only to observe that all of the Japanese people

15

disappeared from the street. When we asked a bilingual dealer what was wrong, he pointed to my 11th Airborne shoulder patch. We had not realized that our World War II paratroopers had been the first U.S. forces in that part of Japan, and they took no prisoners.

As Gene had requested, I reported to General Kemske and Colonel Erickson, who arranged for interviews and tests to see if I could qualify as one of General Douglas MacArthur's Military Government economics investigators. Almost funny, in Tokyo a colonel tried to sidetrack me into being his adjutant. I told him thank you but no thanks, because our 11th Airborne was returning stateside to Fort Campbell, Kentucky, and I was invited. It was kind of him then to vote yes to my qualifying as an investigator.

My final test for the Military Government, nicknamed MG, was in the Kanagawa (one of 46 States) MG Team's Yokohama offices, involving my rewriting the fishing laws of Tokyo Bay. These were accepted, and thankfully I became General MacArthur's youngest economics investigator in the Military Government of Japan. At age 18 more doors were opening and I was finding answers to my questions.

Seeking a quality *interpreter* involved researching stacks of personnel files and interviewing dozens of prospects. One Japanese man stood out above all the rest. His name was Inatsugu-san (san means Mr.), who we finally located south of us in Yokosuka. He was way up an old wobbly wooden ladder, painting U.S. Navy barracks gray. At age 72 he was very frail and short in stature, but with a great smile, and still showing dark yellow skin from cholera. We both felt good vibes and bonded within moments.

Back in Yokohama, those early days also involved getting my first "Off Limits" inspections pass from General Walton Walker. He was one of General MacArthur's top right-hand men. With this pass, one afternoon Inatsugu-san and I were sent to inspect a Japanese movie theater. It was showing a film that portrayed two ancient opposing horse-cavalry armies high on hills. In Japan, some wars like this one were fought to the death only by the leaders.

With swords drawn, each leader raced down his hill, and when they met, one lopped the head off the other. I was told that this was not unusual then, for the loser's family was well paid and highly honored. We ordered a cease and desist to the Kanagawa movie industry in this regard. As with many modern Muslims, the Japanese had not generally been taught Western Law or real Biblical Christianity's Golden Rule from Matthew 7:12 and Luke 6:31, "Treat others the same way you want them to treat you," from the merciful Christ Jesus. Later, our General Walton Walker was killed in Korea, and I wept.

After two weeks of training with Inatsugu-san, and backup work by my number-two interpreter Ishikawa-san, the morning's investigations were arranged. Our fourth one involved Inatsugu-san and me inspecting a factory just east of Mt. Fuji, having lunch with executives in the factory owner's home, and me ignorantly placing chopsticks straight up in my rice bowl. Inatsugu-san softly whispered that this meant someone at the luncheon would die within 24 hours. You learn quickly on the firing line.

During this time, a pal Don and I bought a sailor's 1941 Oldsmobile for $900, which we kept running with baling wire and chewing gum. One of the Japanese paint companies honored us by re-chroming the bumpers and painting the car with a classy black lacquer. There were few gasoline stations then in Japan, and many of the cars ran on charcoal that erupted smoke, which is another story.

Unexpectedly the next Friday morning I received a message in our office to report to General Douglas MacArthur in Tokyo at noon (gulp!). The 38 mile drive in my Jeep from Yokohama to Tokyo was pleasant, and I easily found his office. There he was in his sharp tan uniform, relaxing with his feet up on the desk and corncob pipe in hand. He politely returned my salute, with a warm smile.

Then looking more serious, he said, "Son, I understand that you know how to Dewey Decimal a library. Please tell me about it."

I replied, "Yes, sir, if I can have three books." I named the books and told him about Mr. Zimmerman, my high school English teacher and fighter pilot hero. These three requested books were flown over from the States and arrived the next Monday, which I studied for a

17

day at a small desk beside the general's, with his pleasant pipe smoke lingering in the air.

Following General MacArthur's suggestion to get acquainted with his magnificent library that Friday afternoon, before leaving I asked to borrow two of his books for the weekend. That brought him to his feet, as he growled, "No! People borrow my books and never return them! I can never find my books when I need them."

"I understand, sir," was my reply while starting to put them back, when he changed his mind. But in no uncertain terms he firmly warned me not to lose any of his books. At age 18, and feeling about one foot tall in his presence, I would rather have died than lose even one of his irreplaceable books!

Those that I borrowed for that weekend concerned 2nd century BC Hannibal's military strategies in crossing the Alps on elephants in his bold invasion of Italy, and about 18th century BC Babylonian leader Hammurabi's benevolent dictatorship. Amazingly, the latter had the electric battery back then, and the severe high-level code of "an eye for an eye" law.

Looking down the long rows of General MacArthur's library was almost like viewing the curvature of the earth. We did not count the precise number of his books, but I would estimate it to be somewhere between 12,000 and 14,000, many with strong musty smells from their years in the tropics. He told me that the remainder of his library was still buried in the Philippines from WW II.

Reporting to him daily, we began to bond as he gradually allowed me a free hand with his priceless collection. He told me that he had been given many books by his Medal of Honor winning father and a long list of other great people including his former boss, General Pershing. I studied hundreds of these books over the ensuing weeks, often in a friendly Japanese family's beautiful Hakoni Mountains lodge.

General MacArthur had a superb sense of humor. One of his favorite jokes was about a couple of four-year-old boys waiting for surgery in a hospital. "What are you in here for?" asked the first boy.

"Tonsillectomy," replied the second. "Oh, you will love it!" said the first. "They did my tonsils about a year ago. I got lots of things – pop, ice cream…" "What are you here for, asked the second boy?"

"Circumcision," answered the first little guy. "Oh no, not circumcision," said the second. "Quick, run as fast as you can! I had a circumcision when I was eight days old, and couldn't walk for a year!"

In my opinion, with his brilliant military mind and as a strategist, General MacArthur was unequalled. His fellow general, friend and later President, Dwight Eisenhower, certainly would have agreed. Despite imperfections, both were students of the Bible, to which I saw General MacArthur often referring.

My notes from the general's library show that he had made enemies of influential people in Washington. After World War I, 4,723 U.S. veterans and 1,069 admitted communist infiltrators marched on Washington for promised veterans' bonuses. West Point Superintendent General MacArthur and six hundred troops were ordered by President Wilson to intercede. Wilson's influential chief of staff was the so-called "colonel" Edward Mandell House/Heusman, an apparent (potentially-Canaanite) traitor, who with Europe's Jacob Schiff was instrumental in designing your America-wrecking federal income/excise tax and social security traps. The former's U.S. Internal Revenue Code is amazingly easy to understand, if you carefully study and comprehend all of its tricky definitions, as in our chapter 20.

The above-mentioned 1,069 communist infiltrators were led by 36 others, including Emmanuel Levin, James Ford, and John Pace, who were following orders from Moscow to create a murderous riot. Their goal was to see our side's guns fired and U.S. veterans killed. General MacArthur ordered that not one shot would be fired; and not one was due to his unexpected strategy of using tear gas.

I gradually found that MacArthur's enemy was what is Biblically called the "Canaanite" seed line, which we will thoroughly discuss in chapter 5. They never forgave him, which is apparently why they blocked his potential run for the U.S. presidency. That high-level leadership for America might have been second only to George Washington's.

Of strategy, Pentagon heads turned in World War II when MacArthur instructed U.S. ships and troops to by-pass many Pacific islands held by the Japanese, rather than engage the tens of thousands awaiting them there. Once the enemy supplies were cut off, they had no choice but to eventually surrender. When friends and I later were exploring the jungles of Guam, we found three Japanese soldiers living in a camouflaged cave, with food, arms, tattered uniforms, and the only fresh spring water on the island.

You may be aware of the Philippines' surrender of the Bataan and Corregidor bases during WW II. General MacArthur's *"I shall return"* was announced by Filipino Colonel Carlos Romulo from Corregidor over the Voice of Freedom radio. The general had said *"We shall return,"* but Romulo explained that the word "we'" lacked the needed psychological effect for Filipino people. Then the general, his wife Jean and their son Arthur left the Philippines by PT-41 (torpedo) boat and on to one of four submarines, dangerously slipping through Japanese patrol lines en route to Australia with more important work to do.

The sound of MacArthur's easy laughter still rings in my memory. Always the professional soldier, he responsibly treated me like a son and taught us investigators such pearls as our MG motto, "You are Ambassadors of Goodwill." One of his favorite Bible verses was Deuteronomy 13:14: "You shall investigate and search out and inquire thoroughly." More than once, he reminded us to "Be clean, live clean, think clean." What a role model he was, day after day, thank God.

With his motto of *"No Substitute for Victory,"* it is understandable why General MacArthur was difficult for enemies to overcome, even by President Truman who fired him over his wanting to bomb China's massed troops and win the war. Hoards of North Korean and Chinese enemies were given a rare advantage by Truman and the United Nations. They were allowed to (1) strike our troops in force, (2) then slip back across the Yalu River to China from North Korea, (3) strike our troops in waves again, and then (4) slip back into China and hide – all with the questionable United Nations' blessing. Our victory-oriented General MacArthur demanded that this be stopped.

20

Truman and the UN disagreed, and MacArthur being military property was fired.

Back to the Dewey Decimal library assignment, it took a little over six weeks to complete with the help of two assistants. My relationship with General MacArthur continued through the following months because of my investigations job, until just before Truman's "police action" Korean War.

Retired Marine friend Tom Elliott (wife Dolores) told me of exchanges with the Chinese at the Chosin Reservoir in -20°/F temperature. Enemy troops would fire their bullets into our vehicles' reserve gasoline cans. Not being born yesterday, our guys simply employed American ingenuity by chewing their candy Tootsie Rolls, with which they would plug the bullet holes for an instant freeze, and move on. Most of the loyal military heroics by our Army, Marines, Air Force and Navy occurred after I came home.

CHAPTER

4

EXTRA SERVICE IN THE ORIENT

In Military Government my favorite officer was Katsuki Tanagawa, from Hawaii with Japanese ancestry, who had fought up the boot of Italy as part of the most decorated U.S. Army division in WW II. Katsuki and I did many things together, including a special assignment to observe the Kyoto movie studios near Osaka. That same year of 1949, we were ordered to overcome a dangerous communist uprising in Kawasaki. About 400 potential rioters were coming eight abreast down the main street, aching for trouble. Katsuki brought this to a screeching halt, when he uncovered their large arms and ammunition cache buried in a Kawasaki beer company's barley bins, and called in our U.S. Marines for back up.

One hot Sunday afternoon, Katsuki and I were invited aboard a business owner's yacht. We went for a swim in Tokyo Bay, splashing each other and laughing as we climbed back into the small row boat with its oar at the back. Friends aboard our host's yacht were yelling something beyond our hearing. When we looked back into the water we were shocked to see a vicious school of barracuda-like fish thrashing wildly. As I told Katsuki, we must have guardian angels looking out for us.

"Presentos," meaning gifts from the Japanese to us investigators, were only allowed selectively; and we were strictly on our honor in this regard. I still have a hand-carved wooden ashtray given to this non-smoker one morning by a young artist, with the classic three monkeys' "See no evil, hear no evil and speak no evil." Most often the people were very thoughtful.

This reminds me of the owner of Japan's largest pearl farm, Mr. Mickey Moto. He walked up to my desk when I first joined MG, and kept bowing and bowing, until I realized the need to return his bows. Then we became well acquainted...a nice guy.

Another morning a crate of French wine was delivered to my desk, although I had only sipped green beer and Sake rice wine up to that point. This might have seemed odd, because some of my investigations involved inspecting beer, liquor, and wine factories throughout Kanagawa Prefecture, as we worked with the people to help get Japan's economy purring as successfully as we could.

To me those post-war Japanese citizens were generally cooperative; unlike some of us Americans would be if we had been conquered. In attitudes, unlike in parts of America, most Japanese were educated to benefit their nation and each other. You probably know the saying, *"United we stand, divided we fall!"* Perhaps that is why the Japanese people had never before in its history been invaded.

General MacArthur read them like a book, as he did their primarily-Shinto religion, which I studied (see chapter 8) in night school. Upon first arriving in Japan, he ordered Emperor Hirohito to report to him, respectfully asking that he remain in office as emperor; but firmly without the role of deity. This set the tone for who was in charge. MacArthur wisely saved the whole Japanese nation's "face," and the Japanese people deeply loved and admired him for his real Christian Golden Rule mandates.

I was at my MG desk early one morning, to catch up on work and write letters to Mom, Dad and Miriam – and to the Elliotts who had moved from Evansville to another farm near Jesup, Iowa. Our MG office lights were on dim, when I noticed a cleaning woman rifling through Colonel Erickson's file drawers. Suddenly seeing me, she tried to run but didn't like my drawn .45 automatic pistol. She turned out to be an un-armed, middle-level communist espionage agent under orders from North Korea.

This fact reminds me of my corner MG desk overlooking busy Yokohama Harbor, with its magnificent panoramic view of shipping and the bay. One day, I found 50,000 yen on the captain's desk to the left of mine. Looking suspicious, I reported it as required. General Kemske ordered me to hold on to it, at least until someone asked questions. The captain eventually did inquire, breaking my heart to see him taken to the brig to await trial for allegedly accepting a bribe. That was not allowed by General MacArthur.

If I remember correctly, MacArthur worked with a budget of about $1 million a day during the entire occupation of Japan, which produced a resounding success. Today it is doubtful that the often self-serving politicians and bureaucrats in Washington, DC could do the job for $10 billion a week at minimum, as they have proven in Iraq and Afghanistan. While we feel that our courageous troops there were often unmatched in quality, they are thought of as occupiers and exploiters by many foreigners (as we would feel). They want our side to go home, while the enemy guerilla forces (Muslim al-Qaida with Taliban) are want their suicidal religious war – against the big Satan, with countless recruits.

If the U.S. Congress members would cancel their big pay raises, unbelievable pensions, fully paid medical expenses, chauffeured automobiles as an option, world junkets for relatives and friends, donations from anti-American lobbyists, and then be replaced by firmly-loyal American statesmen and stateswomen, America just might have a chance of surviving. However, that is not likely to happen in view of this world's signs of the times; all of which have been interacting since 1967, as in chapter 18.

I find that *"springtime"* wars are on the horizon, with the West and Israel against Iran, Russia and their Muslim allies. Again, historically Russia prefers to invade its prey in the springtime, and mop up in the summertime. And *"IRAN* also can now produce nuclear weapons" (source: our North County Times, April 9, 2012), with its nuclear missiles to be ready for war by December 2012 to February 2013 (source: Bible prophecy Pastor Hal Lindsey, Daystar TV, October 21, 2012).

Another experience with Japanese presentos happened when I was put in charge of crop collection and food distribution for Kanagawa Prefecture. A shipload of salt-damaged foodstuffs including sugar arrived in Yokohama harbor. I told the Chigasaki Candy Company owner and certain others about this unexpected sugar, for which they were grateful.

A few days later this owner invited up to three of us to go night-time wild boar hunting from their mountain lodge. At about mid-night the hired drummers began banging pots and pans to drive the wild boar up the mountain. General Kemske had fallen asleep, and Sergeant Weeks was relieving himself in the boondocks. Suddenly, a big wild boar raced directly at Weeks, so I had the job of shoot-ing it with my trusty carbine rifle. That helped feed several grateful Japanese families for days.

The next month of August two pals and I climbed 12,388' Mt. Fuji, from dusk way into the night. There were two rest stops on the way up, for tea and brief sleep breaks. A long line of Japanese climb-ers followed us closely because we shared a big flashlight. With my friend carrying it as we were climbing up the dark mountain path, with no ropes to guide us, I felt a strong urge to stop! About five feet ahead was nothing but black space.

We reached the top before dawn. After more rest and a cup of hot green tea, we laughed our way through a friendly snowball fight in the volcano of the mountain's peak, and then took breathtaking pic-tures eastward toward Yokohama and south to Sagami Bay. Running down the west side of Mt. Fuji was another experience, taking up to 20-foot jumps on its small ashes. *Yes, we accomplish by doing!* And it can be more fun as we believe, mature with faith, and trust in the everlasting truth with proofs.

Back to MG, my interpreter Inatsugu-san in his younger years had worked as a railroad design engineer for Russia, before becoming chairman of the board of his own international trading corporation. While traveling on business near the end of World War II, unfortunately he was captured and imprisoned in a Chungking, China concentration camp, where he contracted cholera, also known as yellow jaundice. At the end of the war it and typhus killed many prisoners, in Asia and Europe, with roads out and all supplies cut off. You may know that famous WW II writer Anne Frank died of typhus, not from gassing; and her father made millions re-writing her diary with a ball point pen that was not available until 1951.

As mentioned, when Inatsugu-san and I first met, his skin was still a dark yellow, his stature was short, and he had a smile that would knock your socks off. He said, "At age 72, I am beginning my life all over again, thank you!" He too was hungry and thirsty to learn, even from me, relatively a nobody. So we did it together for what probably became thousands of exciting hours over two unforgettable years.

He was a highly intelligent Buddhist, while I was strongly being drawn toward real Bible Christianity – with proofs of truth. We discussed many topics, often far into the night. At that time, I mistakenly believed that Hell (or Hades, Sheol) was permanent, and thus asked him, "If you die tonight, will your sins be forgiven?"

Somehow, we found Hell's location described in Matthew 12:40 as the "heart of the earth," also Word-pictured in Luke 16:19-31. Years later, I discovered that translators apparently had mistaken Matthew 5:22-26's "*Gehenna*," the ever-burning Lake of Fire, for "*Geenna*" and "*Geennan*," which is temporary Hell (or Hades, Old Testament Sheol) as in Revelation 20:14. Are such mix-ups and leave-outs pitiful examples of why some Christian pastors and theologians, with whom I studied, have been mistaught to avoid key parts of their Bibles, including "the Revelation of Jesus Christ" as in its 1:1+3 with 22:12-19? Our pastors, theologians and lay-people deserve better!

Inatsugu-san did not answer my question right away. We read his Buddhist scriptures as well, which has no belief in "God-anybody." And we saw the Bible's Psalm 2:2–12, which describes the Anointing of the Christ or Messiah or Mashiyach, with some of His miraculous accomplishments previewed in 22:15–18 and Isaiah 53:2–12. Yes, we saw that the real Christ temporarily gave His life for us, as long-before prophesied or promised, to fulfill His required *"once-for-all"* (Romans 6:16) Blood Atonement Sacrifice, and to save spiritually-wandering humankind whom He Created, including you and me. And now He asks us to *pray in His Name*, to really get things accomplished, as in John 14:13, 15:16 and 16:23-26.

We loved His Galatians 5:22–23: *"Fruit of the Spirit —- [Agape]-love, joy, peace, patience, kindness, goodness, faithfulness, gentleness and self-control."* We were learning. It was beginning to make sense. And we appreciated the warning for would-be losers in Gal. 5:19–21: "Immorality, impurity, sensuality, idolatry, sorcery, enmities, strife, jealousy, outbursts of anger, disputes, dissentions, factions, envying, drunkenness, carousing...those who practice such things shall not inherit the Kingdom of God."

In parallel to this, we found that 1 Corinthians 6:9–11 show "the unrighteous, fornicators, idolaters, adulterers, effeminate, homosexuals, thieves, covetous, drunkards, revilers, swindlers... Such were some of you; but you were washed, sanctified, justified in the Name of the Lord Jesus Christ and in the Spirit of our God." Does this remind you of Acts 4:12's "...and there is Salvation in no one else, for there is no other name among men by which we must be saved."

We saw Romans 14:23b, "Whatever is not from faith is sin." And we appreciated Isaiah 1:18–19's "Though your sins are as scarlet, they will be white as snow; though they are red like crimson, they will be like wool. *IF* you consent and obey, you will eat the best... But *IF* you refuse and REBEL, you will be devoured." (Again, all special emphasis is mine, with plenty of help from our God-Someone).

Was it the result of faithless human behavior – and 700 B.C. Isaiah 65:5's "holier than thou" arrogance – that the Christ gave His blood and paid the full price for us, as required by His Almighty Father in

28

Isaiah 53:10–11? "But the Lord was pleased to crush Him…if He would render Himself as a guilt offering …will justify the many, as He will bear their iniquities…He Himself bore the sin of many, and interceded for the transgressors."

You may remember Hebrews 9:22 and Leviticus 17:11: "Without the shedding of Blood there is no forgiveness [by His Almighty Father]." In our spare time, Inatsugu-san and I dug for more insights, and he asked many questions to which I did not yet know the answers.

Thinking of General MacArthur and his brilliant strategy for the later Inchon landing behind North Korean enemy lines, in spite of a treacherous tide, therein was another mark of his genius (some might call it luck). I have no doubt that the general's silent prayers in Jesus' Name helped America decisively in those incredible days of war.

Amazing things were being linked together, such as the General often complaining about America's enemies working feverishly in Washington, D.C. against us; and my remembering the outcast tribes from Genesis 9:25's "Cursed be Canaan;" and condemned as "Canaanite" in Zechariah 14:21c's "And there will no longer be a Canaanite in the house of the Lord of hosts in that day." Were these Canaanite people the same seed line as General MacArthur's enemies, to whom he referred as the *insidious forces working from within* America the beautiful? Were these the satanic enemies, exposed in I Thess. 2:14b-15 that "…both killed the Lord Jesus… hostile to all men [and women]"? With responsible (Agape)-love for all, let's keep on investigating thoroughly and proving, as General MacArthur kindly requested.

CHAPTER
5

HEBREW AND CANAANITE OPPOSITES

Without regular parental discipline in my youth, I enjoyed getting some maturity from talking with many bright people and studying countless books. These included the Bible's Proverbs and Psalms, trying to gradually understand their guidelines, for example concerning *"wisdom."* Who can improve on Proverbs 8:17's *"I love those who love me; and those who diligently seek me will find me?"* This was made even clearer by Colossians 2:2-3's "... true knowledge of God's mystery, that is Christ Himself in Whom are hidden all the treasures of *wisdom and knowledge."*

It seems *dumb to hate other people*, and far wiser to Agape-love (defined below) each. Don't we all make faithless mistakes in this life, called sin, as promised in Romans 3:23 with 6:23?

In order for you to fully enjoy and profit from these pages, please have a Bible at your finger tips. The version may be less important than the proofs that you should find in it; but I prefer the *NEW AMERICAN STANDARD BIBLE* because it uses ancient Dead Sea Scrolls for maximum accuracy and understanding.

With this fact known, Inatsugu-san and I saw Matthew 18:21-35's "Should you not also have had mercy on your fellow slave, in the same way that I had mercy on you? And his lord, moved with anger, handed him over to the torturers until [remember temporary Hell, Luke 12:59, Matthew 5:26, 18:34] he should repay all that was owed him...My heavenly Father will also do the same to you, if each of you does not forgive his brother from your heart." Many people have no idea how merciful and wrathful our Christ can be. For you it depends on you, including the potential Canaanite-Jews!

We delighted in helping each other find more insights, such as Romans 9:6–8's "children of the promise," and the approved Church being *"grafted in"* to the Hebrew-Jews' seed as in 11:17–26. This Salvation will include both lines into the future "Israel" on the future perfected earth. It was also a treat to see Hebrews 11:39–40, with its ancient *"approved"* faithful ones, not yet "perfected" without you, right?

We learned of Abraham's "Ibiru" (Hebrew) tribe from 2100 BC in the lower Euphrates River's Sumerian city of Ur. These historically fierce people became known as Esther 8:17a+c's Hebrew-Jewish "Yehuwdiy," and still later as Romans 2:28–29's and Revelation 2:9 and 3:9's "Iouda."

The opposing "Yahad" *Canaanite-Jews* named in Esther 8:17b get interesting, dreading 8:17a+c's Hebrew-Jews. The Canaanite-Jew seed line of people are subsequently named as Ezekiel 44:7's *"foreigners...they made My Covenant void;"* Matthew 13:25-38's satanic *"tares"* (note 13:30's "Allow *both to grow together* until the harvest..."); Luke 16:8's *"more shrewd;"* John 8:44's half-breed *"of your father the Devil;"* 2 Cor. 11:13-15's *"servants" of Satan;"* I Thess. 2:14-15's *Ioudaikos* "who both killed the Lord Jesus...not pleasing to God, but hostile to all men" (both male and female genders, as in Matt.12:50); I John 3:10's *"children of the Devil;* Jude 4's "marked out for this *condemnation;"* Revelation 2:9's *"synagogue of Satan;"* 3:9's *imposters of our* often-fabulous *"Iouda" Hebrew-Jews*; and 18:11's losing *"merchants* of the earth."

The Hebrews' gradual infiltration by the Canaanites reminds me of a shrewd little infiltrator that I detected in Kawasaki, who was employed by New York's Rockefellers/Rockenfelds. He wanted to buy or steal Japanese companies for profits, while we were trying so hard to get them economically successful. I found it interesting too that the Rockefellers donated the land in New York for the one-world government United Nations headquarters, and that the book, *David Rockefeller: Memoirs*, provides ample proof that David Rockefeller (Rockenfeld) has been an "...internationalist...conspiring with others around the world" to gradually wreck our once-free sovereign America and its Citizens, for their *New World Order Pax Judaica*, as we will review.

History: Again the word *"Jew"* came from the New Testament Koine Greek of Jesus' line, the *"Iouda"* (for instance in Romans 2:28-29, Revelation 2:9 and 3:9); and of Satan's *"Ioudaikos"* aka *"Ioudaizo* (in I Thessalonians 2:14b-15). This word *"Jew"* apparently first appeared in American dictionaries in *1775 AD. It was far too early in my investigations to detect the above Esther 8:17's Hebrew-*Jew "Yehuwdiy" being infiltrated by *foreign Canaanite-Jewish "Yahad."* The latter again were Genesis 9:18–25's descendants of Noah's grandson (also called son in the Hebrew language), the *"cursed be CANAAN."*

Let's see why Canaan was cursed: 1) In the beginning there apparently was a mist-like "firmament" canopy over the earth (Genesis 1:6+14+15+17), partially shielding the sun, so fruit juice from the vine would not ferment. 2) After the world-flood the firmament vanished; Noah farmed, drank his new wine, became drunk and was naked (9:20-21). 3) Grandson Canaan, perhaps typical of Satan's children, committed sodomy, and Noah *"knew what his youngest son [actually grandson] had done to him [9:24]."*

For linguists, I honestly believe that over the centuries Satan's seed line gained control and manipulated the Hebrew language enough, so that today's generally-nice people wouldn't know a Canaanite-Jew from a Hebrew-Jew. Again *it is not my job to hate anyone, and I don't...*

for it is better to leave such "wrath" up to our childhood Friend "God-Somebody." We finites don't need to condemn fellow mistake-makers, okay? There is happiness in helping all other people, as needed. For when you help another up the ladder of life, you are bound to be higher up yourself. Right?

Inatsugu and I were seeing more of Jesus' promises, for example in Revelation 20:11-15 with Matthew 25:31-46 and John 5:29-30, where the real Christ is to perfectly Judge many people for their "*DEEDS*." And yet in John 5:30, "...he who hears My Word, and believes Him Who sent Me, has everlasting life, and does not come into Judgment, but has passed out of death into life..."

You and I can count on this Son taking responsible care of His friends and enemies. I was gradually getting to know more about our Friend "God-Somebody," thank God, and to understand insights such as Hosea 4:6: "My people are destroyed [temporarily] for lack of knowledge; because you have rejected knowledge I also shall reject you from being My priest [note his priests as in Revelation 20:5b-6 and I Peter 2:9, probably dressed in sport shirts]..."

With these facts hopefully you can understand Deuteronomy 7:1-4's bad-"nations," wanting to do their opposing bad-"God [Theos] of this world" Satan's will, 2 Corinthians 11:4, and at times even using his 11:4's "another Jesus." Later in Revelation 21:8 you can see some of his people as part of "...the cowardly and unbelieving and abominable and murderers and immoral persons and SORCERERS and idolaters and all liars."

Let's don't be asleep. Based upon their writings, these satanic Canaanites apparently are determined to either kill or to rule you and yours, with their Pax Judaica's *economic socialism* and *political communism*, and they are right on schedule! To lawfully overcome these in the real Christ, we are to Agape-love all, with 2 Timothy 1:7's no "...spirit of timidity, but of power and [Agape-] love and discipline." For they have a big problem ahead of them, working feverishly to overthrow the proven Creator of the earth, heavens, the universe and infinity.

This reminds me of favorite prose from William Blake's '*Auguries of Innocence,*' "To see the world in a grain of sand, and a heaven in a wild flower; hold infinity in the palm of your hand, and eternity in an hour." Relaxing, yes?

To understand more of mankind's problem, please consider the Canaanites' self-serving *"operation twist,"* a Hegelian trick designed to confuse and destroy you. In this, they may do or say the opposite of what is expected, and even disclaim charges that have been proven against them. The term *anti-semitism* is like that, as thoroughly discussed here. At best, thorough investigating is difficult, because you can get mixed signals. For instance there is the annual Kol Nidre chant on the eve of Yom Kippur, which is an in-advance disavowal of all oaths to be given the following year. Does that sound like a "twist" or what? But then investigating this on the Internet might leave you misthinking that satanists are angelic. What?

By owning or controlling most of the major media and educational systems, it is easy for these predators to mentally control billions of people in this spiritual war with their propaganda. Are you unknowingly on the slippery side of the *"God [Theos, big G] of this world,"* 2 Corinthians 4:4's today, or on the enduring side of simple proven truth? Another factor is to *never confuse the wonderful Hebrew-Jews with the satanic Canaanite-Jews*; and *never feel that you have to judge-to-condemn either line.*

To more history on these two opposing seed lines of Jews, in 70 AD General Titus' Roman legions were destroying Jerusalem. The starving people were even forced to eat their own babies (source: the reliable historian Josephus). Survivors then migrated to the north, west and east. To the northeast many of this mixture settled in Khazaria. They were known as the Khazars, taking the religion of Judaism, and forming the largest nation ever in Europe (source: the Jewish Encyclopedia).

Some others to the west were temporarily victorious over the Roman legions in 132 AD, even gaining Roman citizenship in 212. On the move, by 505 in Constantinople (now Istanbul), Judaism's priesthood consolidated its Babylonian and *Palestinian Mishnah and Gemara* into one voluminous *Babylonian Talmud*. Rome fell shortly afterward.

Eastward in 965 AD the Khazars were defeated and captured by Russian armies of Prince Sviatoslav (source: Harvard Univ's *An Encyclopedia of World History*, Riverside Press). By 1100 they had been emigrated north to Russia and Poland where, with hatred for their hosts, they lived in miserable ghettos. From this their Teutonic-Hebrew "*Yiddish*" language emerged.

Reportedly on May 1, 1776 their leading rabbis and merchants met in Warsaw, Poland, headed by Adam Weishapt, and forming their "*Order of the Illuminati*" – with a world-dictatorship plan whose goal has gradually progressed worldwide ever since. Their global headquarters allegedly has been located in Basel, Switzerland, with its "gnomes of Basel" to whom fellow investigators report that the private "Fed"/Federal Reserve corporation's something-Jewish chairman goes up to ten times a year for instructions. History shows that these powerful "gnomes" financed allegedly half-Canaanite Adolf Shickelgruber Hitler, by way of the Warburg family. But they rejected his suggestion to expatriate "all Jews to Madagascar" in the early 1930s. And you probably know much of the rest, spiced with daily propaganda by way of their Canaanite-owned major media.

ANTI-SEMITISM again has been a clever tool used in their "*operation twist.*" Most Canaanites may pretend that their and Jesus' seed lines are the same Genesis 6:10's "*Semite*," from Noah's son Shem, with his brothers named Ham and Japheth. Repeat: Ham's son was Noah's grandson (also known as son in the Hebrew), on to 9:24-25's cursed "Canaan," who apparently satanically sodomized drunken Noah. Therefore Canaan was a *HAMITE*, not a Semite. Given such confusion in today's government public schools, if asked, most students and graduates today wouldn't know "*Anti-Semite*" (anti-Jesus) from an *ANTI-HAMITE*" or "*ANTI-CANAANITE*," would you agree? This sad fact is the result of planned brainwashing, not education.

Tracing back before Canaan, I find that Ham's wife was one of the Genesis 6:4 bad-God Satan's offspring (Genesis 6:4, 2 Corinthians 4:4), in order to produce the human "filthy" of Revelation 22:11. She apparently carried the satanic seed through the world flood; and you know the resulting mixed-breed mess. Your friends may have also been brainwashed to not believe in that flood, but Jesus does, and He promised its happening in Genesis 7:4, 2 Peter 2:5 and 3:6, always doing His Father's will.

Please be aware too of Proverbs 30:5-6's *"Every word of God is tested..."* and 2 Timothy 3:16's "All Scripture is inspired by God [God-breathed]..." This explains why all 66 books of your Bible were originally mathematically perfect, as in chapter 17.

Today's Canaanites economically influence almost everything in America and the world, as they did ancient Israel. After infiltrating, they have gradually imposed their "dialectical materialism" or "principle of material interests," promoting debt-spending that produces artificial affluence, until many of their enemies are in debt over their ears, including governments. People in debt are easier to enslave. Also this *debt-spending* can become *compounded,* involving *periodic interest* on each loan. And guess who makes most loans, for example to market material goods such as "I just gotta have that little red Toyota?" And in any debate about this, can you detect which side could have *easily doctored its evidence?*

It is also alleged that when a Canaanite-Jew says to you, *"Have a nice day,"* it means that you will be ruled over during their future "Pax Judaica," with 10,000 years of their "peaceful" dictatorship. I am told that similar boasts appear in their voluminous Babylonian Talmud, quoted as accurately as possible in chapter 8 with the assistance of respected scholar and apparently Hebrew-Jew Benjamin H. Freedman.

In fairness, another investigated quotation is potentially wrong, from 10th century AD's Simeon Haddarsen. While consistent with the Canaanites' *New World Order "Pax Judaica,"* he allegedly wrote "When the Messiah comes every Jew will have 2,800 slaves." Don't know...but let's be truthful about it!

It also interests me that in America's 1800s, trading posts were made available for supplies needed by the pioneers. What is not taught in public government schools is that these trading posts were generally owned by one company, nowadays called Goldman Sachs, still controlled by the Rothschilds of Europe. They also own or control most of America's money with their associates, except that now those families own the stock of their private 'Federal Reserve' banks across America, which own the private 'Federal Reserve' corporation stock, which owns America's money supply...imposed in 1913 on this once-beautiful Nation...as in our chapter 5.

Writer and Rabbi Ravage stated in his 1928 article referred to earlier, concerning the infamous *Protocols of the Learned Elders of Zion*, "They are genuine and authentic." He also provides in-advance promises of pre-planned crises and conflicts that have taken place worldwide since 1928. These are real, as apparently are the reported concentration camps now built on off limits areas of U.S. military bases, according to reliable fellow investigators.

Inatsugu-san and I found far better "Good News" for Canaanites, when seeing Matthew 15:22-28 from our merciful Friend God-Somebody: "...A *Canaanite woman*...came saying, 'Lord, help me!' He answered and said, 'It is not good to take the children's bread and throw it to dogs' [check out your dictionary's "*dogs*"]...But she said, 'Yes Lord, but even the dogs feed on the crumbs which fall from their master's table.' Then Jesus said to her, 'Oh woman, your faith is great; it shall be done as you wish.' And her daughter was healed at once." Almighty Mercy? Oh, yes, even for Canaanites!

This reminds me of His Titus 2:13's "...Blessed Hope and the appearing of our great God and Savior Christ Jesus," for you to share now along with 1:1b's "...Faith of those chosen of God and the knowledge of the truth which is according to revering well." I find that most everyone is welcome to these gifts, with a few easy "if" and "because" conditions. But in my early decades of investigating for proofs of truth in thousands of conflicting books, it turned out that Ecclesiastes 12:1 has been right on with "...be warned...excessive devotion to books is wearying..." You may have experienced this, too.

It took me many years to discover that the original of 66-book Bibles have always had the answers to our questions, subject to mistranslations. By narrowing my investigations generally to this most-reliable source, it was possible to get a better handle on Who our Friend "God-Somebody" was and is.

On the contrary, before the American Revolution a Mr. *Meyer Amschel Bauer* (1743-1812) changed his name *to Rothschild, or "red shield,"* after his pawnshop in Hamburg, Germany. He also worked at shrewd *"banking,"* learned from his ancestors, hiding customers' valuables in nearby banks of dirt hills, with the clever idea of issuing paper receipts to his customers in exchange for their gold and silver – always at a profit. He also believed in the Yiddish words *"leolom tickoch"* – *"always take"* – a term still used by Revelation 18's "merchants of the earth" (you probably remember Shakespeare's *"Merchant of Venice"*), who will be Judged for their deeds according to Revelation 20:12-13. All will learn that Agape-loving responsibly is better than taking. Let's never confuse the real Christ's Agape-love versus self-serving philanthropists – where donors' names are prominently on buildings.

John Davison Rockefeller (Rockenfeld) was very much like this; reportedly from Rockenfeld, Germany in the late 1800s; and financed by Rothschild to exploit American oil with depletion allowances, at the Congress' and American Citizens' expense. His publicity agent *Ivy Lee* had photographs taken of John as he handed shiny new dimes to New York children. Lee made sure that the pictures were printed in the associate *New York Times*, and John was instantly made "a kind old gentleman, a philanthropist" (or an often-lying Canaanite, such as to the Congress regarding his Standard Oil?). The Rockefellers had sent Lee to Russia to aid in the communist takeover of that land (source: U.S. Senate Committee on Internal Security, Report #2050, 82nd Congress). In 1946 the Rockefellers (Rockenfelds) donated the land for New York's United Nations' *New World Order*; with the pledge to promote world *"peace and security,"* a term prophesied in I Thessalonians 5:3. And Matthew 7:15-16 warns, "You will know them by their fruits…"

Meyer Amschel Bauer *Rothschild* trained his five sons to run the five banks of Europe, and more. Reminding me again of Luke 16:8's "shrewd," in 1815 his *son Nathan* (1777-1836) earned $17 million in just a few days. England and France were locked in war at Belgium's *Battle of Waterloo*, so Nathan secretly hired horseback riders to let him know which side won (England did). When one rider reported this, and the other independently confirmed it, Nathan simply used dialectic economic psychology – first leaking word that he sold all of his English assets. A majority of English investors then panicked, and sold at a loss...while Nathan was secretly buying these back for a penny on the pound. What seems almost comical, the other English investors didn't know what hit them, and he never let on!

Reportedly by 1850 this house of *Rothschild* controlled nearly half of the world's wealth, with its patriarch's boast, *"Give me control over a nation's currency, and I care not who makes its laws."* He knew what he was doing, temporarily, with Mark 4:19's "deceitfulness of_riches" known, while the current Rothschild patriarch continues as "king of Jerusalem."

A good many early American pioneers spent money at those *trading posts* in exchange for needed supplies; while the government, media and promoter Horace Greeley pleaded "Go West, young man, go West!" Seeing Revelation 18:12+15's "merchants," it is just a tiny step to also see the Canaanites' descendants, now called *"princes,"* multiplying their inherited millions as directors and producers of U.S.— *"a-muse"-"no think" entertainment* – movies, television, sports, parties et al. Note: Beware of such self-serving merchants, whose leaders have controlled America's money for about one hundred years. Oh yes, the word *"wealth"* in Babylonian is "stur," mathematically numbering the Revelation 13:18's famous *"666."*

Pulling every trick in the book, *Rothschild's dream* came true in November of 1910 when the son-in-law of John D. Rockefeller (Rockenfeld), U.S. Senator Nelson Aldrich from Rhode Island, hosted a mysterious group of other powerful men to an exclusive meeting on Georgia's Jekyll Island. His polished black railroad car named Aldrich – with brass hand rails, mahogany paneling, velvet drapes, plush armchairs, a well-stocked bar, porters with white serving coats, and the distinct aroma of expensive cigars – raced southward through the night.

These *seven men* were: 1) Nelson W. Aldrich, the U.S. Senate whip, chairman of the Monetary Commission, associate of J.P. Morgan, father-in-law of John D. Rockefeller/Rockenfeld Jr.; 2) Abraham Piatt Andrew, Assistant Secretary, U.S. Treasury; 3) Frank A. Vanderlip, National City Bank of New York president, representing William Rockefeller/Rockenfeld and the Kuhn Loeb & Company international investment bankers; 4) Henry P. Davidson, J.P. Morgan Company senior partner; 5) Charles D. Norton, First National Bank of New York's president; 6) Benjamin Strong, J.P. Morgan's Bankers Trust Company head; and 7) Paul M. Warburg, partner in Kuhn, Loeb & Company, representative of England's and France's Rothschild banking empire, and brother of Max Warburg who headed Warburg's banking powers in Germany, the Netherlands and financed Hitler (sources: Eustace Mullins' *The Federal Reserve*, and G. Edward Griffin's *The Creature from Jekyll Island*).

These potential Canaanites designed what became the unconstitutional privately-owned *Federal Reserve corporation*, to control America's money supply and interest rates.

This *TOTAL CONTROL OF AMERICA'S MONEY* was finally gained in late 1913 by these owners of the '*Federal Reserve corporation stock*: (1) Rothschild's European family descendants with their associates: (2) the Lazards of Paris, (3) Israel Moses Seifs of Italy, (4) the Warburgs of Germany, (5) Lehmans-Kuhn-Loeb, (6) Goldman-Sachs, and (7) the Rockefellers (Rockenfeld) of New York

On December 23, 1913, with most of the Congress adjourned for Christmas, a quorum of (bribed?) members voted for this shrewd privately owned misnamed "Federal Reserve" or "Fed" corporation. Private, yes the Fed does have to pay property tax, while government agencies do not. The Fed is not federal nor does it have a reserve structure. Its *private ownership is affirmed in 1982's 9th Circuit court decision* of Lewis v. U.S., as in your local county law library. Why hasn't the Congress reversed this blatant lawlessness, do you suppose? Could it be that money still talks, especially for blackmail, bribes and pay-offs in Washington, D.C., which shall be judged for such deeds about 1,000 years from now?

A great study of *$trillionaires* can be enjoyed with the name *David Rockefeller, Ph.D.*, again reportedly whose ancestors came from Rockenfeld, Germany. 1) The real Rockefeller boss was older brother Laurance, whose chief operative from 1940 to the late 1960s was the brutally ruthless French Lazards' chief, *Andre Meyer*. 2) With David then in charge, and paying little or no income-excise tax on mind-boggling profits, he followed brother Nelson's lead in reportedly using sharp lawyers, accountants, farm subsidies, tax write-offs and over 2,000 equity trusts, before Nelson died. 3) David and *Goldman Sachs* (controlled by Rothschild) had control of 1913's New York Rockefeller Center.

4) David allegedly has owned a lavish apartment in Moscow since before World War 2 – as did Occidental Petroleum's Dr. Armand Hammer (also a Canaanite?), who likewise stole many of the former Czar's expensive art treasures. 5) David has been chairman of the *Council on Foreign Relations* founded in 1921 by Europe's Jacob Schiff (pushing self-destructive U.S. foreign aid, U.S. bankruptcy and *anti-USA NAFTA's* one nation North America; founder of the infamous *Trilateral Commission*; and has been a high-level *Bilderberger* with his assistant *Henry Kissinger (Heinz Stern)* from Germany, former head of the U.S. National Security Agency (look out!) and U.S. Secretary of State under President Nixon.

6) David is the founder of Chase Manhattan Bank, which with Morgan gobbled up Washington Mutual S&L and more in the 2008+ housing crunch). 7) An example of satanic greed, before secretive sadistic agent Meyer died in 1979, he was appointed as Chase Manhattan Bank's front man; and then bought controlling interest in the Iran Development Bank, while Chase was a private banker to Iran's government. What brilliant cons! With this arrangement, David could set his own terms and approve his own bids; while Iran's treasury lost over one $billion to David.

8) Our post-war Military Government in Japan had to watch the Rockefeller/Rockenfelds' agents like a hawk, including their senior economist *Alden Whitworth (people do change their names)*, whom they planted as General MacArthur's advisor on postwar construction – to

help himself buy up tempting Japanese assets for a penny on the dollar. I was there.

9) The U.S. Constabulary in West Germany had similar problems, with the Rockenfelds' shifty *John McCloy* having far too much reconstruction control. 10) Age 96 Dr. David Rockefeller has used elevators alone for fear of germs and bacteria, but he is also known for boasting that "We are on the verge of a global transformation. All we need is the right major crisis and the nations will accept the *New World Order.*" 11) Reportedly when giving a speech, president *Obama's skills at psychologically snowing his admiring audiences* were taught to him at Occidental College by *Dr. Zbigniew Brzezinski*, under orders from David Rockefeller via trillionaire Rothschilds (you might take a break now with chapter 21 on Obama's thorough investigations).

12) Dr. Rockefeller (Rockenfeld), again in his *2002 Memoirs*, confesses "...Some even believe we are part of a secret cabal working against the best interests of the United States, characterizing my family and me as 'internationalists'...to build a more integrated global political and economic structure – one world...I *stand guilty and I am proud of it.*"

And 13), his relative Nick Rockefeller (Rockenfeld) in 2007 confessed to Hollywood director Aaron Russo about their wealthy world elite's ultimate goals...*financing Gloria Steinem's women's liberation* to add more taxpayers; *reducing world population by at least one half*; and micro chipping the remaining 50% for *total dictatorial control* (sounds like the Revelation 13...right?). 14) The Rockefellers' mother was noted for her pseudo-Christian remarks, but she honored stealing as part of life. 15) *We pray in Jesus' Name for apparent-Canaanites' forgiveness* while they are living, again remembering Matthew 15:22-28's *MERCY FOR THE CANAANITE* mother and daughter.

But how shrewd can Canaanites get – to cause chaos, and then profit while pretending to correct it with another planned chaos? This is exactly what the world wars, the privately-owned 'Fed' and the various U.S. Treasury secretaries' actions have been about, with economic recessions and crises for well over a century – always for a profit to their tribe – with their goal being to gradually break and enslave the once-strong American middle class Citizens financially... and then the remainder.

The 2008 housing bubble, combined with subsequent trillions of dollars in shrewd government "stimulus bailouts" to banks and other corporations and foreign governments that hate us, appear to be exactly such a preplanned con-game, and it worked! The privately-owned Fed's former chairman, Dr. Alan Greenspan, was a key player who reportedly took his orders from the planners in Europe during his various trips there. Present Fed chairman *Dr. Benjamin Bernanke* is reported to follow a similar procedure, gradually aiming the U.S. economy into a train wreck.

The *2008 U.S. housing meltdown* came from then woman-chaser U.S. president *Bill Clinton* when he, Janet *Reno* and homosexual-sodomite U.S. Rep' *Barney Frank* ordered mortgage lenders to lend money even if unsure of the borrowers. You are right now being conditioned for further chaos, with filth like U.S. Senator *Lieberman's enslaving mis-named Patriot Act's* dictatorship, but by Constitutional Law applicable only to federal U.S. Articles 1:17-18 and 4:3:2, including property and persons.

Millions of America's middle class have been destroyed financially in that 2008 orchestrated housing crunch, which led to carefully planned ripple effects. Have you considered the names of people who were in control of that mess? Have you noticed the millions of home foreclosures, as well as how much smaller the average American car is today compared to 20 years ago? These symptoms mirror terrible economic manipulation, with credit card and other debt-spending traps.

As former U.S. Senator *Jacob Javits'* aid, *Harold Rosenthal*, reminded us that *name-changing* has long been used by their distant relatives in this drama, so it is appropriate to review some famous people who have *changed their names*: Victor Borge (Rosenbaum, one of my all-time favorites, hopefully a Hebrew-Jew), Lauren Bacall (Perske), Irving Berlin (Baline), Charles Bronson (Buchinsky), Charlie Chaplin (Israel Thornstein), Tony Curtis (Schwartz), Kirk Douglas (Demsky), Judy Garland (Gumm), Cary Grant (Leach), Lorne Greene (Leibowitz), Judy Holliday (Tuvin), Harry Houdini (Weiss), Michael

Landon (Orowitz), Jerry Lewis (Levitch), Karl Malden (Sekulovitch), Eleanor Parker (Friedlob), Jan Pierce (Perelmuth) and Warner brothers (Goldenberg). These include some wonderful people.

The August 28, 1966 edition of the San Diego Union named descendants of some 70 AD Jerusalem escapees to the land of the *Khazars* as being Alpert, Caplon, Galpern, Halpern, Halperin, Kagan, Kaganovich, Kaplan, Kogan, and Koppel. For the record again, that year Rome's General Titus and his legions destroyed Jerusalem, described by probably Hebrew-Jew historian Josephus as on your Internet.

Our fellow Citizen, Dr. Stan Monteith (D.O.), writer of *Brotherhood of Darkness* (PO Box 969, Soquel, California) recently shared the facts that fewer than 30 percent of American teens found jobs in the summer of 2011; the unemployment rate for Americans age 18 to 29 was nearly 45 percent in 2010, and about six million Americans age 25 to 34 were living with their parents. Now more millions are faced with crushing student loan debts in an economy where they can't find good jobs. Those under age 30 voted for Barack Obama first in 2008 because they believed that he would "change" things for the better. Dr Stan adds that "Americans are starting to wake up...and they are starting to get mad... about it." But Citizens should be cautious about joining mobs, which can be easily infiltrated and then manipulated.

One of the most obvious strategies in all of this would be for many confused Americans to participate in an armed revolution, with Revelation 13:10's warning not to. This apparently would result in a pre-planned, overnight imposition of *martial law with concentration camps* waiting and more. Reportedly millions of patriotic Americans' names are recorded in the Canaanites' records called the *"Quarantine."*

Their *"Noahide Law"* with its sentencing requirements specifying *beheading as in Revelation 20:4,* was passed as an Act of Congress on March 20, 1991 – allegedly without the members reading it! This was like the *mis-named entrapping Patriot Act* mentioned earlier authored by Senator Joseph *Lieberman*; in parallel with so-called Obama healthcare, reproduced in part in our chapter 21. Have you read these? One

45

reason for our urgent book is to help keep you and yours from the planned *"trap,"* of which I warn readers in our Preface. It appears to be coming quickly. The destruction of America's once-strong middle class of *capable Citizens financially, physically, and spiritually* did not happen by accident. For as president Franklin Roosevelt said of politics, **"In politics nothing happens by accident. If it happens, you can bet it was planned that way."** Meanwhile, a majority of D.C.'s House and Senate sadly appears to remain heavily bought and paid for by key campaign donors, often with the tricky U.S. supreme Court protecting the latter.

A recent watered-down 'audit' of the privately-owned Federal Reserve corporation did not scratch the surface of what you have read here. But it did prove that over $16 trillion have been secretly given or loaned by the private Fed to corporations and foreign banks (source: unelected.org). Why has that foreign-owned Fed loaned or given these assets to bail out banks, companies and foreign governments like foreign aid? The Fed's chairman Ben Bernanke says he *does not remember*, like Hillary Clinton!

Also why do visual-only inspections of Fort Knox's supposed gold overlook digging into the real thing? Keeping the status quo guarantees Canaanite control, assuring them of mind-boggling ongoing profits. Consider how Congress and *We the People* could simply read the 1913 *"Federal Reserve Act,"* and see in its *Sections 30 and 31* how that ruinous Fed's group of private banking corporations could be lawfully eliminated – after they *repay America's $trillions with interest, stolen since 1913!*

I honestly believe it was toward this goal that *President John Kennedy* signed his *Executive Order #11110* on June 4, 1963, which *returned power to issue its currency to the U.S. government* without going through the privately-owned "Fed." This order still gives the Treasury power "to issue silver certificates against any silver bullion, silver, or standard silver dollars in the Treasury..." It brought $4,292,893,815 of U.S. Notes into circulation backed by silver, versus Fed Notes backed by nothing. Kennedy also signed a companion order on June 4th that changed the backing of $1 and $2 bills with gold instead of silver.

I do not know how much of this planning was done by his brilliant comptroller of the currency, James Saxon; but with these 1963 orders, Kennedy recalled 1,000 advisors from Vietnam by that Christmas, and the balance of the American troops out by 1965.

These presidential orders would have severely cut into the profit and control of American economics by the Canaanites of Bible prophecy. In this regard he was a real President in action! Five months later on November 22, 1963 President Kennedy was *assassinated*, not unlike Lincoln, and apparently for similar reasons *about satanic Canaanite money-control*.

In case you haven't seen these two presidents' uncanny *COINCIDENCES*, let's take a look at these with Presidents *Abraham Lincoln* (1809-1865) and *John F. Kennedy* (1917-1963): Lincoln was elected in 1860, Kennedy in 1960; both were killed on Friday. Both last names have seven letters. Lincoln's secretary Kennedy warned him not to go to the theater, and Kennedy's secretary Lincoln warned him not to go to Dallas. Booth shot Lincoln in a theater and hid in a warehouse, and Oswald shot Kennedy from a warehouse and hid in a theater. Both were shot in the head, and both had successors named Johnson.

Regarding money, by hook or by crook the Canaanites of Bible prophecy directly or indirectly own or control a majority of this world's tangible assets, including *what was America's Fort Knox gold* – now reportedly just lead bars painted gold. We have a copy of the 1961 audio interview by the Canadian engineer who allegedly headed the theft, with Washington, D.C. attorney Dr. Peter Beter. They agreed that Fort Knox's American gold was shipped under the cover of darkness to New York's Federal Reserve Bank and to Swiss bank vaults, never to be returned. *To find out* if my investigations of this gold are in error, let there be an honest open physical audit by quality independents and find out now! Why not?

Speaking of *gold*, let's add a word to the wise, who find themselves trapped in the coming seven years of "tribulation" and "great tribulation:" *People will need adequate reserves* of water, food, clothing, medicines, bedding, tools and so forth. During the seven years these can be *BARTERED*, shared or used as needed. Also one may use *GOLD AND SILVER* coins for the same purposes. But be fully aware that the Canaanite powers will plan to confiscate all of these. Their commissioned gangs of mercenaries can be expected to raid every American home to get what they want. So if you are going to store any assets, wrap them in oiled cloth for protection, and write down where you bury them about 2'down, out in the countryside! Helping others may fulfill Matthew 25:31-46, right?

The stolen Fort Knox gold was reportedly added to the Canaanites' hoards, hidden in the New York Federal Reserve Bank and in Switzerland, from which they plan to own and control all...supporting their ownership of banking, commodities, communications, education, energy, governments, media, medicine, money, politics, publications, trade, transportation et al. If you did not know and are just learning about this, remember that Canaanite merchants have also owned or controlled America's mass media since around 1900, and they restrict whatever they choose to by cutting off their opponent's advertising and other income.

Pogo, the Vietnam War's mascot, was wrong. The enemy is not us; it is Satan with his filthy (Revelation 22:11) Canaanite seed line as exposed in Bibles. Their guilt was openly admitted to in the January 1928 *Century Magazine*, in which rabbi *Marcus Eli Ravage* wrote about "the real depth of our guilt...we are intruders...disturbers...subverters...we have been at the bottom not merely of the latest great war but of nearly all your wars...brought discord and confusion and frustration...[our] undue influence in churches...schools...laws...governments...thoughts...no conquest in history can remotely compare with this clean sweep of our conquest over you."

By January 1, 1952 this same rabbi *Ravage* had gained prominence, so in Budapest, Hungary, his keynote speech to fellow Canaanite-Jews reminded them that "You have been called here to recapitulate the principle steps of our program...the goal for which we have striven so concertedly for 3,000[+] years is at last within our reach...our race will take its rightful place in the world, with every [Canaanite-]Jew a king and every Gentile a slave...ten thousand years of peace and plenty, the Pax Judaica, and our race will rule undisputed over the earth...*there will be no more religions.*"

With best efforts, my investigations show that originally the word *"Gentile"* came from the Latin word *Gentilis*, and meant any person not where you are. It then had nothing to do with a vague Gentile-Jew interchange. *People in Jerusalem were Gentiles to all people living in Rome*, for example, okay?

As was admitted by U.S. Senator *Jacob Javits'* 29 year-old administrative assistant, *Harold Rosenthal*, in *an interview with Christian editor Walter White*, before the former was assassinated for this disclosure on August 12, 1976 in an Israeli jetliner over Istanbul, Turkey: "We continue to be amazed with the ease by which Christian Americans have fallen into our hands...naive Americans...we have taught them to submit to our every demand...we promote both sides of the issue as confusion reigns [no, I wish that Rosenthal could have read this book!]....

"*ANTI-SEMITISM, there is no such thing*, it is an expression we use effectively as a smear word, to brand anyone who brings criticism against us [Canaanites]... We can accomplish anything with money...we control every media of expression...newspapers, magazines, radio, television, even your music! We censor...before long we will have complete control of your thinking...we took over the publication of all school materials...people are only stupid pigs that grunt and squeal the chants we give them...an unthinking [remember no-think, a-muse-ment] majority.

"Their escape is the opiate of our entertainment [sports etc.] industry... We pretty much control the UN...amazed at the Christians' stupidity, Judaism is not only the teaching of the synagogue, but also the doctrine of every Christian Church in America...through our propaganda the church has become our most avid supporter... their believing the lie that we are the 'chosen people'...the church defends us to the point of destroying their own culture...through religion we have gained complete control of society, government and economics." [Earlier apparent Canaanite-Jew Vladimir Ilyich Lenin had ignorantly confused man-made traditions of Roman Catholicism (see chapter 8) with real Bible Christianity, and him proclaiming that RC tradition is the "opiate of the masses."]

"They never understand that *through democracy we have gained control*...mob-rule which we control through their *churches, our news media and economics institutions.* These religious puppets' stupidity [such as their *entrapping anti-Christ 501.c.3, replacing 508.c.1.A's freedom*] is only exceeded by their cowardice, for they are ruled easily... *our God is Lucifer.*"

Isn't it *time for America's "We the People'"* to know *the proven enemy, to awaken responsibly*, and courageously share what they find to be simple proven truth now? This tunes to the responsible Agape-love that you are asked to have for your neighbor. *You and yours can do it with this little book!*

CHAPTER

6

HORRIBLE HOLOCAUST

Of deep concern to other dedicated investigators worldwide and me have been attested documents about World War II, such as the extensive 1948 International Red Cross World Report at Volume 3, hopefully in your public library. Its written testimony states that not more than 2 million [Hebrew and Canaanite] Jews were interned by the Germans during the war, and that not more than 300,000 people of all ethnic groups died in those camps.

These deaths were from old age, childbirth, spying, as military prisoners, and at the war's end from starvation and diseases such as typhus – with all food, water and medical transportation brought to a halt due to allied saturation bombing. This left countless thousands of prisoners with no drinkable water, food or medicine. Conditions were much like my Japanese interpreter Inatsugu-san's, when he was imprisoned in Chungking, China's concentration camp in 1945. With no help, he contracted the horror of cholera.

Right after WW II my kid sister and I saw a steady flow of media photos, reported as bodies of Germany's concentration camp victims. No mention was made of the thousands who had died from starvation and diseases; only gassing and ovens were promoted. Later it was found that doctored pictures of the camps' victims included some 20,000 Polish officers, who had been murdered far earlier by Russian soldiers in Poland's largest forest. The countless thousands of pitiful people who had died from *typhus* included the famous *Anne Frank*, and we can certainly sympathize with their surviving families!

But incredibly, *no forensic investigation* into the "six million" allegation had ever been done – until 1988 when the world's top forensic expert on execution technologies, *Dr. Fred A. Leuchter*, completed full forensics studies on alleged gassing at the main camps named Auschwitz-Birkenau and Majdanek. His three written forensic reports to the government authorities concluded that "*There were no* execution gas chambers at these locations." Some were built right after the war, for unknown reasons.

Dr. Leuchter's forensics were agreed to by a leading Japanese magazine *Marco Polo*, which concluded that "*There were no* homicidal gas chambers in Nazi Germany" (source: San Diego Union-Tribune of January 25, 1995). These evidences were so complete that the *New York Times* and the *Washington Post* the next day published that WW II Nazi German prisoner deaths had to be "*changed to 1.1 million* [source: see these on the Internet]."

The mass media charged that deadly cyanide "Zyklon B" gas was used by the Germans to murder concentration camp prisoners; however this was reportedly used *to kill gnats* that were spreading the typhus. *Ovens* indeed were used by hospitals in *cremating* deceased patients to stop disease; not including more ovens that were built right after the war maybe for whatever propaganda purposes. The rows and rows of camps' *dead bodies*, which made our Generals Eisenhower and Patton sick, reportedly included these many thousands of the unburied who had died from that lack of water, food and medicine as WW II ended. Investigating which side still now has the most to gain, from the accusers and deniers about the "6 million," it is tough to *prove* who is telling the truth about such things, and exactly which would and could have presented doctored evidence.

Whatever the number was of prisoners killed in WW II Nazi concentration camps, the government of Germany has reportedly paid related *reparations to 3,375,000 Claimant "survivors."* So who had the most to gain by making non-ending charges? And what do you find is the proven truth about this horrible holocaust so far? While the earlier-exposed lying Canaanites of Bible prophecy continue to play their *propaganda* games to enslave mankind, let's consider that the Germans and the International Red Cross are notorious for keeping accurate records, but liars are not. And let's keep investigating for *truth*.

You may have seen the Johns Hopkins University study, published in 1972 by the American Psychiatric Association, which described people that were suffering from a corkscrew deformity in the proteins at the base of their necks. This can produce a *paranoid schizophrenia* that results in thriving on *twisting* the facts. This may or may not relate to the holocaust, and why weird charges have been made.

It might explain the foregoing *mathematically-impossible "six million"* promotion by the media etc., about Hebrew-Jews and Canaanite-Jews alleged to have been murdered in that holocaust. Investigating this figure further, another report indicates that this figure came from World War I, relating to British Arthur Balfour's plan for Israel to occupy Palestine.

Iran's president Mahmoud Ahmadinejad might smile about his mathematics being more accurate apparently with this figure than at least the Canaanite-Jews of Bible prophecy. He may even benefit from an honest look at his Muslim religion in our chapter 8. Let's keep on investigating.

Let's see more proven truth on the "six million:" On February 22, 1948, the *New York Times* published a review of facts confirmed by the American Jewish Committee and the Statistical Bureau of Synagogues of America. That year the number of people professing

Judaism as their religion worldwide numbered *"between 15.6 and 18.7 million."* The 1947 World Almanac on page 219 shows that in 1939 the number of all Jews *worldwide was 15,688,259*, with about 500,000 of them residing in Germany.

So where did the lost "six million" go to? In 1966 the Bonn government cited the 1945 Nuremberg tribunal as reporting *5,731,000 missing Jews worldwide* in 1945. However, authorities only allowed Jews to register between May 8 and December 31, 1945; again with all roads in Germany destroyed by the saturation bombing as WW II was ending. It is interesting that propaganda has produced such bad mathematics, including on concentration camp "survivors;" while ignoring facts such as the later first European Economic Community lady-president was reported killed earlier in a prison camp (!).

It is also interesting that the WW II's *'Anne Frank: The Diary of a Young Girl'* apparently was re-written later by her father with a *ballpoint pen*, after those were made available to the public in 1951. I am deeply sorry that she and many thousands of other helpless concentration camp prisoners died from diseases such as *typhus*, with no clean water, food or medicine, as the war was ending.

CHAPTER

7

THE APPROVED CHURCH

With Inatsugu-san it was too early for me to know the mysteriously *"approved"* Church named in 1 Corinthians 11:18–19, 2 Timothy 2:15, and James 1:12. We found that it mirrors the diligent faith in Christ discussed in 1 John 5:4; it is motivated by Him; it knows what His Blood, the Cross, and the Resurrection are all about; and it knows what is meant by His forgiving Grace as in Ephesians 2:5–13.

From childhood with these, I had searched for which denomination was the one for us to join. One clue was the ancient believers' *"approval,"* seen in Hebrews 11:39–40. Not having been clear to me over the early years, it was delightful to see that for centuries mankind's Bibles had shown this Agape-loving "approved" status for believers, which I never heard in sermons. Meanwhile 1 Corinthians 11:18–19's "factions" or denominations, sad to say, were competing with each other.

When I was a child, someone said that *"a real church is like a hospital, where hurting spirits are healed with Bible studies."* This echoes John 8:31-32's "If you abide in My Word...you will know the truth, and the truth will make you free." This promise seems to be in harmony with Micah 6:8b's "...And what does the Lord require of you but to *do justice*, to *love kindness*, and to *walk humbly with your God?*" I pray that this book will mirror these requirements, in Jesus' solitary Name, amen.

Future timing for our students: I find that the Christ's real church body will be 1) *gone* at the beginning of Ezekiel 39:9's "seven years," in Revelation 20:5b-6's "first resurrection." If among these approved, shortly thereafter you will be 2) *perfected*; you will enjoy His 3) *"marriage supper;"* and will 4) *return* to earth with Him to win the battles of Armageddon and southward. For documentation of these, our being 1) *gone** Biblically is again the Revelation 20:5b-6's "first resurrection" [20:4 relates to 14:11-13's slightly-later tribulation church] tuned to Rev. 3:10a with Luke 21:36; 2) being *perfected* as in I Corinthians 15:50-57; served at the 3) *marriage supper* in Rev. 19:7-9 ; and then 4) we *return** with Him, as prophesied or promised in Zechariah 15:5b, Colossians 3:4, I Thessalonians 3:13 and Jude 14. Again, *in order to return, you have to be gone first, right?*

My interpreter Inatsugu-san and I found that these insights get simpler when people ask (Matthew 7:7) in the Christ Jesus' Name, repent or change the mind and path, and enjoy Romans 6:23: "For the wages of sin is death, but the free gift of God is everlasting life in Christ Jesus our Lord," thankfully. Keys: This repent decision, along with *1 Peter 3:21's "baptism, an appeal to God for a good conscience"* in Jesus' Name, begins the race. Perhaps this *attitude is easier for us rough-and-tumble youth* of Lamentations 3:27: *"It is good for man that he should bear the yoke in his YOUTH."* It is exciting to see so many thousands of cocky *rebellious youth growing up* and taking a responsible look at great learning and *successful living with chapters 15 to 18's proofs of truth.*

We also discussed mankind's future *Judgment* for faithless *"deeds,"* as promised in John 5:29, Matthew 25:31–46, and Revelation 20:11–15. It seems that many of these rare treasures are *ignored or misunderstood in most churches*, as is the Christ Jesus' Revelation and its "book of life."

When Inatsugu-san was a *Buddhist,* many Christians would have erroneously misjudged him as lost forever. But that is not what your Bible promises! *"Forever" is not always permanent or "everlasting,"* as shown in Deuteronomy 15:17's "He shall be your servant forever." Inatsugu-san was growing in the Word, with his smile shining magnificently.

My younger sister Miriam's and our childhood Friend "God-somebody" in chapter one was now being better understood. He chose to give us *unique Freedom* in Galatians 5:1-6: "It was for Freedom that Christ set us free; therefore keep standing firm and do not be subject again to a yoke of *slavery*...You have been severed from Christ, you who are seeking to be justified by Law [Law of Moses]; you have fallen from *Grace.*" You may remember the 14 year-old Middle East *Muslim* girl, Malala Yousafza, who was shot in the head by the Taliban for questioning Islam! *Do you want that shooter's future?*

Over the centuries *Muslim women* have often been treated worse than slaves within their families and religious mosques. The Christ gave His believers *Freedom, along with His Gospel of Good News*, as *millions of Muslims now gladly learn with proofs of truth*. You too might enjoy relaxing with the *Proverbs 31:10-31, honoring our treasured wives.* Please take a look when you can.

For His Biblical Church, and for Hebrew-Jewish Israel, He fulfilled Acts 13:39's humanly-impossible *613 Commandment "Law of Moses,"* as shown also in Romans 8:1-4 and Matthew 5:13–20. The latter's half-breed Canaanite-Jew scribes and Pharisees had no righteous*ness* (faith) in the Christ, although their pureblood ancestor Abraham had plenty, as seen in Genesis 15:6 and Romans 4:3. Let's never confuse this righteous*ness with trying to be righteous (deeds)*. And never confuse those scribes' and Pharisees' future with yours, coming up in chapter 14.

Inatsugu-san and I considered James 2:10's *"For whoever keeps the whole Law and yet stumbles in* one *point, he has become guilty of all."* Putting this another way, if even one tiny point of the Law of Moses is broken, the breaker is *guilty of breaking all* of its 613 command-ments; for the Christ's Almighty Father is *100% Holy, with no compromises except through His Son.* Again as above, the real also-Almighty Christ Jesus *fulfilled every bit of these tough Laws for His believers*, giving Grace, His Good News or Gospel, first to His real Church and then for Israel's real Hebrew-Jews.

But the unbelieving world will instead be Judged 1,000 years later for "deeds" under that Law. With the promised *"Salvation" or "Redemption" back to His "Ancient of Days" Father* – seen with Him in Daniel 7:13–14. The Son of Man overcame death and your enemy Satan; *while never ever lying to anyone.* Is that truth refreshing in this tough Church-building Age, or what?

So He asks us now to *"be proving all things [examine everything thoroughly]*," 1 Thessalonians 5:21. Our thousands of students worldwide will remember this helpful guideline, from attending our fun *"rap and scrap"* studies over many past decades. Along with this are 5:16–20's additional pearls of *"Rejoice always...pray* without ceasing... in everything give *thanks*...do not quench *the Spirit*...do not despise *prophetic utterances."* I love to get up in the morning, open the shades and *say good morning to our God, with thanks*!

SUICIDE despite daily problems will not make the grade for the approved church. Matthew 24:13's promise applies here: "But *the one who endures to the end, he [male/female, Matt. 12:50] shall be saved."*

Some years ago a group of us psychologists and theologians were invited to the Camp Lejeune, North Carolina *"War Games."* The reason was that the Marines and Navy personnel were having too many *divorces, drug cases and suicides* there and around the world. We completed our work in five days, finding the troops eager to listen as we counseled. They agreed that the men and women would be far healthier *mentally, physically and spiritually* if they were provided *at least a weekly solid Bible study* – with the instructors also teaching *proofs of truth as in our chapters 15, 16, 17 and 18).* The latest word from there is that this plan is now being discussed, along with this little book; and if any so-called "separation of church and state" anti-Christs don't like it, our 1st Amendment does allow that, and a U.S. supreme Court chief justice by the name of ('no public school prayer') Earl Warren appears to have been a Canaanite.

Speaking of *SUICIDE*, the great retired NFL professional football linebacker, *Junior Seau*, comes to mind, with his suicide on May 3, 2012. He attended Calvary Chapel Church where we have visited in Oceanside, California; and he lived with his girlfriend Megan Noderer, who reported his death to emergency 911. (The U-T San Diego of 10/24/12 reported more – his gambling, with financial, alcohol and drug problems.) You and I are not qualified to perfectly judge whether Junior's gun accidently discharged, but if it did not, then despite theories his *soul and spirit Biblically now would temporarily* be in Hell, awaiting John 5:29, Matthew 25:31-46 and Revelation 20:11-13's Judgment for his *"deeds"* some 1,000 years from now. Trusting that his name is still written in the Christ's *"book of life,"* as in Revelation 20:12+15, I have no doubt of his future salvation; for *he did plenty of good deeds*, for children, adults and institutions in which he believed.

NEWBORN BABIES dying in childbirth *are also mercifully provided for Biblically*, I find. For instance, Luke 12:48a gives an insight concerning seemingly-innocent people: "But the one who did not know it, and committed deeds worthy of a flogging, *will receive but few [punishments]..."* The unbiblical Roman Catholic philosophy of *purgatory* might be slightly closer to truth than Protestant guesses that all such babies somehow go to heaven, despite what their Bibles teach.

A fine friend in the church globally is *Senior Pastor Noah Hutchings*, with the Southwest Radio Church Ministries in Bethany, Oklahoma. Noah and I have Agape-lovingly exchanged Bible and other insights for years, so of course he is deeply appreciated here. He as well as *Pastor Hal Lindsey* feel that *ALL* Christians will be taken out before earth's coming "great tribulation," which I do not find to be Biblical. *Our job is to help them*, with James 3:1 understood. Likewise a good associate of Noah's has not answered my reply-essay to his article on the *"Trinity,"* which I find simply shows the *Bible's role relationship structure* of the Father, Son and third Holy Spirit, responsibly clarifying Matthew 28:19. He had been parroting the confusing 'glomp theory,' imposed at Nicaea's 334 A.D.'s Council of Nicaea primarily by Egypt's Athanasius. Colossians 2:8's "philosophy" fits that one like a glove.

Thought: Our Creator Christ apparently felt an unmatched Agape-loving responsibility to care for you and us is *another Miracle*, would you agree? And only mankind would blame you for this Son's murder!

Instead, the guilty Biblically were Satan's "hostile to all men" Canaanite-Jews, charged in 1 Thessalonians 2:14b–15, "who both killed the Lord Jesus and the prophets…" They have a big problem.

This fact is unlike what is mis-taught in many philosophy-filled books, and on television, in movies, in music and Roman art. The Christ does not blame you for His murder Biblically. Instead, He says, "Greater [Agape-] love has no one than this, that one lay down his life for his friends," John 15:13. He did it for you, for us, and for all others, even if some won't accept it until the "Great White Throne" Judgment for their human "deeds," Revelation 20:11–12, John 5:29, and Matthew 25:31–46. – with many current unbelievers "…into everlasting life" because of their good deeds and with their names still then written in the "book of life!"

Related to our Dedication page, Christ's Agape-love is one purpose of this book, dedicated to you and all other readers globally, now prior to Matthew 24:21 and Revelation 7:9-14's coming "great tribulation." Do you want to help? Tell your friends about this book, or try to disprove these results of my investigations, if possible; and let us know the results with your own responsible Agape-love, winner…

Our family will remember the many times that Satan and his minions have tried to block these investigations and this writing. On a much higher level, you will probably remember him tempting the Christ Jesus, as in Matthew 4:1–11. If we are tempted by Satan the ancient Devil, James 4:7 can kick in with *"Resist the Devil* [with your prayer petitions in Jesus' Name] and *he will flee from you."* He does!

Sometimes as mentioned it has been necessary to deal with psychological patients who were manic-depressive and suicidal. For them, a few moments again with Matthew 24:13 puts an end to considering suicide from this life: "*But the one [he or she] who endures to the end, he shall be saved.*" When I have occasionally needed to exorcize demons from hurting patients, this simple prayer does the job: "I command you Satan and your demon spirits, in Christ Jesus' Name, come out now and go back where you came from. Go!" It is amazing, they go, every time.

This reminds me of mankind's opposing religious philosophies of chapter eight, with their followers trying desperately to reach upward to their "God" (Satan, Elohim, Genesis 6:4; Theos, 2 Corinthians 4:4) for recognition of their deeds. We found instead that Biblically the proven God/Elohim/Theos Christ/Messiah the Son was conceived by His Father's Holy Spirit with His mother Mary; came down from Heaven (believe it or not!) as a vulnerable baby and paid the severe price for redeeming us for and to His absolutely Holy Father. And He accomplished this work perfectly, thank God.

Again we read Isaiah 53:1–12's prophecies, which Judaism prefers to hide from its followers, let's remember Acts 4:12's "And there is salvation in no one else, for there is no other name under heaven that has been given among men by which we must be saved." We marveled at the simplicity of 1 John 1:9: "If we confess our sins [to the Christ, and/or to His Father, in Jesus' Name, not to priests], He is faithful…to forgive us our sins." Wow!

Over the weeks Inatsugu-san and I wrestled with other insights, such as Romans 14:23b, "*Whatever is not from faith [in Him] is sin;*" and 10:17's "So *faith comes from hearing, and hearing by the Word of Christ,*" as well as 1 John 5:4's "This is the victory that has overcome the world—our faith."

To my earlier question, asking Inatsugu-san "*If you die tonight, will you be forgiven?*" He had not answered directly. A couple of weeks later he told me of having chosen this simple Bible Christianity, because of its proofs of truth (coming up), good news gospel, freedom, grace, hope, its unmatched God the Son doing His God the Father's Will always, and promises of the future that can blow minds (chapters 14 and 21). So we continued studying together, with Agape-love.

Although I had been aware of the term Agape-love, sometimes being slow it took me 30 or so years to discover our third of *four kinds of LOVE*, storgoi (in Koine Greek). You may recognize these primarily four kinds of love: 1) *"eros"*, erotic or passionate; 2) *"philia"* or "phileo," meaning brotherly; 3) the above *"storgoi,"* meaning family—blood runs thicker than water; and 4): considering Luke 11:30–35's Good Samaritan, I define this *Agape love* as *"responsible for one another as needed, without want of reward from man."* I find that this Agape attitude will dominate mankind during the coming 1,000 year reign of the Christ Jesus on this re-made earth, with His "Rod of Iron" Rule, Revelation 19:11-21, 1,000 years after Armageddon's next-to-last war, the later one being in 20:7-10.

We found that the Christ's number one love is Agape, which *fulfills the 613 Commandments* (the accepted count of the Law of Moses) as in Romans 13:8–10 and Galatians 5:14. Acts 13:39 and Romans 8:1-4 also make this fulfillment clear; while again your breaking even one of them makes you guilty of breaking them all.

We relaxed when reading 1 John 5:3, *"His Commandments are not burdensome,"* and appreciated His new "Freedom" as mentioned above. Romans 8:1–4 make it a whole new ball game: "Therefore there is now *no condemnation* for those who are into (full spiritual submersion) Christ Jesus." This goes along with 14:14's "Nothing is unclean in itself; but to him who thinks anything to be unclean, to him it is unclean." Again let's consider *1 Peter 3:21:'s waterless "Baptism now saves you* – not the removal of dirt from the flesh, but *an appeal to God for a good conscience* – through the Resurrection of Jesus Christ." Is that simple freedom or what?

Acts 9:18 shows this freedom being given to the Apostle Paul (Saul). Baptizo is the *total submersion of one's self*, the soul/mind/psyche/id, the physical body, and the spirit for communicating with our Almighty God, Father and the Son, with the #3 Holy Spirit Helper Teacher Comforter given for the church-building Age – and all in 100% unity. I find Biblically that adding water to this simple baptism dedication, as the ancient Babylonians did and as our Christ fulfilled, is a wonderful option.

Conversely, too many vote-seeking politicians have boasted that they are born again. Indeed, the "new birth" in Christ is a "new creation," described well in Colossians 3:10–17. But the requirement in John 3:3–7, which proves to be mathematically perfect, is that *"you must be born from Above."* To be born "again" is then automatic.

CHAPTER
8

BASICS OF COUNTLESS RELIGIONS

My studies continued in a Yokohama college, completing the first year from night school. This included courses in comparing all of mankind's primary competing religions, and later in civilian life earning the doctorate in comparative theology. Let's consider that all religions can have good and bad points, but our goal is to detect proofs of truth. These religions are given with their chronological beginning dates rounded off for simplicity, with all participants responsibly asked to "COME OUT...so that you will not participate in [suffer consequences of] her sins and receive of her plagues," Revelation 18:4. *These insights are not to pick on anybody; but rather are intended to help save valued minds, bodies, and spirits while there is still time*. Be <u>careful not to want your *"ears tickled,"* 2 Timothy 4:3, rather than truth</u>.

1. From its 2000 BC origin came *HINDUISM*'s philosophies
    that somewhat changed from time to time, with its con-
    flicting superstitions of gods and goddesses, once influenced
    substantially by Europe's nomadic Aryans. Its Upanishads
    scriptures show concern for over one million gods and god-
    desses, all headed by the ruler of gods, Indra, the mid-region
    sky god of storms, monsoons, and war. (Maybe this is where
    some atheists' and agnostics' "sky god" fiction comes from.)
    Another of its goddesses is the greatly-feared fang-toothed
    Kali, described in the Samhita Veda scriptures.

    On one of our few foreign assignments, Inatsugu-san
    brought up the Hindu philosophy of creation, read from
    an Indian drape: "Millions upon millions of cycles ago this
    world came to be, several stories high, resting on the backs
    of giant elephants with their tails turned right, standing on
    the back of a massive tortoise, which sits in the coil of a great
    snake. And when these elephants shake themselves, earth-
    quakes occur." We tried to empathize with our Hindu hosts,
    who were fearful of these superstitions.

    But they could provide **NO PROOFS** of truth. Followers
    of this, **COME OUT**, and join the approved while you can,
    Revelation 18:4!

2. Also about 2000 BC, *PRE-CHRISTIANITY* emerged much
    further back than many scholars have estimated. Beginning
    with the faithful Abraham, "El Shaddai," the "God Almighty"
    of Exodus 6:3 appeared to him for mankind. As Creator the
    "He" in Genesis 1:27 is the "God" (Elohim), often seen by
    mankind. Biblically He is God the Son, remembering that no
    man has ever seen His Father.

    This *SEEN GOD* is affirmed in 16:13, Exodus 6:3 again,
    24:10, 33:11, Judges 6:22 and 13:22. The angel (or messen-
    ger) of the Lord was often this same Christ our Creator as in
    John 1:3, Colossians 1:16, and Hebrews 1:8–10. Dedicated
    archaeologists have unearthed details of father Abraham,
    as in public libraries under his name. His fierce Ibiru or

Hebrew tribes, from the southern Euphrates River city of Ur, dated back to about 2000 BC. And what a dedicated "faith" Abraham had in this real Christ!

Speaking of faith, you may have heard about the small American town with seven *competing denominations* or factions of churches. Leaders among its Baptists, Episcopalians, Lutherans, Methodists, Pentecostals, Presbyterians, and Roman Catholics decided that they should have a town meeting to consider dropping their divisive denomination or faction titles, as in I Corinthians 11:19, and just call themselves "Christians." All was well with their meeting until one of the wealthiest men said, "Nope, I've been a Baptist all my life, and I'm not going to change and become a Christian now!" Unfortunately, the majority felt the same way, and stayed stuck. And they are often what others see.

Inatsugu-san and I noted more about God Almighty, El Shaddai the God of Israel, the Anointed, always obedient to His Father's Will, seen in 1,000 B.C.'s Psalm 2:2–12 with more in John 5:30+. Despite Roman and other artists' theories, you may enjoy the *Christ's PHYSICAL description* in part from the Song of Solomon 5:10–15: ruddy complexion, hair black as a raven, cheeks as balsam, hands as gold, and abdomen as ivory. Genesis 49:12 depicts His eyes as darker than wine and His teeth whiter than milk. Not being under the Nazarite vow, His hair would have been above the collar, considering the guideline in 1 Corinthians 11:14-15 "...that *if a man has long hair it is a dishonor to him*, but if a woman has long hair it is a glory to her..."

Those under the *"Nazarite Vow"* were Samson, Samuel and John the Baptist, who were not to drink wine or vinegar, intoxicating liquor, cut their hair or touch a dead body, Numbers 6:1-6, under the Law of Moses. Some others voluntarily gave shorter vows, such as Paul.

Conversely, we noticed different insights of the *UNSEEN God*, the Father of Jesus, shown for example in Exodus 33:20

is "... no man can see me and live!", and again John 1:18 "No one has seen God at any time; the only begotten God... He has explained Him." Colossians 1:13–15 shows, "Of His beloved Son...He is the image of the invisible God, the first-born of all Creation." And I Timothy 6:16 promises "Who alone...dwells in unapproachable light, Whom no man has seen or can see."

These descriptions clearly conflict with the frustrated Mormon founder Joseph Smith's claim that he had seen both the Father and the Son. Unlike man-made religions with no proofs, some of the Christ Jesus' hundreds of Proofs of Truth will be shared with you in chapters 15, 16, 17 and 18. My yearnings for such proofs began at least by age 12, and now were beginning to be answered.

I discovered that throughout recorded history most of mankind has had a built-in desire to worship "God-somebody," but exactly who they would worship was the big question. A great obstacle to finding this simple, 'narrow Way' of Matthew 7:13–14 was the admixture of Roman, Babylonian and barbarian or pagan philosophies melded with half-truths, apostasy detours, religious fictions and Biblical Truths. The real Christ came down from Heaven for Abraham, Moses, you, us, and billions of others who wallowed in relative-darkness – thank God. He is doing His job, and it is your and our turn now to help. You can practice spreading His Word and Good News, while there is still time. Happy to help...

3. 600 BC *ZOROASTER*'s Zend-Avesta scriptures showed belief in a one-god Ahura Mazda (not the car), an afterlife and a moral, natural order in the universal struggle between good spirit Ormazd and bad spirit Ahreman. Followers were savagely forced to accept Islam's traps, but in both there are NO PROOFS of truth. COME OUT, and join with the approved before it is too late!

4. 500 BC *CONFUCIUS* taught politics, devotion to parents and family, ancestor worship, formal behavior and courteous

principles for justice and peace, but there are NO PROOFS of truth. COME OUT!

5.	500 BC Gautama *BUDDHA* was another religion that Inatsugu-san and I enjoyed studying, of a prince-turned-pauper. Buddha did not believe in "God-anybody," but guessed that right thinking and self-denial would produce a nirvana release from misdirected passions, desires, pain and sorrow, and would provide eternal rest. However, again there are NO PROOFS of truth. COME OUT and join with the approved in time!

6.	In 500 BC China, half-man P'an Ku created the *TAOIST* theories. Over the course of 18,000 years, he separated heaven from earth, formed mountains and valleys, and as he died his sweat became rain and insects that stuck to his body became a mortal man. Again, there are NO PROOFS of truth. COME OUT!

7.	In Israel 500 BC, *JUDAISM* developed as a mix of the voluminous Babylonian Talmud's philosophies along with the Bible's first five books of Genesis through Deuteronomy, the Torah, plus at times parts of the 39-book Old Testament Bible, firmly excluding Isaiah 53:1-12. My investigations show that when the Israelites were enslaved by Babylon in 606 BC, and released in 536 BC after 70 years of captivity, they returned to Jerusalem as a mixture of both Hebrew-Jews and Canaanite-Jews.

They were accompanied by *Judaism's Babylonian priesthood* with the oral tradition, exposed in Isaiah 28:14–15: "Therefore, hear the Word of the Lord, O scoffers who rule this people who are in Jerusalem, because you have said 'We have made a covenant with death, and with Sheol [Hell, Hades] we have made a pact, the overwhelming scourge [great tribulation?] will not reach us when it passes by, for we have made falsehood our refuge and we have concealed ourselves with deception.'"

And Isaiah 29:15–16 says, "Woe to those who deeply hide their plans from the Lord, and whose deeds are done in a dark place, and they say, 'Who sees us?' or 'Who knows us?' You turn things around! Shall the Potter be considered as equal to the clay, that what is made [created] would say to its Maker, 'He did not make me;' or what is formed say to Him who formed it, 'He has no understanding?'" To me, that is maximally-stupid, trying to do battle against the now-proven Creator Christ, and thus His Father!

Voluminous *Babylonian Talmud* texts are the spiritual guide for its followers, without which Judaism and its Pharisees would have a difficult time existing. Rabbis in their synagogues have to study and work with it. President Truman, as a 33rd-degree Freemason (at which level the spokesman leads the group in denying the Christ Jesus), reportedly was given a set of the Talmud when he agreed to the bombing of Hiroshima and Nagasaki. But he felt double-crossed by these backers, according to his personal diary of July 21, 1947 with: "The Jews [Canaanite?] I find are very selfish...when they have power, physical or political, neither Hitler nor Stalin has anything on them for cruelty or mistreatment to the underdog."

Here are some of the Talmud's Hamitic-Canaanite-Jew mis-teachings, which are allegedly taught in preparation for their so-called "Pax Judaica's" 10,000 years of peace and plenty (meaning their merciless world dictatorship):

1. "Five things has *CANAAN* recommended to his sons, 'When you go to war, do not go first...love each other, love the robbery, hate your masters, and never tell the truth'" (Pesachim, F. 113B).

2. "A [Canaanite?-] Jew may do to a non-Jewess what he can so...he may treat her as a piece of meat" (Choszen Hamiszpat, 348).

3. "Jehovah created the non-Jew in human form so that the Jew would not have to be served by beasts" (Midrasch Talpioth, p. 225–L). These predators also teach that Jesus is a liar and Mary a whore!

4. "A Gentile girl who is three years old can be violated [by deranged minds?]," (Aboda Sarah, 37a).
5. "A [Canaanite?-] Jew is permitted to rape, cheat, and perjure himself, but he must take care that he is not found out" (Choszen Hamiszpat, 348).
6. "If a [Canaanite?-] Jew is able to deceive them by pretending he is a worshipper of the stars [who does that?], he may do so" (Iore Dea, 157; 2 Hagah).
7. "The [Canaanite?-] Jews are human beings, but the nations of the world are not human...but beasts" (Baba Meca, 11, 6).
8. "A [Canaanite?-] Jew should and must make a false oath when a Goyim [Goy, Gentile] asks if our books contain anything against them" (Szaaloth Uts-zabot, Jore Dia, 17).
9. "Our vows shall be no vows, and our oaths no oaths at all" [in the annual Yom Kippur's Kol Nidre chant], (Schulchan Aruch, Edit. 1, 136).
10. "The teachings of the Talmud stand above all other laws, they are more important than the laws of Moses" (Rabbis Ismael and Chamar).
11. "Jehovah Himself studies the Talmud standing; He has such respect for that book" (Tract Mechilla).

Overuse of the word *"must,"* and flailing of their *hands* when speaking, often mirror the Canaanite-Jew seed line's deeds for which they shall be Judged by the real Christ. They cannot lose these traits any more than a tiger can lose its stripes. President Richard Nixon's Secretary of State, Dr. Henry Kissinger (aka Heinz Stern, David Rockefeller or Rockenfeld's import from Germany) is a good example of these traits. Speaking of Nixon, you may have heard his tape recording of discussions with Evangelist Billy Graham (honorary Dr.) on this topic of what I have found Biblically to be Canaanite-Jews.

These traits are further exposed in 1500 A.D.'s Martin Luther's Biblisches Spruch U. Schatz-Kastlein's: "Squeezing from us our money and goods...lying, blaspheming and cursing...in the *Three Fables of Aesop* there is more wisdom to be found than in all the books of the Talmudists and rabbis." Henry Ford's 1921 *The International Jew* added, "The [C]-Jews are not the chosen people, though practically the entire church has succumbed to the propaganda that declares them to be so!" Given the above-mentioned examples of man-made Talmudic satanics, believers' teachers (James 3:1) and followers may pay dearly for their deeds about a thousand years from now as in Revelation 20:11–15's "great white throne" Judgment for "deeds"...unless they first repent and are baptized. COME OUT!

You may have noticed the results of the Canaanite-Jews' 70 AD infiltration of Italy, gradually dominating northern-Italy's once-blond people, along with their infiltration of European royal families. My investigations of these are quite thorough. This in itself is a study in shrewd Canaanite-Jews' art. Their dreamed-of *Protocols'* "king" may soon be the abominable "Antichrist," before he double-crosses them, finds himself alone as in Daniel 11:45, and then is physically overcome by the Creator Christ south of Armageddon as He goes through Jerusalem and on into Jordan/Edom to free Petra's Hebrew-Jews.

These facts in part may help explain why U.S. Senator Jacob Javits' administrative assistant, Harold W. Rosenthal, was assassinated in an Israeli jet at Istanbul, Turkey in 1976. The reason was that he confirmed many secret (Canaanite?) details to Christian editor Walter White, quoted earlier here, which ends with "...our God is Lucifer" (Satan). The Canaanite-Jews' "Antichrist" will be doing his own thing, with some signs and wonders, but there are NO PROOFS of enduring truth. Never confuse satanic wonders for truth. Followers of those satanics are asked to COME OUT and join with the approved now!

8. *ROMAN CATHOLICISM's* 325 A.D. Nicene Council decisions replaced parts of simple Biblical Christianity when

Egypt's Athanasius reportedly vocally overwhelmed Antioch's elderly leader Arius, and selling his unbiblical co-equal co-eternal three-way all-the-same God-somebody glomp philosophy – with lots of Babylonian baggage. My records show that, prior to this, allegedly Athanasius had been ex-communicated five times from the Egyptian church. Roman priests write about it being impossible to understand this religious confusion, which may have led to the superb *Mother Teresa's* terrifying problems that she admitted in writing before her death.

Roman Catholic beliefs appear to be a mix of philosophy from ancient Babylon, some facts from the Bible, and many man-made fictions as we will prove. For examples, the pope's carp-mouth hat, or miter, is a tribute to the Babylonian god Dagon (source: the Encyclopedia Britannica). And you will probably know Matthew 23:9's "Do not call anyone on earth your father [religiously]," but they do so anyway, as do some of their offspring protestant factions.

Here are some of many Roman Catholic *precepts* that are not Biblical, including the "priests" title imposed in 200 AD; prayers for the dead, and making the sign of the cross by 300 AD; Roman Emperor Constantine (280-337 AD, baptized by Arius in 324) and his mother Helena wanted all people to be Roman Catholic, although they could keep their pagan beliefs. Mass became a daily ritual in 394, exaltation of Mary was imposed in 431, priests' special clothing came in 500, extreme unction/526, purgatory/593, prayers to Mary/600, first pope, papa/[father versus Matthew 23:9]/610 AD], veneration of relics and holy water/786 AD. The 'mother nature' fits with these dogmas somewhere. There are more:

The college of cardinals was begun in 927 AD, canonization of the dead/995, Friday fasting/998, priests' celibacy/1079, pagan rosary/1090, satanic inquisition/1184, indulgence sales/1190, seven sacraments/1200, transubstantiation mass re-killing of Christ daily, and the confession to priests/1215, the wafer/1220, Bible forbidden to laymen/1229 by the Council of Valencia, purgatory made a dogma/1439, church tradition equal to Bible authority/from their 1545+ A.D. Council of Trent, at which time the Bible was also canonized (thank you!), and the official creed replaced the [non-] Apostles' creed/1560.

The immaculate conception of Mary was promoted next/1854, condemnation of freedom of conscience, of speech, the press, and scientific discoveries then was imposed by the church/1864, assumption of Mary/1950, and Mary was proclaimed mother of the church/1965. The Vatican's respected seer-priest Malachy predicted in 1130 A.D. that the next pope to come after the 111th one, the present pope Benedict, will be Revelation 13's false prophet with Antichrist (sources: ex-RC priests Dr. Bart Brewer in California, and Mountain in Minnesota, etc.).

Meanwhile far too many Protestant (pro-Testament) beliefs, half-truths, precepts and traditions are copied from the above Roman Catholic fictions, beginning with the Anglican/Episcopal basics. Here again I see no enduring PROOFS of truth. COME OUT, and join with the approved while there is time!

9.   Japan's 400 AD, *SHINTO* religion was guessed to be a way to higher spirits or gods, such as the storm god and sun goddess. It involved worship of ancestors who were Ainu people originating from Malaya, Mongolia, Korea, Siberia, and South Pacific lands and islands. With such superstitions held until 1945, it was believed that the emperor was descended from the sun. 500 A.D.'s Korean and Chinese Buddhism had brought it literature, art, and ritual, as well as logic, medicine, and social service. This was chronicled from 620-806 AD in the Kujiki and Kogoshui gleanings. But again, there are NO PROOFS of truth. COME OUT! Join the approved while you can!

10. 600 AD *ISLAM* (to mean submission to God's will) began infiltrating America big time after President Lyndon John-

son's quiet 1960 directive ordered open American doors for more aliens including Muslims to pour in, with little or no opposition or media notice. It is bad enough that D.C. politicians and bureaucrats with lobbyists have unlawfully left America's borders open to both legal and over 12 million illegal aliens...in exchange for their illegal votes. But America is now dangerously infiltrated by these often-nice Muslim/ Moslem (meaning traitor) believers, with their Shiite and Sunni conflicts, their clergy's shari'a law, their dhimmitude program to systematically control the USA, and their jihad all-out war, each using their clever cordoba procedures.

Good or bad, their loyalty is to an orphaned Arabian camel-driving illiterate businessman, who gained wealth and time by marrying his cousin Khadija. His name was Mohammed ibn Abdullah ibn Abdelmottalib ibn Hashim (570–632 AD). After marrying Khadija his life became one of leisure, with time to question Christian and Jewish travelers and to refine his moon-God Allah-philosophy of love that brought very few followers. He then changed his *"LOVE"* idea to *"JIHAD"* warfare, enticing hopeless males by writing about dreams of a fictional paradise and 72 dark-eyed virgins per warrior dying for his cause. And so it is sadly today; with his human "suicide bombers" destructively wallowing in man-made ignorance. Let's remember that Satan is the deceiving "God" [Elohim] of Genesis 6:4 and "God [Theos] of this world," 2 Corinthians 4:4.

The Muslim philosophies evolved from this self-proclaimed prophet, while today his polygamist Muslim couples (up to four wives per male) compete with illegal aliens and rabbits in producing babies. Incredibly charismatic president Barack Hussein *Obama allegedly admitted on a video we have that he is a Muslim*, and on his third finger the ring that he wears is Muslim. He also hints that he is sort of a Christian (doubtful, you shall know them by their fruit!), among the four levels warned of in Mark 4:15-19.

In accord with his Columbia University training, he reportedly was also taught at Occidental College by Dr. Zbigniew Brzezinski in dialectic mob psychology etc. Add to this the pro-Black prejudices of Jesse Jackson, Al Sharpton and Maxine Waters; two decades of brainwashing by Obama's hate-America pastor Dr. Jeremiah Wright; more brain-washing by Chicago's political machine; plus that of communist Saul Alinsky (*"Rules for Radicals,"* demonizing anyone who disagrees, an Obama favorite tactic); and more from Tony Rezko (now in jail), would have left Obama and his wife with some weird theories such as *misthinking that everybody has the same God.* Also-Black General Colin Powell, formerly of the Joint Chiefs of Staff etc., has the same ludicrous theological conclusion with NO PROOF. Reportedly when Obamas went on vacation their dog Bo flew in a smaller jet, but that could have been because their B-47 was too huge for Bo's small airport.

IRAN apparently is now the most threatening of Muslim nations, with its anti-Israel president Mahmoud Ahmadinejad's fundamentalist's goal being to provoke a nuclear war...to usher in the 'second coming' of ancient Persia's Shiite "Hidden Imam," to supposedly reveal obscure secrets of the Quran, and to restore ancient Persia's Shiite Islam religion worldwide. They teach that their Hidden Imam was five year-old Muhammad ibnal-hasan al-Mahdi, the 12ᵗʰ Imam, who vanished into a well in 941 A.D. But they provide NO PROOFS!

Barack Obama's alleged double-religion is as impossible as the duo-philosophy called "Chrislam" (Christian-Islam), reminding me of the latter-day apostasy warned of in I Timothy 4:1, 2 Timothy 3:1–7 and 2 Thessalonians 2:3-12. Despite modern Islamic mullahs' propaganda, nowhere did Mohammed Hashim write that *Jerusalem* belongs to Islam, or that he even mentioned that car-honking loud but wonderful city. His so-called shrine of Medina seems to be legitimate, even though he had been evicted from there before he enshrined it for himself. You probably know of the mostly-Roman Catholic crusades to recapture the Holy Land, as man preys upon man in the name of so-called 'Christianity' ad nauseam.

Later by 1856 A.D. Muslim *SLAVE TRADERS* were capturing whole villages in France, Italy, Greece, and Spain, taking white slaves to serve in Arab harems and fields. Angry Muslims still can't understand that their ancestors started the anti-West war with their *piracy on neutral seas*, feeling that those waters belong to them alone. The U.S. Navy and Marines answered in the Mediterranean, from which comes the Marines' Hymn "…to the shores of Tripoli."

You may also remember the 2006 Muslim riots in Denmark over an offensive anti-Muslim *cartoon*. But you may not know that the cartoon was commissioned and published by Flemming Rose, a Jewish colleague of Jewish artist Daniel Pipes who drew the cartoon. Pipes is a Polish descendant of Professor Richard Pipes, a Middle East analyst for CNN.

The *Muslim Brotherhood* was reportedly formed and financed by England during World War II, to help overcome the German forces in Africa; and after the war the rights to it were sold to the U.S. government, which has financed it for years. It is important to note that the Muslims' Islam, with its merciless al-Qaeda leaders and trained Taliban guerillas globally, provides NO PROOFS of truth either. COME OUT, and join with the "approved" while you have time!

11. 1500's A.D. *SIKHISM,* developed in northern Asia as a mixture of Hindu and Muslim philosophies, with beliefs in one god; rejection of the old Indo-Aryan caste system, idolatry and ritual; and for inward moral sincerity. Again, this has NO PROOFS of truth. "COME OUT!" Join with the "approved" while you still can, before it is too late.

12. *OCCULTS, SECRET CULTS and SECTS* by the thousands worldwide are probably not limited to 1 John 3:10's "chil-

dren of the Devil," but many appear to be descendants of Satan's children. Of occults, you are probably familiar with the black and white magic sorcerers, such as pagan nature-worshipping Wicca (Wiccan) followers. These are not to be confused with the more thoughtful American Indian tribes – who will also miss the Revelation 20:5b-6's "first resurrection" unless they qualify with the "approved" with (Romans 8:1-4) the Jesus Christ/Messiah and His Romans 8:1-4 walk.

The foregoing Devil's children were apparently founders in the 1776 AD Warsaw, Poland Canaanite-Jew's first "*Illuminati*" meeting, chaired by journalist Adam Weishapt. In 1910 their relatives met on Jekyll Island, off Georgia State, and planned the unconstitutional privately-owned 1913 Federal Reserve Act to control money and interest throughout America. Then in the 1920s their *Council on Foreign Relations,* instrumental in infiltrating the U.S. Government, was founded by Europe's Jacob Schiff with Paul Warburg, followed by David Rockefeller/Rockenfeld's *Bilderbergers* and *Trilateral Commission* interacting with the top level of *Freemasonry*, each smacking of treason.

Trilateral Commission founder David Rockefeller's (Rockenfeld) *Memoirs*, mentioned previously, leave no doubt that he and his clans are *one-world-government traitors to America.* Apparently of Satan's Canaanite-Jew seed line, their 4,000+ year-old goal is merciless world dictatorship, and they are right on schedule. This reminds me of Matthew 4:1–11's conceit by their lying boss. I define such conceit as "confidence without enduring power," but have often wondered why Dr. David Rockefeller (Ph.D.) and Occidental Petroleum's chairman Dr. Armand Hammer (Ph.D.) owned apartments in Moscow throughout World War II, with some of Russia's most-prized art collections, and now we know. They will apparently get theirs in the real Christ's perfect Judgment for "deeds," as in Revelation 20:11-15, 1,000 years in the future. This can possibly be with you helping to judge, as in 1 Corinthians 6:2–3 with Revelation 2:9 and 3:9.

13. *JEHOVAH'S WITNESSES* often have fine work ethics; but may be well-meaning semi-Bible people using their *New World Translation*, who can be unwittingly using II Corinthians 11:4's "another Jesus." Following dedicated Brooklyn, New York theologians with whom I have worked, they are supposed to believe that their John 1:1b's "a god" Jesus is not Theos/"God" the Son, nor 1:3's Creator (with Colossians 1:16 and Hebrews 1:8-10). Reportedly they believe that since 1914 He has been in some atmospheric apartment, trying to figure out who among their faction's humans are doing what, why, how, where and when, with their 144,000 priesthood. Their worst error is in finding Jesus' Father to be the only "Jehovah," with the real Creator Christ Jesus placed far lower (sources: their publications, Brooklyn's JW theologian Dr. Savage, and earlier friend Dr. Leograndis among their 144,000). How man-made can they be?

14. *MORMONS* generally are also hard-working well-meaning family people, who tend to miss Matthew 7:14's narrow way. Allegedly its founder *Joseph Smith* claimed to have seen both Jesus' Father and the Son, in direct opposition to Exodus 33:20, John 1:18 and I Timothy 6:16. He was excommunicated from Freemasonry for stealing its signs, rituals, grips and symbols for his Mormonism. The Mormon Doctrines & Covenants have required over 2,000 changes since Joseph first wrote or copied them in 1829.

Reportedly Mormons are taught to believe that 'God the Father' has many wives and more spiritual children, male and female, each of whom will someday become a 'god' over his/her own 'star-planet.' And Biblically their using the Hebrews 7:11 Mosaic Law's order of Aaron is directly opposed to the real Almighty Christ's Order of Melchizedek in 7:17. Being of high interest, it is worth mentioning the 2012 U.S. presidential race. I agree that Mormon Mitt Romney and potential-Muslim Kenyan Barack Obama know similar wealthy potential-Canaanites of Bible prophecy for political and social gain. To better guide America, I honestly believe that Romney should have won the 11/6/12 presidential election (please see "Obama" exposed late in our chapter 21).

With Utah State populated by 70% Mormons, their *SUICIDES* are real concerns. Female suicides there especially appear to be from *lack of personal accomplishment* and from too many children not unlike the Muslims. Their male suicides tend to be from Mormon *doctrinal requirements of perfection*, having to be perfect in this life's priesthood or else they cannot get to their planet-heaven.

Acutely aware that all of us humans need *security, variety, recognition and response*, participants in the magnificent *Mormon Tabernacle Choir* satisfy some of these needs, and the young men get fulfillment with required *missionary efforts*. But is there much *accomplishment* enjoyed by the remaining Mormons? (Sources: Utah Department of Health, lifeafter.org, Mormon Bishop Phelps, Dr. Cheeseman, Investigator Texe Marrs, *Book of Mormon, Doctrines & Covenants*). In deviating from the original mathematically-perfect 66-book Bible, the *Book of Mormon* etc. detour from it with NO PROOFS of everlasting truth (see our chapters 15 through 18). "COME OUT!" Join with the "approved" in time!

Unlike man-made religious speculations with no real proofs of truth, we share with you many of our Creator Christ Jesus' hundreds of Proofs of Truth in chapters 15, 16, 17 and 18. My yearnings for such proofs began by at least age 12, gradually being answered in full over these many exciting years.

Again, *these insights are not to pick on anybody, but rather are intended to help save valued minds, bodies and spirits while there is still time.* Are you "OUT? Are your best friends? Revelation 18:4 warns, "Come out of her, my people, so that you will not participate in her sins and receive of her plagues."

To our next investigation topic, *SLAVE SHIPS* of 1661-1774's America are another mysterious topic for our investigations here.

Slave trading was forbidden by Christian Colonial Law, until persuasive slavery petitions by immigrant merchants from Holland – Wooman, Sandiford, Benezet, and Solomon – promoted that merciless satanic money-making filth.

A few years earlier, sample families of West Indies and American Indians were found to be too lazy for brutal slavery, so they were gradually replaced by getting African tribal chiefs addicted to cheap rum. Taking advantage of their drunkenness, whole villages could then be ravaged. Black slaves could be sold for huge profits, up to $40,000 for a healthy black male. The ocean voyages were terrifying, with these slaves chained to the decks or below the decks of the ships all the way. Documents at Pittsburgh, Pennsylvania's Carnegie Institute and Washington, D.C. show that the wealthiest slave ship owners were:

Moses Levy, owned slave ships "Nassau," "Four Sisters," and also "Abigail" with

Aaron Lopez and Jacob Franks.

Isaac Levy and Nathan Simpson owned "Crown."

Justus Bosch and John Abrams owned "Anne" and "Eliza."

Henry Cruger and Jacob Phoenix owned "Prudent Betty."

Nathan Marston and Abram Lyell owned "Antigua."

William DeWoolf owned "Betsy."

James DeWoolf owned "Polly."

John Rosevelt (grandfather Claus Rosenvelt/Roosevelt owned China's opium trade!) and Jacob Rosevelt owned "Expedition."

Jan De Sweets owned "White Horse".

Sam Levey owned "Caracoa" together with #1 Moses Levy and #3 Jacob Franks.

These are the main slave ship owners, making me wonder what they are doing now, if they didn't repent or change their minds and pathways in time and COME OUT!

"False prophets" also have been necessary to investigate, as seen from pulpits and television screens with their soothing "give"-"give," voices begging for *money*. One insight about this has been Deuteronomy 18:22's "When a prophet speaks in the Name of the Lord [Father and/or Son], if the thing does not come about or come

true, that is the thing which the Lord has not spoken. The prophet has spoken it presumptuously." Matthew 7:15-20 and 24:11 leave no doubt concerning these slick con artists. God willing, this little book can help straighten out the pathways of many false prophets.

Speaking of them, again President Franklin Delano Roosevelt/ Rosevelt taught two main ideas: (a) Own real estate, they're not making it anymore (this may prove to be wrong because it is not portable when barter is necessary); and (b) nothing in politics happens by accident; if it happens, it was planned that way. As an insider, he should have known.

Still investigating and studying with my interpreter Inatsugusan, we found that Bible Christianity has no command for *tithing*, which was Old Testament law for Israel's survival. Instead, we found that our Almighty God, Father with Son, own 100% of all things everywhere, and the Son delegates some talents to us in order to see what we will voluntarily do with them. These for example are His unequalled Good News/Gospel, His unique Proofs of Truth as shared in this book, His miraculous Prophecies likewise, and their future with you as in the Revelation 21:22 and 22:1+3+5+ to Their Honor and Glory.

Isn't that relaxing? Also, when we honor the Son, we automatically honor His Father, with the third Holy Spirit Paraclete always in perfect Unity, as Matthew 28:19's threesome and *non-co-equal Trinity*. What an Almighty Team to love, to enjoy, to appreciate, and to thank in Jesus' Name through this unique church-building age.

We chalked up the man-made religions as being more of Colossians 2:8's sometimes well-meaning but dangerous "philosophy," failures going you know where. Then we compared those in chapter eight with 2 Timothy 3:16:'s "All Scripture is inspired by God [that is, God breathed] and profitable for teaching, for reproof, for correction, for training in righteous*ness* [meaning *faithfulness*]."

By now you may know that this righteous*ness*, as in Genesis 15:6 and Romans 4:3, has a far different meaning than the word "*righteous*," which relates to "*deeds*" as in 3:10–12, 1 Peter 4:18 and the Revelation 20:12's future Judgment thereof. Furthermore Proverbs

30:5–6's "every word of God is tested" (and originally was mathematically-perfect), providing more insight, as does Revelation 22:18–19's warning, "…if anyone adds to them… [or] takes away from the words of the book of this prophecy, God will take away his part from the tree of life and from the holy city, which are written in this book…"

Isn't it great to be *forgiven* for being imperfect mistake-making people in this fleeting life, due to the real Christ's love and work to set us *free?*!

CHAPTER

9

OUR FRIEND "GOD-SOMEBODY"

While using the patient process of elimination in disproving the most-known man-made religions, I was also guided to investigate detouring religious "philosophy" as part of Matthew 7:13's deadly "broad way," also warned of in Colossians 2:8.

These investigations are a reminder that there are three named as "God" (OT Elohim and NT Theos) in Bibles. Of the definitions among Jesus' Semitic people, spirits that possessed a high degree of power or dynamism were given the singular name *"El" or the plural name "Elim" or "Elohim,"* applicable at times to both major and minor divinities alike and also applied to demons. Watch out for the latter's bad-"God" number three, exposed below, and people who say that they "believe in God"-anybody.

#1 is the Invisible Almighty Yahweh Lord and God, the Christ's Father, Whose "face" has always been *UNSEEN* by man (John 1:18,

Colossians 1:15, 1 Timothy 6:16, I John 4:12 and Exodus 33:20 (note the "Rock" for refuge). He has delegated all authority except Himself (as below) to His also-Almighty Yahweh Lord God the Son, the Anointed Christ, with the two shown together in Daniel 7:13 as the "Ancient of Days" and "Son of Man," among other Word-pictures in *a perfect Role Relationship*.

We see that in 1 Corinthians 15:27–28: "[The Father] *He is excepted* Who put all things in subjection to Him [the Son]. When all things are subjected to Him, then the Son Himself also will be subjected to the One Who subjected all things to Him." *So much for apostasy's man-made "co-equal" confusion*. You now can see how this Role Relationship gets the job done, and you can understand John 9:31's "God [Christ's Father] does not hear sinners," because He is 100% "Holy." He delegated that miraculous job of interceding for us to His always-obedient Son, our real Christ Jesus.

These insights make it easier to understand Who are meant by the "Us" in Genesis 1:26 and 11:7. Again the Father has never been seen by mortal man. *He is "greater" than His Son,* John 14:28, and indeed He is also with the "Lamb" in Revelation 22:1–3. Their Almighty relationship is also Word-pictured in John 3:16's "God so loved the world that He gave His only begotten Son, that whoever believes in Him shall not perish, but have *everlasting life*." You are not expected to look up or memorize these jewels of knowledge, understanding and wisdom…except when you want to.

#2 is this same "Son of Man," the Biblical God Who was often *SEEN* by mankind, as Genesis 16:10–13's "angel of the Lord" or Messenger of the Lord (17:1, 32:30, 35:19); seen by man in Exodus 3:6, 6:3, 24:10, 33:11, Judges 6:22 and 13:22. Are these enough? He was first seen as the Messiah, the Masoretic Hebrew word "Mashiyach" (see Strong's Concordance at #4899), or the Koine Greek word "Christos" or Christ at #5547). He would have enjoyed the 1,000 B.C. Psalm 2:2 and 2:7's Anointing, with 2:12's warning 1,000 B.C: "Do homage to the Son…take refuge in Him!" What a privilege it is to do so.

He is also our "God" with "God," Elohim with Elohim, as in Psalm 45:6–7, Theos with Theos in Hebrews 1:8–10, "Lord" with "the Lord," and *YHWH*/Adonai with *YHWH*/Adonai in Psalm 110:1, Isaiah 44:6–7, Zechariah 10:12 (and Matthew 22:44). This Role Relationship is so simple that it may be far easier for Matthew 18:2–10's "children" to grasp, than Matt. 11:25's "wise and intellectual."

Also mankind's ultimate Judge is this Son (John 5:22–30), Whose Name we are required to go through to reach His Father. Is that so difficult? His faith-filled followers or disciples of John 8:31-32 are not in that Judgment as promised in 5:24. When we pray *"The Lord's Prayer"* from Matthew 6:9–13, let's remember that Jesus is also called our *"Father"* in Isaiah 9:6–7, for He is the Father of His Church, while always voluntarily subject and obedient in turn to His "Ancient of Days" Father.

We found the Son too in Titus 2:13's "...Blessed Hope and the appearing of the Glory of our great God and Savior, Christ Jesus." Inatsugu-san was spiritually very hungry, as he kept us digging, gaining new insights, and getting us to Titus 1:1b's status: "...the faith of those chosen of God and the knowledge of the truth which is according to revering well." We found Romans 8:15's *"Abba"* or *Daddy* can be applied to Both.

Again we were reminded that "...there is *Salvation* in no one else; for there is *no other name* under heaven that has been given among men, by which we must be saved," Acts 4:12. This is why we can be Matthew 18:3-4's humble "children," praying in our Creator Christ Jesus' Name for His Almighty powerful results! Here is Romans 5:1's "peace" from His Gospel or Good News of Salvation and the promise of being redeemed back to His Father. It will happen. But this earth will not enjoy enduring "peace" (Luke 12:51, Ezekiel 13:16), until He takes command over His enemies for everlasting truth.

This is true and meanwhile Isaiah 28:11–13 promises that His Word is given as in a mystery" – "...*a little here, a little there*" – prayerfully with daily digging. Also this is why Proverbs 25:2 applies so well, "It is the glory of God to conceal a matter, but the glory of kings is to search out a matter;" as with 8:17's "I love those who love me; and those who diligently seek me will find me." Acts 17:11's Bereans were like this, "These were the more noble-minded...for they received the Word with great eagerness, *examining the Scriptures daily*, to see whether these things were so."

Considering earth's estimated 10 or more billion of earth's people who have died, and the present living population of over 7 billion, this totals to at least 17 billion people, of course. Applied to Matthew 7:13–14's "... the Way is narrow that leads to Life, and there are *few* [relatively] who find it;" would these few mean that millions have found everlasting Life with the real Creator Christ, do you suppose?

Jude 14's count of "10 thousands of 10 thousands" can help us. But note Matthew 24:37–39's promise, "For the coming of the Son of Man will be just like the days of Noah...they were eating and drinking...marrying...*they did not understand* until the flood came and took them all away [13:40-42's *fire* this time] so shall the coming of the Son of Man be." Are you, your family and best friends ready for Luke 21:36's promised *"escape"* and Revelation 3:10's *"keep you from"*? Please enjoy these.

We are respectfully dealing with our Almighty Merciful God the Son, Who will Judge those *"many"* others about 1,000 years from now. They will win only because of their good *"deeds,"* and if their names are written in our God's *"book of life,"* plus the Christ's all-important *Blood sacrifice* (Leviticus 17:11 with Hebrews 9:22).

A majority of Christians apparently have ignored this later Judgment by the Son, as clearly promised in John 5:29, Matthew 25:31-46 and Revelation 20:11–15. Maybe this is because they have ignored His Mercy – not being able to accept seeing so many others ultimately enjoying this subsequent Salvation! I think of our atheist brother Jeff, as in our Dedication page; one of the nicest guys you would ever know!

As reviewed here of tempting and competing "religions," again Roman Catholic Emperor Constantine and most other participants in 324-25 AD's *Council of Nicea compromised* with the vague God philosophy of Egypt's Athanasius. Many other man-made compromises are exposed in our chapter 8, including 1229 AD's Roman Catholic Council of Valencia that outlawed the Bible for laymen and listed it on Rome's terrible *"Index of Forbidden Books,"* not unlike Judaism forbidding the Bible's Isaiah chapter 53.. What do you think they were they afraid of?

It is worth repeating that the Roman Catholic "mass" is a non-Biblical *substitutionary transubstantiation-communion*, in which maybe 2 Corinthians 11:4's "another Jesus" is to physically atone for mankind's faithless sins again every day; in blatant opposition to the real Christ's Hebrews 9:12 total accomplishment *"once for all."* In 1965, because Roman Catholics like my younger sister Miriam were reading Protestant Bibles, the 1229 AD '"forbidden" edict was ended by the Vatican II council.

To me such man-made restrictions are as erroneous as again the so-called *"Apostles Creed."* Due to its apparent origin of around 300 AD, when Roman creeds were taking the place of Bible promises, I do not find that this one was composed by the Christ's' first century apostles at all. And again, Biblically He did the Creation, as in John 1:3, Colossians 1:16 and Hebrews 1:8-10; not His Father as erroneously stated in that man-made creed. So why do pastors and congregations parrot it?

With all of churchism's *non-Biblical baggage and sacred cows* from centuries of theological wandering, it is no wonder that the loving Roman Catholic *Mother Teresa* wrote that "she was deeply tormented about her faith" and "suffered periods of doubt about God" (source: San Diego Union-Tribune, August 25, 2007). How sad, as are the many frustrated celibate-predator-priests with eros-love passions for helpless little boys.

#3 God Biblically is the *BAD God (Satan),* also shown as "Elohim"/God in Genesis 6:4 just before the worldwide flood, and "Theos"/God as 2 Corinthians 4:4's "God [capital G!] of this world." He is Revelation 12:9's deceiving Satan the *Devil*, the great *dragon*, the *serpent* of old, with his own filthy seed line in I John 3:10 called *"children of the Devil."* This bad God's offspring are also warned of with Jude 4's "...long beforehand marked out for this *condemnation;"* in 2 Corinthians 11:13-26 as his "false apostles...servants...*false brethren;"* in John 8:44's "...of your *father the Devil;"* as in Luke 16:8's "...more *shrewd;"* and as Matthew 13:25–30–38–40's satanic "...*tares*...sons *of the evil one."* These are now clearly exposed to the light of day and proven truth. Let's be alert to this Zechariah 14:21c "Canaanite" seed, along with their propaganda and *unbiblical "brotherhood of man* under the fatherhood of God"-anybody (as in Freemasonry etc.)!

Satan's skids are greased as in Isaiah 14:12–27, aiming for the Revelation 20:10–15's everlasting sulphur-stinking *"lake of fire,"* also known as Matthew 5:22's *permanent "Gehenna;"* and never the temporary *Geenna* (NT Hell, Hades and OT Sheol), as sometimes mistranslated by scholars. Why aren't these vital differences regularly taught in church?

His son is this world's near-future *"Antichrist,"* promised in 1 John 2:22, 2 John 1:7, also as 2 Thessalonians 2:3-12's *"man of lawlessness;"* the "beast" of Revelation 13:3+4+12 and 14:9, back to Zechariah 11:17, miraculously recovering from his *"fatal" head wound,* with his right eye blinded and arm totally withered. He will miraculously recover from this fatal head wound (Revelation 13:3+12+14). With him is his *"false prophet,"* who was predicted, by the great 1130s AD Roman Catholic seer-priest *Malachy*, to be Rome's 112th "pope" after the present one, Benedict. I am only the reporter, so please don't be mad at me for these insights (Galatians 4:16).

Next, many Christians mistakenly think that the *third "Holy Spirit"* is a co-equal in Matthew 28:20's blessed 'Trinity.' I honestly find Biblically that this wonderful Comforter, Helper (Paraclete) and Teacher as the #3 Holy Spirit *is only for the Church-building age*. Please notice that He was given this job in Acts 2:4+38, never to be confused with the *Christ's Holy Spirit #2* as shown in Isaiah 63:10 with 1 Peter 1:11, and 2 Peter 1:19–21; nor confused with *His Father's Holy Spirit #1* named in Matthew 12:18; nor is #3 a fiction in the Old Testament; nor is He with Revelation 22:1-3's "God and the Lamb" whatsoever!

In review, you can see the Almighty Christ's "Holy Spirit" is named in Isaiah 63:10, with 1 Peter 1:11, and II Peter 1:19–21, and certainly His Almighty Father's Holy "Spirit" in Matthew 12:18 is "Holy." These add to the importance of 2 Peter 1:19–21 re Bible prophecy: "So we have the prophetic word made more sure, to which you do well to pay attention…know this first of all, that no prophecy of Scripture is a matter of one's own interpretation…" There is no interpretation needed from us imperfect mortals. Just read it as is. This is supported by our Christ in His 1 Corinthians 10:1–4 insight of Exodus 13:21: "For I do not want you unaware…all passed through the sea…drinking from a Spiritual Rock…and *the Rock was Christ.*"

CHAPTER
10

YOUR BIBLE OR MINE?

A bit of history: Back to our Military Government team in Japan, it was peaceful to study one evening by the light of the moon, out on the large patio between our barracks and Club Shebang. After a day of investigations, it was relaxing to leaf through my small King James Version, as reviewed below.

Again, Mom and Miriam had given this "KJV" to me near the Christmas of 1941, with the loving comment, "Mom's way is not always right, but God's is infallible...keep your face to the Light, and the shadows will fall behind." Oh, yes, they cared. I received another KJV from the 11th Airborne Rangers in Japan, and still enjoy each copy when comparing them with over 20 other Bible versions.

Today's often-conflicting Bible *versions* (not translations!) tend to parallel factional sacred cows, which have divided Christian believers throughout the Church's history. Who pays attention to the KJV's proven errors, such as its Genesis 1:28, where the word "replenish" is erroneously used in place of "fill the earth;" or 1 Thessalonians 5:3, where the KJV's "safety" is erroneously used in place of the mathematically most-perfect "peace and security"? Sadly nice KJV-only believers want to ignore errors.

The KJV of Acts 12:4 *erroneously shows pagan "Easter"* in place of the accurate "Passover," which comes from the original Koine Greek word "Pascha." This should always be *"Passover,"* as it is properly translated the other 28 times even in the KJV. So why not this 29th time? Just as we finites are all imperfect in this life, so are the KJV and all other human versions. But of interest, both sides of such opposing arguments often show scholarly data that should be considered, and then if possible should test their side again with chapter 17's mathematics.

After substantial research, and with no ax to grind, for what it is worth I am respectfully convinced that the 1611 KJV was a revision of the earlier Roman Catholic Vulgate and Bishop Bibles, as were the Tyndale, Coverdale and the great 1560 Geneva Bible (of which we have a very used copy). Despite philosophy, none of these were translations from the original mathematically-perfect Masoretic Hebrew and Koine Greek manuscripts. Only our God's original 66-book Word for us was and is mathematically perfect, as in chapter 17.

On the other hand, most KJV-only friends intensely reject what they feel are erroneous Alexandrian texts. I find these to be equally useful when testing all available versions for accuracy, with II Timothy 2:15's "Be diligent to present yourself approved to God as a workman who does not need to be ashamed, accurately handling the Word of truth." This is why using *God-breathed most-perfect mathematics* testing can help all of us as one (John 17:11+21).

As he was growing up, our son Mike loved to throw stones into water and across land. Probably with a similar passion, in 1947 south of Jerusalem a Middle East Bedouin boy was throwing stones into high caves near the Dead Sea's area of Qumran. Some stones hit large pottery vases, which fortunately were hiding the ancient *"Dead Sea Scrolls."* This was vastly important because they held copies of every

Old Testament book of the Bible, for example, including four complete sets of Isaiah, and even bits of the book of Mark. They had been hidden there prior to Jerusalem's 70 AD destruction by Roman General Titus and his legions. And no new discoveries of Bible scrolls had been made for centuries prior to this.

Belated to this important find of the scrolls, you can see on our copyright page the name "The Lockman Foundation." Made available in 1960, and including these Dead Sea Scrolls' invaluable insights, its dedicated theologians and their associates produced their more accurate easy-to-read version of scripture named the *NEW AMERICAN STANDARD BIBLE*. Studying from all available versions of the Bible, I enjoy the NASB's simple modern language and non-paraphrasing accuracy, when comparing its verses with over 20 other Bible versions, side-by-side, including the KJV as well as the *New King James*.

Romans 13 is a good example of conflicting Bible version interpretations (with 1 Peter 2:13–17 and Titus 2:13–15). In my opinion, for many centuries the sincere global church has been thrown additional curves because of *man-made Bible mistranslations*, such as in the former. I have not found extra time to be a scholar of Masoretic Hebrew and Aramaic (Old Testament), nor of Koine Greek (New Testament); so please join me in using a Bible Concordance, Bible Dictionary and Lexicon for looking up meanings. These research texts should still be available at your nearest Christian bookstore.

In the controversial Romans 13:1-7 (with I Peter 2:13-25), mathematically the original Koine Greek word *"EXOUSIA"* simply means "power," but instead it is often translated "authority." The Greek word has at least 12 different definitions, including "power of choice," "right" as in Hebrews 13:10 and Revelation 22:14, and "liberty to do as one pleases." While we all should pay the taxes owed in all jurisdictions applicable to us, do you really find that "exousia" means IRS' dictatorial "power" over *excised U.S. federal citizens* due to their receiving *voluntary government benefits and privileges*?

Or is this more accurately applicable to the approved Christian's reverent and loyal "power of choice?" After enjoying our chapter 20 on lawful taxation, you too may richly benefit from following our

"Law of the Land" Constitution *for our USA* as in its Preface, with our U.S. supreme Court rulings in accord.

Of Bibles, my Agape-loving caution is to *beware of paraphrased Bibles*, and avoid them if you want to follow 2 Timothy 2:15's guidelines. One such paraphrased version is *The Living Bible* series, although years ago I did enjoy this for further understanding the Old Testament's Minor Prophets. Another popular paraphrased version is the *New International Version*, somewhat less accurate than those that use the Dead Sea Scrolls; and I am told that its next version is to be sexless.

The NIV paralleled the King James Version in *not capitalizing pronouns* regarding the Father and Son, which seems to be less reverent to me. Again 2 Timothy 2:15 can guide us on these topics with "Be diligent to present yourself *approved* to God as a workman who does not need to be ashamed, handling *accurately* the word of truth." Let's try to do all things to glorify our Almighty God, Father and Son, Who have done so much for each of us and promise to do so in all of the exciting future...with no lies.

Over the past 70 years there has often been a silent inner-voice saying "Keep learning - We will help; keep learning - We will help." I must have heard these silent supporting words over a hundred times, thank God. That 1949 night with a full moon shining on our MG patio, I was guided to study the promised future Millennium, as in -500 B.C. Zechariah 14, with 14:21c's *"And there will no longer be a Canaanite in the house of the Lord of hosts in that day."* This showed me that obviously somebody called *Canaanites* have to be around in the meantime, too. Are these the same *satanic people* also as Matthew 13:30's *"tares,"* who grow together with the Christ's "wheat" until the harvest (first resurrection)? These insights helped to open the door further in better understanding our Friend of chapter one, "God-somebody," and His Agape-love.

CHAPTER
11

KATSUKI TANAGAWA
AND GENERAL MACARTHUR

My favorite officer, Katsuki Tanagawa, a highly decorated Hawaiian U.S. soldier who had fought his way up the boot of Italy in World War II, asked if I would join him at General MacArthur's request for a 30-day pre-war assignment in South Korea. Our work would be primarily to search and destroy North Korean vehicles and guerillas that were dangerously infiltrating *South Korea*. You may know of the general's deep concerns about the untrustworthiness of the Russian, United Nations, communist Chinese and North Korean leaders. So he had asked his magnificent Honor Guard and some others of us who were trained for combat to help stop a pre-war guerilla takeover of South Korea. This was about a month before I was shipped out from Yokohama to the States.

Shortly before Katsuki and I left to fulfill our assignment in Korea, a Russian general had been trying to bully General MacArthur, but without success. After one more arrogant tirade from this man of rank, our general invited him to take a taxi ride in Tokyo. (I would have loved to be listening in that car!) Apparently this Russian general got the point, with nothing left out, ending with something like "If you do not keep your mouth shut on these matters, you will find yourself in one of our darkest prisons, with no communication whatsoever!" Rumor had it that this would-be Russian bully suddenly became instantly cooperative.

My wife Fran's wonderful sister, *Marion*, reminded me to share with you about one of the evenings in South Korea. Katsuki and I had seldom found chances to shower and change uniforms during our three-day and night trips for engagement north of Seoul. Rain left our uniforms wet and dirty, and after many months overseas I was getting lonesome for the dozen homes where I grew up.

He and I talked about having a *hot turkey dinner* with mashed potatoes and gravy, vegetables, cranberry sauce, with pumpkin pie and whipped cream. He joked that he'd rather have K-rations (dried food), so we pulled them out of our packs. I began opening a package of cookies, when on the plastic cover was printed *"Hello from Waterloo, Iowa"* – where I mainly grew up! At age 20, I just sat in the cold mud and cried.

Back in Japan after those 30 wild days, Katsuki and I attended *our final Military Government banquet* (by then called Civil Affairs), personally sponsored by General MacArthur, at the *Trade Winds Club* in Yokohama. He reviewed what our MG team had accomplished successfully in the occupation of Japan. After a few other speeches and a delicious dinner, with our feeling that he might be retiring again as he had in 1936, the general came over to where I was seated, put his hand on my shoulder, smiled his fatherly goodbye and gently added, *"If you want to do a service for our God and Country, investigate thoroughly and prove who is knifing America in Washington, and why..."* Those indelible words took me a good 20 years in which to accomplish their basics, often with prayers going in the Christ Jesus' Name.

Of the United Nations, according to its regulations every one of General MacArthur's Korean War (Truman's "police action)" plans had to be cabled to Washington, DC before their execution. Then each plan was cabled on to the UN military commander, always head-quartered in Moscow; thus exposing our side's strategy every time. So throughout the Korean War the communist enemies knew in advance where our side was going to strike; meaning that they could evacuate primary targets before the strikes. This bothered MacArthur to no end, short-circuiting his *"No substitute for Victory!"*

In one of his valued speeches, General MacArthur stated "I am concerned for the *security* of our great Nation; not so much because of any threat from without, but because of the *insidious forces working from within* [DC+]...What...is our greatest menace? End invisible government based upon propaganda, and restore truly representative government based upon truth." He often talked about the hidden identity of this enemy; exposed for you now with many thanks to our Bible's Zechariah 14:21c.

These are named as this world's *"Canaanite...children of the Devil,"* and seen from Genesis 9:24–25 through at least 1 John 3:10, which the general had softly asked me to *"...investigate thoroughly..."* You may know them by their *other tribal names* besides Canaanites, such as Amorites, Arkites, Arvadites, Girgashites, HAMathites, Hittites, Hivites, Jebusites, Sidonians, Sinites and Zemarites – who loved to enslave other nations economically (just like today), and to religiously sacrifice their children by fire.

This book is the least that I can do for our General MacArthur, for you, for truth and for all with concerns about their present and future. It is an honor to responsibly expose your dedicated satanic enemy, *proven* to be destroyers of our once-free America.

In 1941 I did not know about their 1776 Illuminati, their 1913 non-federal privately-owned Federal Reserve banking corporation (against which President Kennedy gave his life), their later Bilderbergers, David Rockefeller's Trilateral Commission, Jacob Schiff's and Paul Warburg's Council on Foreign Relations, or Schiff's and president Wilson's so-called 'colonel' House's criminal nation-destroying IRS (please see chapter 20). Or that the 1950s U.S. Senator Joseph McCarthy would be proven accurate about these traitors...even if he did not know a satanic Canaanite-Jew from the more trustworthy Hebrew-Jew. It would take some decades to unscramble these things for you, many long-hidden in silent books and shrewd minds.

CHAPTER
12

THE SEARCH CONTINUES

Back in the States, after passing my freshman year of college overseas, in 1950 my 12th family the Elliotts knew that I needed more college education. They opened the doors to *Winona State University* in Winona, Minnesota. Its student population was kept at about 1,200, which allowed for small classrooms and intimate interchanges with its superb professors. For example, my first (sophomore) class on the English writer John Milton (1608-1674 AD) consisted of three female students and one male – me, plus the professor, *Dr. Augusta NELSON*. She opened class with, "Ladies and gentleman, in the future you may not remember me, and you may not remember this university, but you will remember how to *THINK*!" She taught us to do exactly that. And Dad amazed me with 21 new dollar bills for my 21st birthday!

For whatever reason, in the next year (1951) local *YMCA* executive secretary *Herb Johnson* asked me to be the *Aquatics Director* at

Winona's brand new Y.' I had no Water Safety Instructor training, but he said that it could be done later. This part-time job was teaching swimming, diving, rings, judo and karate. For this I was paid $1 an hour, and received some GI Bill for my college costs, thank God. Herb also helped me join the *Toastmasters* dinner club, for additional speech training and memorable fellowship.

Among hundreds, one of my favorite students for swimming and practice-teaching the 6th grade was *Lanny Doner*, who later was accidentally cut in half while ignorantly playing under nearby railroad cars. Another favorite student was *Roger Young*, a 15 year-old guy with a great attitude, handicapped as a Mongol. His single mother had asked me to *help him learn how to swim*...a wonderful challenge.

One Saturday morning, about two hundred boys in my swimming classes excitedly climbed the nearby Sugarloaf Mountain, which had an elevation of maybe 2,000 feet. We all reached the top, amazingly including Roger. But his short legs swelled badly from the strain of holding over 200 pounds, so I had no choice but to carry him down the mountain. About a year later, on a special parents' night he swam his first full length of our 40-foot pool – to the loud cheers of many parents and students. I can still hear Roger's voice as he hugged my legs and shouted, "I wuv you, I wuv you!" The next year, after I was graduated, Roger went on to win the men's and boys' city chess championship. How about that?!

At one point in college, our speech professor, *Dr. Dorothy Magnus*, decided that I should be the male lead in an in-the-round production of *"Washington Square"* (aka *"The Heiress"*), for which I had zero extra time. But she knew her stuff, and it was a *success*...again to me meaning *the accomplishment of a pre-set goal*. Hopefully you have an important goal, such as sharing this urgent little book in time.

After summer schools my jobs were back in Waterloo, where I drilled 117-pound D-cylinder heads for John Deere tractors, worked on the assembly line and in the freezer at the Rath Meatpacking plant, and worked as a lifeguard at the Olympic swimming pool.

My senior college year in 1952 was preceded that summer with a memorable 4,200 mile *MOTORCYCLE trip* on a like-new 1951

Harley-Davidson, visiting friends all over America while following Lait and Mortimer's book, *Confidential U.S.A.* This described almost every place of interest from coast to coast. For example, led by the book I went into St Louis' Kingshighway Hotel, asked to see winning professional boxers' owner Ralph Calico, and said that Minneapolis' Fred Osana wanted me to give him best wishes. In a minute two gangster-like men with shoulder-holstered guns came out, said a curt hello, and added that Calico and Osana had been deadly enemies for 20 years. They added that I was to take my *motorcycle "bike"* down the highway to their white-columned restaurant on the right, have an unforgettable dinner and dessert of my choice, and then get the h' out of town forever or I would be dead!

On July 4th, as planned overseas, I arrived at our hotel in New Orleans in time to meet my three Army Ranger buddies for an old-time's sake dinner celebration. The next day involved a meeting with Delta Airlines' official top-scoring commercial jet pilot, *Gene Bradstreet*, who counseled me to *never get stuck in life's "ruts."* That was consistent with my life's goals and planning, and superb advice!

After seeing other friends in Dallas, Oklahoma City, Kansas City, Des Moines, Waterloo and Minneapolis, I was hired from a newspaper ad to be *Personnel Recruiter* of construction specialists. These ranged from steamfitters to airbase superintendents for North Atlantic Constructors, then building in Greenland and Saudi Arabia. This involved wonderful work with an FBI supervisor and new friend *Jack Bills.* My NAC boss was Charlie Kopald, who had been personnel director for WW II shipbuilder Henry Kaiser.

Back at college Dr. Nelson had asked us students to write an *essay on what we did over that summer.* When I turned my essay in and she read it aloud, with a twinkle in her eye she said, "English majors just don't do this sort of thing..."

That fall I was paid for being the regular evening and weekend escort for our gorgeous *Miss Minnesota.* She was such a smooth dancer that at St. Mary's College in Winona all of the other couples cleared the floor, as we swirled doing our thing.

During the final college year, thankfully, *Danforth Foundation's* Dr. Brown in St. Louis telephoned to say that I had won the foundation's national essay contest about President *Eisenhower*, in 3,000 words or less. You may remember that General Eisenhower had been my hero in Army basic training days, so I studied everything possible about him – which made winning the contest easy.

Dr. Brown then flew from St. Louis to Winona, and described what winning this contest involved. They would pay all expenses including toothpaste, tuition and transportation for up to three doctorates. I could attend the schools of my choice, near wherever our future family might live, with this to be coordinated by the Neotarian Fellowship of Kansas City, Missouri. I told Dr. Brown that one of my goals was to learn as much of Hosea 4:6's hidden *"Knowledge"* from these studies as possible, adding that the schools could keep the honors. He agreed, and we became long-time friends.

From Winona State University, thankfully I was graduated with honors in 1953, majoring in English, Speech, and Education. Then after a three-week canoe trip with five buddies, shooting Canada's rough Drowning River toward Hudson Bay, I went with Chicago's *Continental Can Company* (CCC), in its two-year sales management trainee program, which was another fabulous experience. Basic training in Chicago's CCC was followed by four months of grueling 110-hour work-weeks with CCC in Mankato, Minnesota, after hiring and training two very alert secretaries. Our overall job was to coordinate the routing and shipping of thousands of railroad cars, filled with Continental cans, to customers' plants all over America. It was a responsible challenge, with full awareness that the previous year's trainee had been fired for routing a trainload of cans right into the Kansas City flood.

The next assignment was further training in CCC's Omaha, Nebraska. On weekends at my age of 25 it was exciting to drive to and from *Minneapolis to date Sandy*, who had been my best friend when I had worked there with North Atlantic Constructors in 1952. Sandy was a sensational model, her shocking beauty captivating all the guys who looked her way, who in turn stalled traffic while others took a look.

On one drive back to Omaha, after a full weekend with Sandy and her folks, I fell asleep at the wheel. Thankfully tall grass on the highway's left side and my Guardian Angel awakened me, about 40 feet short of a cement culvert. Another weekend, when preparing for the drive, there were warnings that all highways looked like sheets of ice from cold rain and sleet, but Sandy was more than worth the effort. We continued dating for a couple of years, until 1957 when I met my unmatched Fran. Although Sandy was a wonderful friend, I knew prayerfully that she was not for me, and never looked back.

During those times in Minneapolis I had become especially well acquainted with the same *FBI* supervisor Jack Bills and his wife Helen. You may remember that Bill and I had worked together when I was with North Atlantic Constructors, and we became close friends. With my 2-year Continental Can sales management training program nearly completed, Jack sponsored my application to join the FBI as an agent. However, a few weeks later he was ordered to assist on a case in Texas, requiring his being there for nearly a year – with little or no family communication. That lifestyle was not for me, so I canceled my FBI application, preferring instead to be much nearer my then-future family.

After the Omaha training I returned to Continental Can in Chicago, reporting to its marketing vice president Wills Larkin. He ordered me to arrange for prostitutes to service his executive-level customers, so I quit. Fortunately, our Dad needed assistance in his *Waterloo*, Iowa insurance and real estate business. So I joined him for some months, while awaiting additional speech training by scholarship at the Pasadena Playhouse in *California*. This had been arranged by Winona State University's Dr. Magnus, feeling that I could add to my public speaking techniques. During the time in Waterloo, as a sideline it was fun teaching dancing at *Arthur Murray's*. The term at Pasadena Playhouse was highly educational, even if I did not care much for wearing the silly leotards that were required for fencing and for many of Shakespeare's and other great plays.

With that schooling completed, General Telephone in Santa Monica agreed to hire me daytime as a personnel traffic engineer.

During evening hours my music-loving friends Tom Powers, Pat Dougherty, Mike Campbell and I practiced our close-harmony *"Bonaires Quartet"* songs, often with choreography. Singing part-time in clubs from California to New York, we each averaged $600 a night in earnings, but not often enough. We also recorded long-play albums at Hollywood's *Capital Records*.

One night the famous Frank *Sinatra* charged into our Studio, yelling and mad as a wet hornet about our great pianist, Sam Mineo (uncle of then-actor Sal Mineo), taking away the music "mixer" from Sinatra's group. Later it was flattering to be invited to replace the great Hi-Lows quartet's bass singer, but I honestly did not feel fully qualified. Those were delightful times, singing and meeting talented people.

As mentioned in late 1957 I met the love of my life, the *phenomenal beautiful Fran*, a registered nurse from Toronto, Canada. After being graduated from nursing school there, and then doing several months of private duty nursing in Vancouver, British Columbia, she and another nurse, *Anne*, hitchhiked over 1,000 miles from Vancouver to Santa Monica, California. We met on a blind date, and she was everything I ever dreamed of in a girl. I told our mutual friend Doug Campbell that *"She is the girl for me,* bright, clean and game to hitchhike all that way!" After we dated for over a week, she and Anne left for Toronto; driving an auto-transfer company car and taking my broken heart with her.

My telephone headset, with permission from Santa Monica General Telephone, provided global telephone service. So Fran and I were able to talk by telephone almost daily after 3 o'clock in the afternoon her time when she awoke from sleep after each nursing shift. When she overslept, her mother and I visited, so we got well acquainted too. The next spring in 1958 Fran flew out to visit me, I put her *engagement ring* on her precious finger, and she agreed to be my wonderful bride after her loving parents flew in from Toronto — intent on protecting their youngest of six daughters. I won.

We were *married* at their Toronto St. Timothy Anglican church that fall, thank God. Then after special months in our new Santa

Monica apartment, initially with the bathroom and closet plaster still damp, in late 1959 we prayed in Jesus' Name for baby #1, which resulted in Fran conceiving our wonderful daughter *Sally that same month*. With Sally aboard, I quit our Bonaires Quartet and again never looked back. 21 months later, in mid-1961 we prayed in Jesus' Name for baby #2, resulting in Fran conceiving our marvelous son, *Mike, that same month*. Soon we bought our first home, a small bungalow in nearby Pacific Palisades. Yes we were blessed.

These years also were spiced with visiting our *SUPER FAMILIES* in Canada and America: Our Mom, Dad, Helen and her Les, Jim, Alice, Jeanne, Larry, Pat, Jo and Barb; Jeff and his Faye, Jud and Joel; Miriam and her Sue, Mike, Kim and Tom; Fran's Mom and Dad and her five sisters and husbands, Marg and John with Mary Ellen, Ian and Barb; Marion with Jim, Bob, JoAnne and Ron; gracious Joannie, Betts with Louise, Doug, Bob, Guy and Tim; anonymous family, and all of their families.

We also love and appreciate *LIFELONG FRIENDS*: General Dick & Ann Abel, Wally & Jennie Butts, Mike & Mel Campbell, Fred & Sheila Carpenter, Jim & Betty Cary, Tom & Laurie Daane, Gerrit & Lori Dragt, Dr. Dick & Dee Eastman, Barbara Dee Ehrnstein, Phil Elliott, David & Ronnie Friedman, Dr. Kathryn Hanes, Bob & Joan Heitger, Senior Pastor Noah Hutchings, Jan Jensen-McGaughey, Phil Kosh, Free Lazor, Dr. Dom & Rita Maga, Bill & Shirley Mundt, Gordon Perry, Marjorie Semensow, Dr. Doug & Susan Shaw, Tommy & Cindy Stuart, Rick Turner, Rick Webb, Peter Wood — and more other special friends than we can count. Hopefully you too will count yourself as our special friend, whom we can meet soon, or in the coming Millennium under the Almighty Christ's perfect rule, as described in chapter 21.

CHAPTER
13

A CAREER JOB AND PROVE UPS

In 1959, feeling a need for specific *career guidance*, I took tests at the California Employment office, which showed that I had a natural ability *to help people with their insurance and investment needs*. Further training provided the little edge to out-perform worthy competition. My clients were provided with complete estate planning, and written reviews of each one's social security and related provisions. It always helped to remember Christianity's *Golden Rule* in Matthew 7:12, *"... however you want people to treat you, so treat them, for this is the Law and the Prophets."* This book shares the same attitude for you.

Gradually maturing, I found that this pearl of wisdom parallels the powerful *Agape-love*, unmatched in Romans 13:8-10 and Galatians 5:14, as being *responsible for one another as needed*, without want of reward from people. Christ Jesus did this plus-quality love for you. Fun! With this it is again wise to remember our simple and powerful definition of *Success... the accomplishment of a pre-set goal...*

That December was devoted to the job as chairman of Santa Monica's YMCA Christmas tree sales – successful for the "Y," but there was no earned income for our family. Another challenge was to serve on our Santa Monica Junior Chamber of Commerce's Board of Directors, with its many committees.

This had led to my friendship with *A&W Root Beer's* (Allen & Wright's) personnel director, Brent Cameron, headquartered in Santa Monica. A&W executives needed help in improving the relationships with their 2,000+ franchise drive-in owners, who did not enjoy giving part of their profits to A&W as a slice of their franchise cost. So I was given the opportunity of developing what became highly successful nationwide insurance and investment programs, using then-new and unique Group Insurance Trusts.

These became *"DIGIT"*/for A&W Drive-In Group Insurance Trust, for Major Medical, Life and Disability Income protections; *"DIFACT"* for A&W/Drive-In Fire & Casualty Trust, and *"DIART"* for A&W/Drive-In Association Retirement Trust. These utilized unusual group purchasing power and resulted in superb relationships for all operators and headquarters. It was delightful to give hundreds of speeches all over America regarding these financial benefits at A&W's national, regional and district conventions including in key cities such as Chicago, Las Vegas, Los Angeles, Miami, New Orleans and San Francisco. At Las Vegas' Sahara Hotel I asked the staff for good ideas, so the bell captain suggested that we hire a half-dozen beautiful models, dressed in mink bikini outfits with gold colored boots, to hand out these Digit, Difact and Diart Group Insurance brochures at each doorway. Everybody loved it, except for a few overly-concerned wives.

Meanwhile other finance specialists and I were building a national team of about 40 insurance and investment brokerage houses, each with our own clients. I honestly don't remember losing one important case to tough competitors in Beverly Hills, with the Christ Jesus in our corner. Many of these excellent brokers often contacted our office on South Beverly Boulevard, for high-quality products on behalf of their own clients. These very special investments, often with written IRS tax advantages, involved client-ownerships of working solar panel operations, gold and silver mining, Kentucky oil and gas, and Federal Communications Commission's cellular telephone license applications.

Besides these, my work also involved ownerships of Beverly Office Equipment Company on South Robertson in Beverly Hills, half-interest in a printing company, and half-interest in our 45 apartment units with pool in Glendale. *I wondered if there was anywhere outside America with such great opportunities*! Meanwhile we upgraded our home in *Pacific Palisades* to three bedrooms, providing for our four-member family, dog and two cars.

Vacations were treasured by our family. About every other summer we reserved a *houseboat* for a wonderful week at *Lake Shasta's* 365 miles of shoreline, north of Sacramento. With no electricity or newspapers we just relaxed, read, swam, fished and visited. When Sally and Mike were small they would awaken us early for help baiting their fish hooks, reminding us of each Christmas morning's thankful freedom to laugh, play and exchange modest gifts. Our kids also loved jumping from the houseboat roofs into the water, maybe 10 feet down, while our Cocker Spaniel Shadow barked and finally learned to jump in too.

Sometimes they were invited to bring along a friend each, which was memorable. One Sunday we were treated with a fun visit by friends who lived nearby, Dawain and Jan *Jensen*, for whom I had been best man at their marriage. Another gorgeous morning we cruised up the Sacramento River to its beginning trickle, with *Shadow's barks producing echoes* on the way from each side's high cliffs, and her wondering if she was going to be able to play with the other thousand imagined dogs. That evening we tied up to a cove's shore, enticing three baby deer to have some lettuce, while Shadow went berserk. As we were leaving for home that Sunday, Shadow chased some ducks into the lake, whereupon Mike in his good suit waded in after her...

Back home, UCLA was only a few miles east of our Pacific Palisades home, so with it and other schools there were excellent opportunities to study and audit courses part-time between business appointments, while working quite close to home and Beverly Hills. Thanks to the tremendous *colleges' staffs,* including those in Japan, Iowa, Minnesota and Michigan, I was provided with exceptional opportunities for learning and for these investigations.

Back to our 1941 and earlier experiences there was an eagerness to find psychologically, theologically and economically *why our Mom and Dad had divorced.* In 1967, with many years of additional courses completed, we decided to ask the Neotarian Registrar where I stood toward the first doctorate. She listed the few remaining requirements, so after these and the dissertation and prove-ups were accomplished, my earned doctorate in Psychology was granted on December 21, 1970. Now I could assist mental patients.

About the same time, one Saturday night we were enjoying dinner at home with a couple from New York, when our *45-unit apartments'* manager telephoned in a panic. He said that a big group of tenants and their friends had been drinking beer that afternoon, stacking the empty cans into a huge pyramid; and they were jumping out of our 2nd story window into the swimming pool. You might enjoy such a liability risk, but not this brother. Off I drove from Pacific Palisades to Glendale, prepared with my Ranger weapons, just in case someone wanted to have at it. Only one young man did, just for a moment, and he backed down unhurt, thankfully.

Due to too much overwork, after upgrading the 45 apartments, our accountant and co-owner Ralph Smith and I sold that challenge for about a break-even, thank you! I also sold the printing company, and resigned from 10 of the 11 civic organizations that were burning time, staying only with our Santa Monica City College Citizens' Advisory Board presidency, servicing A&W Root Beer of course, and the other insurance and investment consulting work that was growing by leaps and bounds.

Also it was a delight to help one evening a week in Santa Monica as a graduate-assistant for the *Dale Carnegie Institute* using the speech training. A young *psychological patient lady* was painfully shy; so much so that it was wrecking her life. I invited her to the next Carnegie

112

session, asking her to say hello to the group, tell about her family, school and hometown, and hit the podium with a rolled-up newspaper every time she made a major point in her talk. Within two minutes this timid young girl matured like a flower in bloom, as she demolished the newspaper...and found her future husband!

Meanwhile, my Saturdays had been mainly devoted to teaching recovering alcohol and drug addicts, mostly from nearby beaches, often invited by fellow UCLA students to Pastor Fred and Pat Hiltz' modest *Venice* church for bed and food. We met in the basement for Bible *"rap and scrap"* discussions, as our students called them, following a breakfast of pancakes, eggs and bacon. We prayerfully shared our best efforts with proofs of truth, tuned to each addict's questions and their still-unknown futures.

These addicts were rough, but generally gracious. One was a once-beautiful 24 year-old Linda, with a deep razor scar on her face, and her lovely three year-old daughter Sherry. Then there was Indian Joe, from an Indian reservation, who told us that he had been conned into participating with a coven the night before, and feared that he had blasphemed the Holy Spirit. So we read Mark 3:28–29 together, where scribes had falsely charged that Christ Jesus had an unclean spirit, the unforgivable sin. Indian Joe was relieved that he had not blasphemed the Christ's Holy Spirit, named so in Isaiah 63:10 with I Peter 1:11.

When I first arrived that morning, Fred had asked me to slowly open the door of a classroom, where a drug addicted American Hindu man with long dirty blond hair and tan leather clothes was sitting on the dirt floor. He had apparently spent the night in the Hindu position, in need of being exorcised, which I did in Jesus' Name. After the rest of us had breakfast and began a discussion, he came out and sat on the only vacant chair, to my immediate right. To answer another student's questions, I went to the blackboard after laying my open Bible on the Hindu's lap. To the other person, my answers included 1 Corinthians 11:14's "...if a man has long hair, it is a dishonor to him."

The Hindu was surprised by that, but it got his attention, followed by Acts 4:12's "...*there is no other Name* [only *the real Jesus*

Christ/Messiah]...by which we must be saved," leading us to Romans 8:1–4's "Therefore there is now no condemnation for those who are into Christ Jesus." After reading these the young Hindu walked down the hall, flushed his Hindu headband down the toilet, and then came back and studied with us until into the evening. That was one long day.

Also there was unforgettable *Isaac,* a giant black Merchant Mariner, who came for that Saturday breakfast, intent on disrupting our studies. But he became interested instead. Later that evening as I was walking to the car, with books and a briefcase in hand, a loud threatening Venice gang was stopped cold when Isaac shouted to them, "No! Nobody touches that man but over my dead body!" They didn't.

One early evening on our patio in Pacific Palisades I was teaching *Judo and Karate to* Sally, Mike and half-dozen other youngsters from the neighborhood. Showing them how to stop a would-be robber, who looked like he was going to attack from behind, I asked 18 year-old Frank Frisch to pretend that he was the robber. He was to duck to his right side, because my bare foot would be going at his left jugular. On count he ducked to his right, my foot missed his jugular okay as planned, but it went on and split the back of our house's 25-foot stucco wall from the cement up to the roof.

Fran and I vividly remember the moment after midnight of *June 30, 1972*, when I sat straight up in bed and shared with her an incomparable vision, *seeing our childhood Friend*, "God-Somebody." He was standing about 30 feet from me, in a white robe, with more than 40 others in robes facing Him. His eyes met mine, followed by His silent but unforgettable command, *"The Time Has Come!"* He made it clear that it was then time to consolidate all of the facts that I had learned so far. These were to be included in our first hardcover book, which was copyrighted in 1976, as a preview for this present one that is far more complete. Even the title of that book was given to me in advance, *Lukewarm and Tender*. I found later that its name is from the Revelation 3:16 and Isaiah 47:1-15. L&T's writing began early the next morning.

Some readers may be helped by knowing how I was guided then *to learn faster* than usual, by copying each interesting topic on a *lined 3x5" index card*. First the alphabetical topic is printed in the card's upper-left corner, for example if I want to learn all about the Biblical *"Abraham."* Then the topic's teachings, gained from whatever sources, are printed on that card. Some of my topics have more than a dozen index cards Scotch-taped together for easy reference. One of our 12 year-old students, David Wheeling, found this idea so effective that he became the town's expert on three topics, giving speeches on these to the local schools and civic clubs – Rotary, Kiwanis et cetera – at $15 per talk. Some of our other students, desperately struggling in school, matured to straight-A grades with this marvel. It works.

Meanwhile, many of my psychological patients had desperate needs but little money, so they were often served without charge. But we had bills to pay and children to raise. Therefore with more guidance from the Fellowship's Registrar, and completing the remaining courses, dissertation and prove-ups, my second earned doctorate was granted on November 6, 1972, in Comparative Theology.

Four months later, we were strongly guided to sell that home and *"go east" to parts unknown*. Delegating my business work to trusted associates took a few weeks. I remember then tearfully putting our garden hose on the huge Mayflower moving van, while feeling like a minor Abraham with this guidance, after which we drove off in our pre-owned Cortez motor home with a *"Have Jesus, Will Share"* sign on the back window. After weeks of prayerfully driving around northeastern USA and southeastern Canada, both our daughter Sally and I knew the moment that we reached the beautiful 7,000-population town of *Lapeer, Michigan*, it would be our next home for awhile. Then for 16 months I worked on *Lukewarm and Tender*'s manuscript while completing studies at Michigan University's branch in Flint, about 20 miles west of us.

The first weekend after we arrived in Lapeer, while trying to locate a rental home we were driven around the countryside by a nice real estate lady. East of town we all saw *a dark threatening tornado*, maybe 200 yards away, twisting right at us. The real estate lady was about to faint, when I commanded the tornado to *"Turn and go back where you came from, in Christ Jesus' Name!"* It did. She could barely believe her eyes, although our family had no problem with that.

Our adorable *Cocker Spaniel, Shadow* (black and tan with white boots and chest), helped us through that memorable 1973 winter. She often barked freely as we put a sleigh to good use, riding around Lapeer in the deep snow, pulled by Sally's registered Quarter Horse, *Chipper* (Chipper's Pride II). Nearby kids enjoyed riding with us, sitting on the soft hay, with lots of singing, laughing and the sleigh bells jingling.

For taking our kids out of their California schools, I offered to buy a horse for each of them, then ages 12 and 10. Sally had worked part-time for several years at Will Rogers' State Park in Pacific Palisades, grooming the polo ponies and loving them. The four of us bought Chipper for her, and then bought *Cricket* for Mike...only to find that she was one-fourth donkey. After too much work staying on his donkey, Mike said of Cricket, "Who wants a horse anyway, I just want my bike." They were good kids.

Sally boarded Chipper at McGregors, who had a farm about a mile southeast of us. She commuted to Chip by riding her bicycle, which involved a dangerous half-mile of busy highway. Sure enough, one afternoon a young driver was reportedly going way over the speed limit, and he lost control of his dad's car – hitting Sally's bike, resulting in her flying into a clay ditch and the car straddled over her unconscious body. After an overnight stay in the Lapeer hospital, she remained bruised and shaken but okay, with her *Guardian Angel watching out for her, thank God (*the Psalms 91:11-12 teach about this).

We had become well acquainted with loyal friends Tom and Laurie *Daane*, who even loaned their Pontiac sedan to us for the 16 months that we lived there. Tom let me use his bank's photocopier while I compiled our book's manuscript, and he insisted that my name was to be "(*Doc*)" after we received the second doctorate. He and I made time to play winter golf, with snowdrifts on the sides of the fairways, among the picturesque rows of white birch trees. Together our families and others enjoyed unforgettable Bible studies, too. And we Scotts often made time to enjoy visiting Fran's family in Toronto.

One day a local pastor in Lapeer, Arnold Bracey, knocked on our door when I was gone. He mistakenly thought that I did not have earned doctorate degrees. Fran patiently found the documentation from our files, after which he apologized to his entire congregation for his unbelief. After the required prove-ups and dissertation were accepted my third doctorate, in Economics-Philosophy, was granted on October 15, 1973. The Neotarian Fellowship Registrar had been great in coordinating my many courses' credits, with a good number applying to all three degrees. Looking back, these were no big deal, with the Danforth Foundation's assistance, making those guided efforts seem easy. After the 16 months in Lapeer, *we considered California again*, with our Cortez motor home, horse trailer, horse, dog and furniture.

So in 1974 we telephoned lifelong friend, *Wally Butts*, a real estate agent among other talents, to see if he could locate a rental home with stables for Chipper. He reported that there were no house rentals available in Oceanside, California, let alone one with stables. Fran and I kept on praying for guidance, when a Chamber of Commerce flier that we'd ordered came in the mail. I had an urge to telephone the office number shown on its upper left corner, to find our next rental home in Oceanside.

A nice lady named *Marge Love* answered. As I wrote in chapter one, *Miracles Still Do Happen*. She seemed to be a real Christian, planning to attend her prayer group's session that night. There she met a new guest named Barbara Davy, whose U.S. Navy parents were being transferred from Oceanside, and who planned to list their home for rent – with community *stables* for Sally's Chipper! Yes, childlike prayers in our Creator Christ Jesus' Name do help plenty. You may have experienced this.

Over the years, there has always been enough money to pay all *bills* and just enough left over to buy an ice cream cone or something for each of us. The learning continued, while deeply appreciating Hebrews 10:22: "Let us draw near with a sincere heart in full assurance of faith, having our *hearts sprinkled clean from an evil conscience.*" This reminded me of Jesus' ancestor, 1,000 B.C. King David, and how he was forgiven of his faithless sins, which included setting up the death of Bathsheba's husband, faithful Canaanite Uriah, in combat, after David had sexual intercourse with her. David confessed directly to our God and sincerely repented, changed his mind, was forgiven, and won big time.

My dumb human mistakes, or *faithless sins*, have been many. All have been confessed to the Christ in Jesus' Name, and all have been forgiven as promised. This total forgiveness brings the unique "peace" promised in Romans 5:1 with Philippians 4:7 – "...*justified by faith*, we have peace with God through our Lord Jesus Christ," and "... the *peace* of God, which surpasses all comprehension, will guard your hearts and minds in Christ Jesus." These have been true through all of our stormy times and calm, ever since that December 1941 evening when my brave kid sister Miriam and I thankfully were helped miraculously with a thin dime by our childhood Friend "God-somebody," as in chapter one.

Having discovered that all of this world's well-known religions except one have proven to be man-made, some with deceitful satanics, my testing increased in finding Acts 9:2's "*Way*," Romans 8:1-4's "walk," Matthew 7:14's "few," James 1:12's "approved," and so much more. Our upcoming chapters would have helped, on the historic, scientific, mathematical and signs of the times' proofs of truth in the original Bible; but they were not generally available in the beginning. So this little book involved interviewing many very bright people and studying perhaps thousands of additional books.

One of the valuable studies was by Dallas theological seminary graduate, pastor and Bible teacher Hal Lindsey, and his former professional writer Carole Carlson, for their "*Late Great Planet Earth.*" Hal signed our copy in 1971, with its review of amazing Bible prophecies, all of which to date have proven to be right on target. It was fun for us that Hal, Carole, her husband Ward, our men's Bible teacher Bill Counts, and our family all attended Pacific Palisades' Calvary Church. Sometimes I sang before Hal preached at special services, and I remember well getting teary-eyed half way through about our Christ Jesus with the unforgettable *"How Great Thou Art."*

The church's pastor, Ralph Herrick, suggested that my decades of investigations should be ended, since he felt that the early church fathers had "settled these topics long ago." They certainly had not!

Back to the books, another investigative finding at that time was Dr. *Stoner's* Pasadena City College computer study, in which he asked his students to research 8 prophecies out of hundreds about the Messiah Christ. The question was, could any eight prophecies that the class chose be fulfilled by anyone born after 70 A.D.? Mathematically the chance of this being fulfilled is one out of a nonillion (one plus thirty zeros). Would you like to take on those odds?

These many studies, including those during our 16 months in Lapeer, Michigan, ***basically completed my investigations*** of man-kind's topics in this book's Contents. I had tried to follow General MacArthur's request to "investigate thoroughly," in the meantime sharing our first book *"Lukewarm And Tender,"* then our study of *"Proofs to Win – While There is Still Time,"* then *"Free At Last – From the IRS [Using And Never Abusing American Law],"* then *"Who Is Going To Tell Them"* and other writings. I remember bowing in prayer to our intimately-known Friend, "God-Somebody." Oh, yes, with thanks.

He had proven Himself to be our real Almighty God, the Angel Messenger of the Lord, the "I Am," our Savior, Jesus Christ the Messiah, God the Son of God, our Blessed Hope. You can easily recognize Him, and share with others that *He is also our Creator*, as promised in the mix of His Genesis 1:27, John 1:3, Colossians 1:16 and Hebrews 1:8-10 with 1,000 B.C.'s Psalm 2:12 and in this little book, thank God. These 70+ years, from 1941 to 2012, have been extremely rewarding, and I am thrilled now to share this winning achievement, *An American Christian's World (with exciting proven hope for your future!),* with you and yours. And now to your future:

CHAPTER
14

YOUR PROVEN FUTURE!

With these investigations accomplished for General MacArthur and you, it is right to share the results of what I found about your *future* for your benefit. Please pick your choice from the following seven:

1) The real *"approved"* Church (as in chapter 7), will experience its silent "escape" of Luke 21:34b-36a, the "keep you from" of Revelation 3:10, involving 20:5b-6's "first resurrection." Remember that the latter event comes physically before Rev. 20:4, 7:9-14, 13:7-10 and 14:12, which concerns what I think of as that period's *"Great Tribulation" Church*. Again these are not necessarily chronological, but rather "a little here, a little there," as the Word of prophecy is promised in Isaiah 28:11-13.

This Revelation 20:5b-6 promise occurs just before earth's "seven years" of "tribulation" and "great tribulation" – Word-pictured also in Matthew 24:21 (24:29 comes later) with Ezekiel 39:9 and Rev.

7:9-14. At the beginning of these seven years the "approved" Church members are given immortal bodies, I Corinthians 15:53-58, and the real Christ's long-promised marriage supper or wedding feast, Rev. 19:9.

At the end of the above seven years this Church body will return with Him, as in Zechariah 14:5, Colossians 3:4, I Thessalonians 3:13 and Jude 14. Due to Him they will win the massive battles against the Antichrist's forces and destroy them at Armagedon, Jerusalem and southward, with the blood flowing up to the horses' bridles. After the earth is perfected, the "approved" will be given their assignments of authority, reign with Him for Rev. 20:5b-6's "1,000 years," and then "forever" as in 22:5. Our chapter 21 will be sharing what your abundant life will be like then; assuming that you choose to be in this approved assembly, and you might even want to go fishing as in Ezekiel 47:10!

2) As an alternative to the approved, earth's *lukewarm and cold* in attitude toward the Creator Christ, Revelation 3:16, not "eagerly awaiting Him for salvation," Hebrews 9:28b – will "suddenly," I Thessalonians 5:3, find themselves in Luke 21:34b-35's "trap," also known as Revelation 3:10's "test."

Several couples who are dear friends of ours refuse to study and show themselves approved, 2 Timothy 2:15, although they attend their churches every Sunday. They seem to be too busy to enjoy this easier way.

Other couples choose to be "preterit" (preterist), erroneously guessing that all Bible prophecy was fulfilled when General Titus' Roman legions destroyed Jerusalem in 70 A.D. They would have a hard time with the Christ's Zephaniah 1:2-3's "I will completely remove all things from the face of the earth," declares the Lord... man, beast, birds, fish [when re-making earth for His future 1,000 year reign]. When did that ever happen before? These great friends have free choice now, while we pray and ache for each because we love them deeply.

Besides Ezekiel 39:9's "seven years," this coming period is also known as 3½ plus 3½ years, or 42 months plus 1260 days (3½ years) in Bibles. Examples are in Revelation 13:5, Daniel 9:27 and 12:7, with "time, times and half a time" in the Hebrew meaning 1 year, 2 years and ½ a year.

3) Many of these rejected people will later change their minds, choosing the Christ Jesus' Way, preferring *martyrdom* instead of the beast Antichrist's "mark" and the computerized world dictatorship of Revelation 13:4-17, 20:4 and 14:12-13 ("sea" in 13:1's prophecy means human turmoil). People will not want to be caught in earth's increasing tribulation, where 13:17 promises that "...no one will be able to buy or to sell, except the one who has the mark ..." So we find that Matthew 25:31-46 will involve the survivors' BARTERING of goods for water, food, clothing, bedding, shelter, tools, bicycles (no gasoline available?) etc. This is where gold and silver coins can be used, if they and other goods are being traded.

4) Those living in *Middle East Israel* will instantly be caught in *"war"* against Ezekiel 38:3-16's Russia/Rosh and Magog, Iran (Persia until 1934) and their many allies, ending with 39:9's *"Israel will... make fires of the weapons...for [the same] seven years..."* This shows that Mideast Israel will not be totally destroyed in these wars. Please also notice 39:6 about additional "fire" on Russia's Magog people and the "Coastlands," which with Isaiah 13:5's "furthest horizons" I find will involve Russia and the large unnamed westward nations including America.

Of Israel burning the weapons of war for 7 years, very interesting is the fact that Russia's armed forces use lots of *"lignostone"* for its light weapons. I first investigated this in the 1960s. It weighs less than aluminum, is stronger than steel and burns hotter than coal. Russia's invasion of Israel gets more acute when realizing that it has more horses for this than any other nation on earth, Ezekiel 38:15.

Half-way through the seven years a remnant 1/3rd of Israel's popula-tion, probably Hebrew-Jews, will escape to Jordan's Petra (Edom's hidden stone city) as in Zechariah 13:8 with Matthew 24:16-22, to later be rescued by the Christ personally. The remaining *2/3rds of modern Israel will be killed*, as promised also in Zechariah 13:8, appar-ently consisting dominantly of Canaanite-Jews.

123

In prophecy a majority of *the invading Muslim and Russian enemies will be destroyed* by Israel's dozens of U.S.-built F-15 and F-16 jet aircraft, intermediate range ballistic missiles and submarines equipped with nuclear-tipped cruise missiles. Israel reportedly has up to 400 nuclear warheads, with the capability of wiping out much of the world, thanks to the U.S. generosity. Its nuclear and neutron weapons of "FIRE" include 50 top-secret neutron "Jericho" I (1,000 mile range) and 50 Jericho II missiles ready to fire from limestone caves southeast of Tel Aviv – which will burn people's rotting flesh "while they stand," according to Zechariah 14:12 with cross-references. These begin the list of Israel's weaponry for striking Iran, Russia and their allies, while U.S. forces simultaneously also strike beyond its *furthest horizons* (again Isaiah 13:5).

5) When people *die on earth during this seven years*, Biblically their souls (psyche, mind, thinker) and spirits (communicator with their God) will either go to *Hell temporarily*, Matthew 12:40's "heart of the earth," or *Heaven temporarily* if they are *"approved"* by then. It is impossible for us to perfectly judge which place dying people will go, considering last moment decisions, and reportedly now with hundreds of millions of Christians living in communist Russia and China...where we have strongly supported Every Home For Christ's and International Students' building of "home-churches" since 2001.

The second-phase faithful also become "approved" due to their diligent faith in the real Christ, Revelation 20:4; joining those of 20:5b-6's who are in Heaven waiting for the return to earth. When the seven years of tribulation and great tribulation on earth are finished, then both approved groups, the real Church, return to earth with Christ (see chapter seven), to win at Armageddon, Jerusalem and south into Edom's Petra. Could our Creator Christ accomplish all of this for proven truth? You betcha!

6) Hell's former humans will await their *final Judgment for "deeds" 1,000 years later*. They showed no real faith in our Creator Christ, as in Revelation 20:11-13, John 5:29 and Matthew 25:31-46; but will have "paid up the last cent," Matt. 5:25 and Luke 12:59. With this done, "Every knee shall bow to Me," promises the Christ in Romans 14:11

with Isaiah 45:23 and Philippians 2:10. Aren't you glad that we have a patient Almighty Merciful God, Father and Son, helping you and us?

7) The satanic enemy *Canaanites* and their pitiful accomplices will also die, with the Revelation 19:19+21's timing, just after 13:12's world dictator Antichrist beast and his false prophet are thrown alive into the lake of fire, 19:20, and before many of the Canaanites' later final Judgment for "deeds."

Of these prophecies, 2 Peter 1:20 applies with "...*no prophecy of Scripture is a matter of one's own interpretation...*" The filthy [Revelation 22:11] Canaanites' self-centered destroyer "God," also known as the satanic "Elohim" in Genesis 6:4 and "Theos" in 2 Corinthians 4:4, Satan/Lucifer the Devil deceiver, will finally get what he has earned. This will be perfect justice in accord with Isaiah 14:26's ancient "plan," executed 1,000 years in the future with Rev. 20:14-15's "lake of fire," described even further in 21:8 and 22:15.

Let's see that key prophecy: "*Outside are the dogs* [please see your dictionary], and the *sorcerers* and the immoral persons and the murderers and the idolaters, and everyone who loves and practices lying." Meanwhile Revelation 22:11, in accord mathematically from the most-perfect original Koine Greek (see chapter 17), shines some marvelous insights of the future: "The one doing *unrighteously* [unfaithfully], let him *do* unrighteously yet; and the *filthy* one, let him *be made* filthy yet; and the *righteous* [deeds] one, righteousness [faithfulness] let him do yet, and the holy [approved] one let him *be made* holy yet."

As relatively a nobody, I would be honored to serve the real Christ anywhere, as I'm sure our General MacArthur would, in the future everlasting reign; and with you if you choose to. 1000 BC's Psalm 2:12 now applies to all of us: "Do homage to the Son, that He may not become angry and you perish in the way, for His wrath may soon be kindled. How blessed are all who take refuge in Him!" And to paraphrase Joshua 24:15, 'As for my house and me, we will serve our Creator Christ Jesus,' which in turn means also serving His Ancient of Days Father, with both named so in Daniel 7:13-14. Don't you love the Almighty delegation of power there, as in 1 Corinthians 15:27-28 etc.? I sure do.

So just take your pick from 1) through 7), as they fit. You and your friends will be in one of these choices for the future; for as Job 34:33 promises, "...you must choose, and not I."

Meanwhile, to the more immediate potential future for America again investigations indicate that *IRAN* considers firing its Chinese Silkworm and Russian Sunburn anti-ship missiles at the West's oil tankers in the Persian Gulf. *Perhaps you can help get the following to the busy U.S. Joint Chiefs of Staff:*

But potentially more effective, it wants to place a specially-armed freighter in the Gulf of Mexico. When the time is right, which may indeed be 2013's "*springtime*," it expects to fire 12 nuclear missiles 250 miles above some Midwest American State, for example Kansas. These are to carry high altitude electromagnetic pulse (HEMP) explosives to penetrate the atmosphere from east to west coasts, with a goal of neutralizing America, southern Canada and northern Mexico. (Thank you for sharing this insight, Senior Pastor Noah Hutchings, Southwest Radio Ministries.)

This is intended to reverse the surviving people's lifestyles back to that of the early rural 1800s...and make them ripe for the satanic Islamic Muslim dictatorship. These nuclear missiles will probably be either the "Scud," costing Iran about $100,000 each, or its less-expensive "Shahad" ...both allegedly about ready to go. Time is ticking, as in the San Diego Union-Tribune of May 26, 2012, page A-6, on Iran's hundreds of newly-installed nuclear centrifuges underground with purified enriched uranium.

This attack would easily encompass all of America, and produce field strengths of 7,000 to 60,000 volts of electricity. This would disable all newer cars, trucks, planes, trains, motors, communications equipment, computers and also other electronic devices, transformers, military electronic capabilities, command controls, and power grids across the continental United States, southern Canada and northern Mexico. Iran's goal is to take America out as competition and promote its Islamic world dictatorship with its very own fictitious messiah with no proofs of truth.

Water, food, and other shipments by transport would be brought to a halt, while again survivors would go back to rural 1800s living standards. *Bartering* with gold and silver coins and other tangibles would be helpful for survival. Iran has had Russia as an ally for nearly a century, with each expecting its missiles to burn American cities and mountains. While outsiders are not expected to know Iran's above plan, I believe that American offshore military units will have a window of time in which to strike back, especially at Russia – which will be devastated by Israel's and the West's actions in accord with the Bible.

If these surprise strikes are accomplished, the U.S. economy, banking and fund transfers will also stop. Iran's freighter would be sunk, supposedly leaving no evidence of who owned it or who launched the missiles. A substantial American, Canadian or Mexican land counterattack could hardly be carried out *without electricity*, especially without proof of which enemy to attack. Meanwhile Washington's many intelligence agencies unfortunately have a track record of too much competition with each other.

Voters who brought in President Obama and his dozens of unelected "czar" specialists, thanks to support from trillionaires and billionaires Rothschild, Rockefeller, Bronfman, Soros, Strong etc., should be *screaming*. Among other things, Obama and his bureaucrats have weakened meaningful defenses against such a HEMP threat, as well as missile shield defenses for Poland and Czechoslovakia at the insistence of Russia's ex-KGB chief and again president, Vladimir Putin. See chapter 21 for more.

The mass media will not help Americans to accurately understand what is going on, being owned or controlled by our chapter 5's satanic "Canaanites" of Bible prophecy. If that media does not like what is being exposed against it in other news, it persuades the opponent's advertisers to take their business elsewhere, cutting off income and killing it financially.

On a broader scope, *you and I need not take any credit* for what has happened in our lifetimes. We need to be aware that there is a far greater drama now taking place, as mankind races for either proven truth or proven enslavement. Such realities and the future deeply interested my former boss in Japan, General Douglas MacArthur.

CHAPTER
15

HISTORIC PROOFS TO WIN

Time is ticking by quickly, as the next springtime Passover and Pentecost celebrations get nearer. I recently heard a superb pastor remind his people, "In the big picture it's not about you. It is about the everlasting proven truth, for you to enjoy and share!"

Our family found that *these perfectly fulfilled Bible prophecies helped to fortify our faith* in the real Christ, so we trust that you and yours will be enriched likewise. *My hope is that you test these "proofs"* for your own benefit and share them. You also may want to test the man-made religions discussed in chapter 8. It might be helpful for you to highlight your favorite teachings in this book, to more easily retrieve them when needed. And please help us spread the word with others, to "COME OUT" (or be trapped) – the sooner the better, before it is too late!

What follows are samples of your *Creator Christ's HISTORIC prophecies*, all fulfilled on target:

1.   500 BC's Micah 5:2, the Messiah/Christ had to be born in tiny Bethlehem-Ephrathah (He was).
2.   1300 BC's Genesis 22:18 and 49:10, the Christ of Abraham's seed, tribe of Judah (Hebrews 7:14).
3.   700 BC's Isaiah 9:6-7 and 53:2+10-12, to be King David's heir, without royalty (Luke 3:23-38).
4.   700 BC's Isaiah 7:14, He had to be born of a virgin (see Genesis 24:16 and Luke 1:34–38).
5.   1300 BC's Deuteronomy 18:15–22, to speak all that was commanded of Him (Matthew 12:18).
6.   500 BC's Zechariah 11:12 and Psalm 41:9, He had to be betrayed by a friend (John 18:2).
7.   700 BC's Isaiah 53:7, He had to be silent before His accusers (see John 18:2).
8.   700 BC's Micah 5:1 and Isaiah 50:6, He had to be rejected, slapped and spat upon (Mark 15:19).
9.   1000 BC's Psalm 118:22 and Isaiah 53:8, He had to be tried and rejected (Luke 23:1–25).
10.   1000 BC's Psalm 69:21, He had to be given gall and vinegar (Matthew 27:34, John 19:28+37).
11.   500 BC's Zechariah 12:10 and Isaiah 53:5, He had to be pierced (John 19:34).
12.   700 BC's Isaiah 53:12, He had to be killed with criminals (Matthew 27:38).
13.   1300 BC's Deuteronomy 21:22–23, He had to hang on a tree/stauros or stake/skolops (Gal.3:13). The *World Christian Encyclopedia* shows this to be a stake or cross (which helps explain Jer. 10:2–5).
14.   1000 BC's Psalm 22:18, gamblers had to cast lots for His clothing (John 19:23–24).
15.   1000 BC's Psalm 34:20 and Numbers 9:12, none of His bones would be broken (John 19:33).

16. 700 BC's Isaiah 53:10, His Father was pleased to crush Him...if He would... (Romans 8:1–4).

17. 700 BC's Isaiah 53:4–12, He'd atone for what He had Created (Isa. 53:10–12).

18. 1000 BC's Psalm 16:10, He would be resurrected bodily (Luke 24:1–7).

    Biblically He was killed on Preparation Day, a Wednesday (John 19:14); Thursday was the annual Sabbath Passover (Leviticus 23:5); On Friday the women could shop for spices (Mark 16:1–6, as no shopping was allowed on the Thursday and Saturday Sabbaths); Saturday was weekly Sabbath (Luke 23:56), despite philosophy. Biblically His resurrection was on Saturday afternoon, <u>fulfilling Matthew 12:40's full "three days and three nights.</u>" Yes, and <u>Biblically He was long-gone before Sunday!</u>

    Pagan "EASTER" in the 1611 A.D. King James Version/ KJV again is a mistranslation of Acts 12:4's "Pascha" meaning "Passover," while the KJV otherwise names this as "Passover" 28 of the 29 times that Pascha is used in the New Testament. Why does the KJV mistranslate Acts 12:4's "Pascha" to "Easter," falsely honoring the Roman pagan vernal dawn goddess Oestre/Eastre, when even the 1560 A.D. Geneva Bible (used by Pilgrims) is accurate with regard to "Passover" in Acts 12:4? *"Easter" has badly detoured Christianity, led by often man-made Roman Catholicism!* Let's see more here:

19. 1000 BC's Psalm 68:18 (Ephesians 4:8), He would take believers from the heart of earth's Paradise to His Heavenly one (Luke 23:43 with 16:19–31); and they are still not yet perfected (Heb. 11:39–40).

20. 1000 BC's Psalm 110:1, He'd be at His Father's right hand (Hebrews 1:3, 8:1).

21. 100 AD's Matthew 16:18, He'd build His "approved" Church (1 Cor. 11:19 and 2 Timothy 2:15 with James 1:12).

22. 100 AD's Revelation 20:5b–6, He'll provide His "first resurrection" for His "approved" true believers. "No one knows"

in Matthew 24:36 is a mistranslation of *"no one has known"* *mathematically*, with 24:25 and Amos 3:7 in full accord.

100 AD's Revelation 16:16 and 19:14-21, He and His cavalry will win at *Armageddon, then Jerusalem and southward* over His enemies. You will probably remember our discussion in the Preface about "going" and "returning" with Him. He will then take over instead of taking sides. "…There is no other name under Heaven …by which we must be saved" (Acts 4:12). He is our Almighty "I Am" Creator, from front to back in Bibles, obedient to His Father's Will, thank God.

It is worth repeating mention of Dr. *Stoner's* Pasadena City College computer study, in which his students were asked to research hundreds of Bible prophecies about the real Messiah/Christ. The question was, could any eight selected prophecies be fulfilled by anyone born after 70 AD? The answer is that the chance of this happening is 1out of 1 nonillion (1+30 zeros). The *coming Antichrist will have no chance* of beating these odds, boastful though that abomination of desolation will be.

CHAPTER
16

SCIENTIFIC PROOFS TO WIN

Here are just some of your *Creator Christ's SCIENTIFIC prophecies*, as more Proofs to share:

1. 1300 BC's Job 38:31, scientists agree that the "Pleiades" (7 stars) hold earth in its universal circuit.
2. 900 BC's Proverbs 8:27 and -700 BC's Isaiah 40:22, scientists now also agree that the earth is round.
3. 1300 BC's Job 38:25, they agree that a tiny dart precedes each lightning bolt.
4. 500 BC's Jeremiah 33:22, they agree that the total number of stars still cannot be counted by man.
5. 1300 BC's Job 26:7 and -700 BC's Isaiah 14:13b, they agree about the north's "empty space."

6. 1300 BC's Job 26:7 and they as you also see that this earth "hangs on nothing."

7. 1300 BC's Genesis 1:16 could make moon-worshippers ask how Moses knew the sun was greater.

8. 1300 BC's Leviticus 13:46's quarantine overcame England's 1800s leprosy. How did they know?

9. 1300 BC's: Genesis 2:21 used deep sleep for the patient when undergoing major surgery.

10. 700 BC's: Isaiah 40:12 countered ancient ideas, by using precision to combine elements.

11. BC's: Genesis 2:7, scientists have found our bodies' elements to be like Middle East dust.

12. 1300 BC's: Job 38:7, they have found that stars make beautiful music together, instead of static.

13. 1300's BC: Job 28:25, they also found that wind does have weight, $1/773^{rd}$ that of water.

14. 1300 BC's: Job 28:7, how did Moses know that the eye of the vulture ranks among creation's finest?

15. 1300 BC's: Genesis 41:54–57, modern archeologists have found proofs of Joseph's seven years.

16. 1300 BC's: Genesis 6:14–16, regarding *NOAH'S ARK*, three European schools proved that samples of the white oak, or gopher wood, brought down from Turkey's Ararat Mountains in 1955, fit all Biblical requirements for Noah's Ark – even though no white oak or gopher wood has ever grown within 300 miles of Ararat. These three schools are:

    a. The National Museum of Natural History in Paris,

    b. Madrid's Forestry Institute of Research and Experiments, and

    c. The University of Bordeaux in France. This was accomplished by French business executive Fernand Navarra, his son and his team (*Noah's Ark: I Touched It*, c/o 84 Boulevard George V, Bordeaux, France).

On the *HUMAN EYE*, Researcher Mark *Cahill* did a good service in sharing *One Second After You*. In this he quoted research by Lawrence

O. Richards' *It Couldn't Just Happen*, Thomas Nelson, 1989, pages 139-140. We did not hear back from Nelson, but Mark honored my request to quote his work, for which we will give a copy of our book to him:

"The human eye is the retina, pupil, iris, cornea, lens and optic nerve. The retina has approximately 137 million special cells that respond to light and send messages to the brain. About 130 million of these cells look like rods, and handle the black and white. The other seven million are cone shaped and allow us to see in color. The retina cells receive light impressions, which are translated to electric pulses and sent to the brain via the optic nerve.

"A special section of the brain called the visual cortex interprets the pulses to color, contrast, depth etc., which allows us to see 'pictures' of our world. Incredibly, the eye, optic nerve and visual cortex are totally separate and distinct subsystems. Yet together they capture, deliver and interpret up to 1.5 million pulse messages a millisecond! It would take dozens of Cray computers programmed perfectly and operating together flawlessly to even get close to performing this task."

Some agnostics, atheists and others might ignore these great miracles, preferring their macro-evolution nonsensical impossibilities. Are you having as much fun with these *Proofs to Win* as I am?

CHAPTER
17

MATHEMATICS PROOFS TO WIN

And third, your *Creator Christ's MATHEMATICS* is another delightful way to prove that you and we are on the accurate track to enjoying the everlasting truth. You probably know of the Latin numbering system in which Roman numerals are used, with I = 1, V = 5, X = 10 etc. Your Bible's original Masoretic Hebrew and Aramaic (the latter in books of Ezra and Daniel) Old Testament, and Koine Greek New Testament had a number for each letter, too, so each letter had a perfect prophetic math' value.

For examples, in Masoretic Hebrew the letters' math' values are: Aleph = 1, Beth = 2, Gimel = 3, Daleth = 4, Hei = 5, Vav = 6, Ziao = 7, Cheth = 8, Teth = 9, Yod = 10, Chaph = 20, Lamed = 30, Mem = 40, Nun = 50, Semoch = 60, Ayia = 70, Phe = 80, Tasddi = 90, Kooph = 100 and so on. Similarly the Koine Greek letters' math' values are: Alpha = 1, Beta = 2, Gamma = 3, Delta = 4, Epsilon = 5, (no 6), Zeta = 7, Iota = 10, Kappa = 20, Lambda = 30, Mu = 40, Nu = 50, Xi = 60, Omicron = 70, Pi = 80, Rho = 100 etc.

Next, if we apply this basic math' to the letters in each word in Genesis 1:1, we will find that the math' total of its Hebrew letters is divisible exactly by both 7 and 11. Here's the kicker: Likewise the entire 66-book original Bible is miraculously this way!

The total vocabulary used in the original 66-book Bible is exactly divisible by 7, as are all words that begin with vowels and all words that begin with consonants, as is the total of all of the letters, as are words occurring more than once, and only once, as are nouns, and non-nouns, as are the numerical values of all male names, as are all female names, as are all words beginning with each letter in the original 66-book Bible, as are all the total references to the Christ's true followers called "holy" ones (mis-translated saints).

The Old Testament books quoted in the New Testament are exactly divisible by 11, as are all letters in the 21 epistles and 45 non-epistles, as are letters in the 26 writers' names, as are letters in the 22 anonymous books and the 44 non-anonymous books, as are letters in the names of writers of a single book, and of more than one book.

Mathematical odds against these perfect multiples of 11 occurring in the 66 books are 214,358,881 to one; while the odds against these perfect multiples of 7 run into billions to one. However, *you and I could not manually compose a 300-word paragraph with math perfection like this if we worked on it for six months.* Yet thousands of proofs show that the original 66-book God-breathed Bible (2 Timothy 3:16) was all composed with mathematical perfection – yes all divisible by 7 and also by 11, from Genesis 1:1 through Revelation 22:21!

The world's greatest specialist in this field was Dr. Ivan *Panin,* a brilliant agnostic mathematician who left Russia in 1872 and was graduated from Harvard University. He accepted the Christ due in large measure to the original Bible's mathematics. He devoted fifty years to this study, producing over forty thousand pages of computations in support of his findings – that the Bible was originally mathematically perfect. Dr. Panin died in October 1942. (Parenthetically, let's not confuse this math' with so-called Bible codes and other such studies.)

The staff at your local public library may be able to help you locate copies of Dr. Panin's books and pamphlets, as our family purchased:, including his *Bible Numerics*, *The Numeric Greek New Testament*, *The English New Testament*, *The Last Twelve Verses of Mark*, *The Verbal Inspiration of the Bible Scientifically Demonstrated*, and *The Writings of Ivan Panin*. His books also mirror earlier works on this topic, such as Dr. Browne's *Ordo Saeculoreum*, Dr. Grant's *Numerical Bible*, and Dr. Bullinger's *Numbers in the Scriptures*.

Another excellent and relatively easy-to-understand study on these Bible numerics is Dr. David L. *Brooks' Absolute Mathematical Proofs of the Divine Inspiration of the Bible*. For potential inquirers, my records show his mailing address as 7600 Jubilee Drive, Niagara Falls, Ontario, Canada [L2G 7J6]. Mathematics and devoted prayer in Jesus' Name seem to have plenty in common. Both are certain; and the second with John 8:31-32's "if…" also brings unmatched peace, truth and freedom.

Campus Crusade for Christ's Dr. Bill Bright shared his "four spiritual laws" with us years ago. But when I asked for permission to quote these here, his nice people required what appeared to me as a volume of paperwork that would have taken hours away from completing this book, so I said no thank you with good wishes.

We appreciate such real *CHRISTIAN PASTORS ETC.,* so you may want to join us in encouraging:

Dr. Pastor Chuck Baldwin (http://chuckbaldwinlive.com) — Pastor Irvin Baxter, Jr. (800/363-8463) — Pastor Matthew Booker (858/231-9152) — Dr. James Dobson (800/232-6459) — Dr. Dick & Dee Eastman, Every Home For Christ (719/337-9528) — Dr. Billy Graham (Montreat, N.C.) — Dr. Franklin Graham (800/631-7141) — Pastor John Hagee (800/854-9899) — Dr. Billy James Hargis II (www.christiancrusade.com) — Sr. Pastor Noah Hutchings (800/652-1144) — Dr. David Jeremiah (800/792-1355) — Pastor Ron & Dorothea Joling (541/396-4183) — Pastor Greg Laurie (800/821-3300) — Pastor Hal Lindsey (www.hallindsey.com) — Bob Livingston

Letter (800/773-5699 — Pastor Texe & Wanda Marrs (1708 Patterson Road, Austin, Texas [78733]) — Richard J. Maybury Report (800/509-5400) — Don McAlvany, Intelligence 877/622-5826) — Dr. Stan+Barbara Monteith (831/475-6651) — Dr. John D. Morris, ICR (800/337-0375) — Pastor Joel Osteen (800/565-0772) — Pastor James & Betty Robison (800/947-5433) — Dr. Doug & Susan Shaw, International Students Inc. (719/576-2700x103) — Pastor David Smith, Newswatch (972/937-2227) — Dr. Charles Stanley (intouch. org) — Dr. Pastor Tom & Judy Theriault (760/504-6787) — Dr. Jack & Rexella Van Impe (800/603-7766) — David Kapelian & Joseph Farah (at Worldnewsdaily.com) —- Of course there are thousands of additional real Christian Pastors etc. in America and worldwide as you know, thank God.

Earlier in chapter 8 we were seeking any time-tested prophetic PROOFS to support man-made religions, but there were none. So with Agape-love I responsibly asked all followers to "COME OUT!"

Why do you suppose there are no such solid PROOFS to support the often well-meaning Hinduism, Zoroastrianism, Confucianism, Buddhism, Taoism, Judaism, Roman Catholicism, Shintoism, Sikhism, Islamism, or other man-made religious philosophies mired in Matthew 7:13b's often-wandering and dangerous "broad" way?

CHAPTER
18

SIGNS WITH PROOFS TO WIN

"When you see all these things...this generation [ranging Biblically from 25 to 70 years] will not pass away until all these things take place" Matthew. 24:33–34. And 16:3–18 add insights, "[3]...cannot discern the signs of the times... [4] except the sign of Jonah... [[see 12:40]]...[16] you are the Christ, the Son of the living God...and... [18] you are Peter, and upon this Rock [Petra, bedrock, Christ; not petros, Peter, little stone] I will build My Church; and the gates of Hades shall not overpower it."

Here are *Creator Christ Jesus' promised SIGNS OF THE TIMES prophecies*, interacting since 1967:

1. 500 BC Ezekiel 38:8...Would you agree that Middle East Israel is now "gathered," as prophesied?
2. 500 BC Zechariah 8:8+12:6...It won control of Old or East Jerusalem on June 7, 1967.

3. Measuring from Jerusalem, Ezekiel 38:12's "center of the world," do you find four geographical confederations of nations? – North: Rosh or Russia, Ezek. 38:3 and 15; South: Arabs and Africans, Ezek. 30:3–5; West: Europe and the Americas, Daniel 7:19-25, Rev. 17:9-16; and East: Asia, Rev. 9:14-16+16:12.

4. Do you live in "difficult times," with media agreement (65 AD, 2 Timothy 3:1–7 and 4:1–4)?

5. Do many people "fear" life, HIV and AIDS, the IRS and other worldly pressures (Luke 21:26)?

6. Have you too been hearing of "peace and security," KJV's erroneous "safety" (1 Thess. 5:3)?

7. Are you hearing of "wars and rumors of wars" and extremes of weather (Mark 13:7)?

8. Do modern jets and space "travel" seem thrilling and easy nowadays (500 BC, Daniel 12:4)?

9. Doesn't the world's "knowledge" nearly double every year or so (Daniel 12:4 as above)?

10. Don't world almanacs show "earthquakes" substantially increasing in this century (Matthew. 24:7)?

11. Aren't droughts and "famines" striking large areas of the earth, leading to the coming Rev. 6:5-8?

12. Aren't "plagues" such as influenza and Aids spreading dangerously in various places (Luke 21:11)?

13. Doesn't the Canaanite-owned or controlled mass media thrive on promoting "terrors" (Luke 21:11)?

14. Would "great signs from heaven" include UFOs, space shots, and satellites (Luke 21:11)?

15. Can you detect "false prophets," who thrive on taking people's money (Matthew7:15–23)?

16. Aren't many 'Bible studies' really social "philosophy" meetings (Colossians. 2:8)?

17. Doesn't "apostasy" test to be common within Christianity's 20,000+ denominations (2 Thess. 2:3)?

18. Aren't there many of the media's and society's "mockers" of Christ's simple truth (2 Peter 3:3)?

19. Unlike Rome's early Christians' saying a firm "no" to state licenses, which puts the state's status over Christ, isn't the U.S. IRS' "501.c.3" license now chosen by pastors over 508.c.1.A's freedom?

20. Does "Babylon the Great" of Revelation 16:19 involve 3 parts – political, religious and economic?

21. Isn't this computerized world ready for Rev. 13:16–18's economic dictatorship by 13:3's "beast?

22. Did you know that your driver's license "ID" is now encoded in the UN's aviation computer system?

23. Did you know that the next "sign" will be Luke 21:35b's "trap" of earth, as in our Preface? In chapter 8 I tried to expose this world's man-made religions and cults, with responsible Agape-love. Doing so is vital now, for otherwise the danger is similar to you flying in a space capsule, but finding yourself off-target by at least one degree – meaning that it is nearing too late to "COME OUT!"

As an additional "sign," giving credit where credit is due, mankind's well-meaning efforts may have been accomplished by *Satan's "tares,"* exposed in chapter 5 potentially as *"children of the devil"* Canaanites. It is not always easy to prove who really did what to whom and when; but history indicates that many **BIG NAMES** have stolen other people's productivity.

For example, the 'great' admitted atheist Dr. Albert *Einstein* told his first wife, Mileva Maric, as proven in his 41 letters to her, that when he was a Switzerland patent office clerk, he stole the "theory of relativity" from Germany's physicist-inventor *Max Plank* (1858–1947). Einstein's pushy-shovey associates, the Ullstein brothers, promoted giving the 1921 Nobel Prize award to Einstein.

For such false acts, in Isaiah 29:16 they are promised that "You turn things around," while they wait for Revelation 20:11-15's "great white throne" Judgment 1,000 years from now for their "deeds," also promised in John 5:29 and Matthew 25:31-46.

Other victims of fraud included America's famous inventor *Thomas Edison*, who patented over 2,000 inventions. He produced his General Film Company's "Kinetoscope Projector" for motion pictures, but in 1903 Jack *Warner* (formerly *Goldenberg*, his father emigrating from Poland to the U.S. in 1887) and his brothers, Albert, Harry, and Sam stole this projector invention. Edison sued and won in a New York court, but the tricky Warner brothers skipped town to Los Angeles and its "Hollywood" to escape enforcement. Other victims of theft/fraud include *Lee De Forrest* and *Theodore Case* with their talking machines inventions, stolen in like manner.

Our family knew the original *"Three Stooges"* (friend *Dick Hakins* and his two partners), who for decades entertained Europe's royalty and other audiences around the world. Even their stage names were fraudulently stolen by the potential Canaanites for movies that you may have seen.

And here's a bigger one: When Bill *Gates* was age 19 at Harvard University, before he dropped out, he and his family paid $50,000 to *Tim Patterson* for the "computer software" technology invention that made Microsoft huge. Did you know that Patterson invented his software in four months? Hopefully all of these people are enjoying the fruits of their deeds while they can, and had better change their pathway in time.

It is not my job to condemn or judge any one for his/her "deeds" or "faith," because our proven Creator Christ will do that perfectly, again as in John 5:29 with the Revelation 20:11–15 and Matthew 25:31-46. Instead, I do ask all of you who are not among chapter 7's "approved" to change your minds now, called "repent;" be "baptized" as in 1 Peter 3:21; and learn all that you can from your Bible's simple truths. You can help share these facts and proofs too, if you care. But do not be like the Dead Sea, where non-flowing water rots; but rather be like the River Jordan, where clean water flows clean and the Christ Jesus' baptism fulfilled the ritual or Law of water baptism for the approved Church.

CHAPTER

19

LAWFUL ECONOMICS

You may be aware that there are basically three opposing types of economics in human societies. #1) is often used in many homes, and essentially follows the concept of Austrian von Mises' free enterprise. This works best where everyone is honest, the government is small, and all can enjoy general prosperity. It also is how conditions tended to be in 1776's American Colonies, with few exceptions.

#2) is used by many governments wanting to gain control, often operated at least partially on the basis of Keynesian *economic socialism*, in parallel with *political communism*. #3) can be total dictatorship, as with 18th century BC's benevolent emperor Hammurabi (with his "eye for an eye" punishments). The weakness with the latter is that when he died his weak successors could not hold the empire together. The real Creator Christ's everlasting reign (Daniel 7:14, Luke 1:33) will not have that problem, right?

Allegedly, Germany's psychopath, apparently one-half Canaanite-Jew Adolf Shickelgruber *Hitler* (1889–1945), Italy's overstuffed Benito *Mussolini* (1883–1945), and Japan's nationalistic Hideki *Tojo* (1884–1948) were wannabe opportunists in comparison. Likewise, Soviet Russia's communist mass-murderer Joseph *Stalin* (Iosif Vissarionovich Dzhugashvili, 1879–1953, who allegedly had a half–Canaanite-Jew mother) and China's equally-cruel communist mass-murderer Mao *Tse-tung* (1893–1976), seemed to get their kicks from hurting people.

What a difference those five were from the real everlasting Jesus Christ/Messiah of Bible prophecy. Those cruel predators, who are now paying their own price (Luke 12:59) for terrible deeds, deserve to also have those same "deeds" fully reviewed in His Revelation 20:11–15's "white throne" Judgment, about 1,000 years from now on this then re-made and perfected earth. Whichever way, economics is the science that deals with production, distribution, and consumption of wealth in relation to labor, finance, taxation, and politics.

The Canaanites' *economic socialism*, melded with their *political communism*, is a pathway to their cruel Pax Judaica's 10,000 years of 'peace'...meaning their long-planned merciless dictatorship. Put another way, Keynesian economics is a road toward socialistic dictatorship, which is exactly what the satanic Canaanites plan to have.

IRAN's president Mahmoud *Ahmadinejad* dreams of an Islamic world dictatorship, but it will fail badly *if its cargo freighter in the Gulf of Mexico launches the 12 nuclear missiles* to go 250 miles over middle America, countered by Israel unleashing its arsenals (see chapter 14). Do you suppose that his Islamic "Amadi"-messiah and the Canaanite protocols' "king" will be prophecy's same Antichrist in one suit for Daniel 9:27's week of *seven years?*

As you probably know, many governments but not all have been enemies of their people, for example purposely destroying their currency with controlled *inflation*. In the 1920s England's John *Keynes* (Keynesian economics) wrote, "By a continuing process of inflation, governments can confiscate, secretly and unobserved, an important part of the wealth of their citizens. There is no subtler, no surer means of overturning the existing basis of society than to debauch the currency. The process engages *all the hidden forces of economic law on the side of destruction*, and does it in a manner which *not one man in a million is able to diagnose.*"

Keynes' philosophy was for *socialist* government to artificially pump up the economy when it was weak, then back off when it was stronger, all the while ignoring the power of a free enterprise economy that over time will tend to heal itself. I agree with England's former Prime Minister *Margaret Thatcher* who, speaking to Parliament, said that "*socialism* always has a problem – eventually you run out of other people's money."

Other economists have estimated that the present Federal Reserve's debt-note, called a paper "dollar," is now worth about 1¢ of its $1.00 value in 1941. You might think of primarily blaming the Canaanites' financial power, and their global "banking" control for starters, with greedy accomplices; and I find that you would probably be right, with *unbelievable $trillions in profits for them.*

Thomas Jefferson (1743-1826), one of America's Founding Fathers and 3rd President, who designed the "Bill of Rights" at self-taught lawyer Patrick Henry's insistence, was wisely skeptical of private banks. He realized that the shrewd banking "*system*" can be *owned and controlled by enemies* of America, as is the case right now (proven in chapter 5). His current enemies have tried to paint him as being as filthy as they are, with no meaningful proof behind their accusations. And the great Patrick Henry's name has been eliminated from modern American textbooks, so we re-introduce it quite thoroughly in chapter 21!

Jefferson said of (now the Canaanite-Jews' Federal Reserve's) private banking, "I believe that banking institutions are more dangerous to our liberties than standing armies…If the American people [We the People, as in the Constitution's Preamble *for* our USA] ever allow private banks to control the issue of currency…the banks and corporations that will grow up around them will deprive the people of all property until their children will wake up homeless on the continent that their fathers conquered."

You might consider re-reading chapter 5, where we discuss how Mr. Rothschild's procedures have gradually seized control of America financially. Two of his keys to conquest are still the *power of debt and compounded interest*, which is exactly America's #1 cancerous economic problem today. In opposition to such a predator is, as our Foreword by Jim Evans reminds us, "the high level of Citizenry and [Republican self-] Government prayerfully designed by our Founding Fathers." This reminds me of the first U.S. s̲upreme [small 's' in the original Constitution] Court ruling, in 1793's Chisholm v. Georgia 2 Dall. 419 at 471, that we private Natural Born Free American and State Article III Citizens are *"sovereigns without subjects."* Do you realize the responsibilities involved in this assignment?

Coming out of the Continental Congress, *Dr. Ben Franklin* (with several honorary doctorates) was asked by a lady-Citizen what kind of government America has. He replied to her, "You have a Republic, madam, if you can keep it!" (Bartlett's Familiar Quotations).

In 1972, the Court ruled in Laird v. Tatum 408 US 1 that "Those who already walk submissively will say there is no cause for alarm. But submissiveness is not our heritage. The First Amendment was designed to allow rebellion to remain our heritage. The Constitution was designed to keep government off the backs of the people. The *Bill of Rights* was added to keep the precepts of belief and expression, of the press, of political and social activities free from surveillance [such as by Obama and his lawyer-czars]. The Bill of Rights was designed to keep agents of government and official eavesdroppers away from assemblies of the people. The aim was to allow men to be free and independent and to assert their rights against [increasingly-usurping] government."

Please be aware that COURT RULINGS are shown first with the names of the opposing parties, then the court (if a U.S. s̲upreme Court case, it will show "US" or "SCt"), and then the page numbers.

Unlike propaganda often seen in Canaanite-owned movies and television etc., it has been proven that *in 1776* a majority of America's women and children felt more secure than today; their men were generally industrious, strong physically, mentally and spiritually, with many educated in the Biblical Christian faith, and all concerned were glad of it.

Untaught in modern government/public schools, when lovely *WOMEN* finally won their right to vote, they accidently made themselves chattel, and thereby they lost both their basic freedoms and protection from lawsuits. Head-of-household voters were men at work, and they were expected to protect their families! Then they all can enjoy the security, variety, recognition and response that all of us need.

Speaking of protection, I am generally against *armed rebellion*, where *mobs* of men and women can be easily manipulated (please see the Revelation. 13:10). The exception is necessary self-defense.

So again, *economics is the science that deals with* the production, distribution and consumption of wealth, in relation to labor, finance, taxation and politics. American families do this with the management of their income and expenditures; while governments most often use vote-seeking career politicians and bureaucrats to spend other people's money and pass on big problems to the next self-servers.

Unless *We the People strongly demand enforcement of the Constitution* (America's "supreme Law of the Land," Article 6:2), even well-meaning governments will continue to run rampant over this nation and your freedom – due to political pride and greed. This is in accord with Romans 3:23's "*for all have sinned* and fall short of the glory of God;" and the third law of thermo-dynamics about any matter, left to its own devices in a closed or open system, will always tend toward decay. *Lord Acton* added another reality – that "*power* corrupts, and absolute power corrupts absolutely" (Bartlett's Familiar Quotations).

And you might want to remind Hillary Rodham Clinton and Obama that "*treaties*" are NOT equal to our Constitution, as in 1957's Reid v. Covert 354 US 1 at 17, referencing their "Treaty of the Sea."

You may have heard about Europe's nations with horrendous *debt*, which is basically the result of their *people demanding economic socialism*. France, as one example, voted out its president, because he wanted to trim that nation's debt. With it everything at first seemed to be without cost. Nobody seemed to be paying for their artificial affluence; but quietly most everybody became enslaved economically by Revelation 18's wealthy "merchants of the earth" – who very often proved to be the Canaanites of Bible prophecy. It was not much different economically with ancient Israel, and will be until Romans 11:26.

The federal U.S. government, often with destructive advisers like Dr. David Rockefeller's (Rockenfeld's) shrewd minion Dr. Henry Kissinger (Heinz Stern, from Germany), has followed ancient Rome's economic patterns like a map. One warning came in 55 BC by *Cicero*: "The budget should be balanced, the treasury should be refilled, public debt should be reduced, the arrogance of officialdom should be tempered and controlled, and assistance to foreign lands should be curtailed lest Rome become bankrupt. People must learn to work, instead of living on public assistance." Is this also America today?

Speaking of *"WORK,"* great guidelines are given in Ecclesiastes 9:10, "Whatever your hand finds to do, verily do it with all your might;" Colossians 3:23, "Whatever you do, do your *work* heartily, as for the Lord rather than for men;" and 2 Thessalonians 3:10, "If anyone will not *work*, neither let him eat." It is the job of the church to assist *widows and orphans*, and the job of government to govern!

Europe's Greece, Italy, Portugal, Hungary, and Spain are experiencing horrendous economic problems as a result of their socialist self-serving overwhelming *debt*. Yet the federal U.S. government reportedly has more debt than all other nations combined, totaling at least $16 trillion of current debt, plus another estimated $45 trillion of unfunded future obligations such as pensions. That is *$61 trillion* (13 zeros) of planned U.S. government incompetence debt! And some people wonder why American Citizens find that their politicians act like idiots! But be careful about replacing them, and getting worse ones...

The Congress of the federal U.S. government, last incorporated 6/11/1887, is restricted in its TERRITORIAL JURISDICTION or authority Constitutionally by Articles 1:8:17–18, "To exercise exclusive Legislation [over *federal property only*, please read it!]..." – and 4:3:2 likewise restricts Congress' [and its agencies'] to "Rules and

Regulations respecting the Territory or other Property *belonging to the [federal] United States...*" Usurpers tried to have the *1940 Buck Act* overlay the 50 States, but that is not organic Law!

Did you notice that all of the Congress' [and again its agencies'] laws and regulations must be in accordance with our Constitution, or they are null and void? My *documentations* for this are wrapped in the mix of 16 American Jurisprudence 2d 1 p. 315; 1900's Lima v. Bidwell 182 US 176 @ 179; 1905's South Carolina v. US 199 US 437 @ 448; 1920's Eisner v. Macomber 252 US 189 @ 205-206; and a zillion cross-references! Plus the classic is 1803's Marbury v. Madison 1 Cranch 137 @ 180: "...all laws which are repugnant to the Constitution are [still] null and void..." Hear this, Congress and President!

You can count on it that some slippery politicians and bureaucrats will try to get around these lawful restrictions, including law-evasions using the so-called "commerce clause" of Article 1:8:3. It would be refreshing to see a golden-throated attorney *squarely challenge* presidents' circumventions of the_Congress' authority, using his slick executive orders and directives in excess, as did Abraham Lincoln and Franklin Roosevelt in war.

And it would also be refreshing to see the same lawyer *squarely challenge* the Congress' unlawful delegation of America's money supply and control to the Canaanite's mis-named "Federal Reserve" corporation (unlawful as proven in our chapter 5). My *references* to proper American law in this are 1935's Schechter Poultry Co. v. US 295 US 495, and 1936's Carter v. Carter Coal Co. 298 US 339, ruling that the Congress cannot lawfully delegate "Constitutional powers to non-government entities."

Re friendly judges and other lawyers, some have reviewed this book's manuscript, and added that they had wanted to write a book about their profession, but would get in trouble doing so. You may have heard the one about the busload of *LAWYERS* going to a convention in Las Vegas. The good news was that their bus went over a cliff. The bad news was that there were three empty seats. Here is more good news:

1) Plato wrote of lawyers as "small and unrighteous." 2) Keats classed lawyers "in the natural history of monsters." 3) Shakespeare's Henry IV Part ii 86 added, "The first thing we do, let's kill all the lawyers." 4) Former Los Angeles Deputy D.A. Terry Fisher concluded her famous "L.A. Law" series with "...the U.S. legal system is just a big game...lawyers do little more than create income and little games for lawyers..."

Factually, the so-called *American Bar Association* was gradually planted by 1878 in America, funded by Europe's Rothschilds' for themselves and lawyers; then it was organized by 1909 as their monopoly in Chicago. Under orders, the Rockefellers wooed the University of Chicago into agreeing to this power-grab, for a $40 million dollar donation, and by 1927 even California was under the ABA yoke.

Today if you *retain a bar lawyer*, according to their Corpus Juris Secundum §4 with 7 CJS at paragraph 2, you become a "ward of the court," like an imbecile of slavery. That is far different from your birthright as a Natural Born Free private Citizen of America and Article III State of your location.

But as a once-famous Robert Welch warned, "The average American is so inherently honest and decent that he cannot believe that his leaders [often lawyers] are *almost totally evil*." No wonder that your Bible teaches insights such as Luke 11:52's "Woe to you lawyers!" and Romans 3:23's "For *all have sinned* and fall short of the glory of God."

A nation of law-abiding tax-paying Bible-believing real Christians, as our forefathers envisioned, would have forbidden the Congress' and Presidents' economic suicide with *usurpations of the laws*; as well as D.C. allowing millions of *illegal aliens* to invade America (breaking Article 4:4:1) in order to get *illegal votes*. The Congress of the U.S. government has not done its Constitutional duty. Furthermore, the proven-*fraudulently ratified Amendments 14, 16, and 17* to the Constitution for the USA should be properly ruled "null and void" by Law, but the U.S. supreme Court, citing the fraudulent 14th, also has been too weak to properly protect the Republic, as its *50 million murdered-aborted babies* should agree!

Of legal antics, the *"ACLU"* or American Civil Liberties Union is another example of apparently-Canaanite infiltration. My investigations show that the root of this came in 1909 from anarchist Emma Goldman, whose inflammatory talk persuaded wealthy but simplistic Roger Baldwin to form the ACLU in 1920. You may want to look up its 1988 "Policy Guide," including anti-American goals on its pages 4, 18, 81, 84, 92, 210 and 242…before you vomit.

Law-abiding taxpaying Citizens (in accord with the Constitution) should be as *well educated* as their American ancestors were; know that their proper status is natural born free American National and Article 3 State Citizens by Law. This marvelous status should be kept without need of any voluntary government benefits, franchises and privileges, unlike federal U.S. citizens with buckets of them! In 1776 almost 100% of America's private Citizens were home-schooled, with nearly a 97% literacy rate as a result. We have copies of the famous 1690's *"New England Primer"* from which America's Founding Fathers learned to read and spell, 1836's *"McGuffey's Readers"* and the superb *"Pilgrim's Progress."*

But the federal U.S. had to impose its government-owned-public school system, with its infiltrated and revised 1913 *NEA*/National Education Association, to help brainwash and dumb down even our magnificent Citizens. Instead of powerful strength in unity, referred to as "out of many one," too often private Citizens "think that they know it all." These can be reminders of ancient Israel's scenario, seen in Judges 17:6 and 21:25: *"…everyone did what was right in his own eyes."* That to me constitutes national stupidity, and is downright ignorant from lack of high-level quality leadership.

The *state driver's license* is an example of this. It was gradually promoted for America's private Citizens, who then *voluntarily* applied for theirs after the controlled media, government, schools and dumbed-down parents falsely warned of a non-existent requirement. Nobody needed such a license when driving a horse and buggy, except for commercial people – such as delivery wagon drivers of ice, milk, butter etc. and chauffeurs. This law has not changed to this day! Then came the Roosevelt administration's 1935 *"social security" dependency…*

When families repeatedly spend more than they take in, financial disaster replaces their security. Assisting in this is subtle government inflation by its paper currency. Economist *Merrill Jenkins* Sr. states in his book *The Greatest Hoax On Earth* that "The writers of the Constitution knew exactly what they were doing when they wrote... Article 1:10:1... People able to *BARTER with gold and silver coin* [can] control government and are free...the loss of the right...enslaves people to the creators of psychological [the privately-Federal Reserves'] 'money.'" Investors in gold and silver coin need to be aware that the prices or values can be manipulated, so enjoy yours for the long-range, not caring about day-to-day prices, for wise bartering when you and others (Matthew 25:31-46's deeds) need to do it.

Confiscation of private assets by a criminal government is always possible; although if you read FDR's 1933 gold seizure acts carefully, his words *"continental" U.S. meant only federal property!* Besides gold and silver, Canaanites enjoy their Federal Reserve paper money, costing them *less than 2¢ per Fed' Note for the ink and paper* to buy each one and lend them to the federal U.S. government, *earning annual interest* as long as each Note is in circulation worldwide! Citizens who believe the infiltrated federal government's propaganda that its annual *inflation* is now under 3% are not watching product price increases. Just compare 1960 prices with those now, and understand what inflation is. Likewise check with your library for real U.S. unemployment, reported to be exceeding 15%.

In accord economically the *criminal IRS/Internal Revenue Service* (see chapter 20) is doing everything possible, often far beyond its restricted territorial federal jurisdiction, to prohibit lawful barter. Meantime its employees are shocked to find out that they have *NO lawful written Delegation of Authority to act for the IRS WITHIN THE 50 STATES.* The equally usurping *FDA*/Food and Drug Administration wants to prohibit you and other private American Citizens from even growing your own crops and purchasing your own garden seeds, vitamins, and minerals. Why? Whose side are they on?

For another example, reportedly the IRS has tried to require American coin dealers to report (to it) all private Citizens who sell

$600 or more of gold, as of January 1, 2012 (so far it is only partly effective). And the FDA has reportedly been seeking the authority to put you in jail for owning the garden seeds! How is that for the once- "land of the free and the home of the brave?"

On the other hand, if you are a *federal U.S. citizen with voluntary government benefits*, you'd better comply! But have you ever been told that, if you volunteer, you can be waiving your Constitutional Rights? Or have you been told that the 1970's Brady v. US 397 US 742 @ 748 may reverse such a waiver? And has government shown you the status of Title 26 Code of Federal Regulations Ch. 1 §1.1-1(c)'s *"Who is a [federal U.S.] citizen?* Every person born or naturalized in the [federal] United States and subject to *ITS* jurisdiction is a [federal] citizen."

I honestly believe that all the legislators and bureaucrats and lob- byists who have introduced such entrapping anti-American slavery should be charged, tried, and if found guilty by a lawful jury, *exe- cuted for treason*...be they "Canaanite" or not. Did government public schooling really dumb them down?

In Lawful Economics the *cancer of inflation* should not exist. This could be achieved with the proper use of electronic transfers backed by gold and silver coin (Article 1:10:1 Constitutionally), with silver as the basic backing of the currency. President Kennedy was assassi- nated for this as his Executive Order #11110, as in our chapter 6. The satanic alternative that Citizens have to use today – paper money that is non-government, privately owned and loaned to the federal U.S. government at annual interest by the Federal Reserve corporation – is killing free America financially with debt.

Add to this the fact that this annual interest paid to the private Fed' corporation is the #1 item to be paid each year by the federal U.S. government, which is what your CEG income-excise tax is all about (President Reagan's 1984 *Grace Commission Report*, pages 21-22). *Lawful economics* would require that the private Fed' be bought out with Law, that President Kennedy's Executive Order #11110 be fully enforced as written *(it is still in effect!),* and that America's money supply be based upon the net population count, adding new births and subtracting new deaths. Is this simple economics or what, to kill inflation? The following three paragraphs are to summarize these facts for you to share.

Unfortunately, in America, the Fed's 'paper money' will continue to be used to buy apples and oranges for a while, with no meaningful alternative, thanks to the ever-campaigning self-serving Congress. Parenthetically, with American private Citizens' wealth slowly disappearing due to that slippery Fed,' you may want to be reminded again that the word "wealth" in Rome's Latin language is "euporia," numbering "666;" as are the words "Stur" for "Rome" in Babylonian, the pope's title "vicarius filii dei," and the Latin "paradosis" for "tradition" (of which the Vatican is loaded, as in chapter 8).

Economically the status quo of the Fed's seemingly-innocent terms tends to entice people into believing in its satanic privately owned "system," which is not backed by a nickel of meaningful substance (gold and silver; Article 1:10:1). Again this current anti-Constitutional system is owned and controlled 100% by the Canaanite enemies of your once-free nation, as exposed in chapter 6 here.

Equally important is the fact that 100% of your individual federal income tax is an excise tax in exchange for government privileges, used only to pay this *ANNUAL INTEREST* on the federal debt, to those mainly-foreign Canaanite trillionaire and billionaire Fed' owners also shown in chapters 5 and 6, plus *WELFARE* payments, again as exposed in President Reagan's 1984 *Grace Commission Report*.

You should have a clear picture now. Except for sharing this book widely and your simple prayers in Jesus' Name, it is doubtful that you can do much to overcome Washington, D.C.'s *"insidious forces working from within,"* as warned of by our Military Government commander General Douglas MacArthur. Meanwhile, America, Mideast Israel, Russia and Iran are getting ready for earth's 'global bubble' to blow, as prophesied and as discussed in chapter 14 and the Foreword of this book.

CHAPTER
20

LAWFUL TAXATION

Every loyal private American Citizen and public U.S. citizen should want to pay proper taxes for the common good, do you agree? That is not in question here. What is in question is the *IRS Misapplication of the Law and Constructive Fraud*, to fulfill its designers' boasts of gradually enslaving the once-free American people. The IRS's proven tricks are as unlawful as the *unconstitutional direct "FLAT TAX,"* which some ignorant politicians promote to get votes from naive voters.

That (flat) "direct tax" is forbidden unless it is apportioned evenly to each State and then paid by each State's population, as was ruled in 1895's Pollock v. Farmer's Loan & Trust Co. 158 US 601 @ 624-625. That flat tax rubbish would be another nail in America's coffin, like giving blank checks annually to the ever-spending generally incompetent self-serving Congress and State legislators.

Little ladies from Pasadena may think that the federal U.S. individual income excise tax helps to pay for good government, but that is a lie! Instead, again "100% of what is collected in personal income taxes is absorbed solely by *INTEREST* on the federal debt and by federal government contributions to transfer payments [*WELFARE*]." Again this is quoted from President Reagan's 1984 *"Grace Commission Report"* (pp. 21–22), and that has not changed, Citizen. Most of this annual interest is reportedly paid to the Canaanite owners of the privately-owned Fed' corporation, again exposed in chapters 5 and 6 with Agape-love, which explains why your payment is endorsed to it. Time is ticking, as global pressures build.

Another example of terrible loopholes in the U.S. federal tax system is the fact that, thanks to the Congress, corporate General Electric's net profit for 2011 was estimated to exceed $8 billion, on which it paid next to nothing in federal income taxes. Also in past years, if cars imported from Asia arrived without their wheels attached, the manufacturers paid almost no import tax. Such games are part of why the Congress and its federal U.S. government go deeper and deeper in *debt, by not following the Constitutional tariff guides*. Loyal government would require charging import taxes or tariffs that would price foreign-made products in accordance with our American-made products!

Most people are used to paying for what they use. Tax for using U.S. government items is called an *"EXCISE" tax*. When people properly pay for what they use, and foreign nations likewise pay for what they export to your Land, the U.S. government budgets can be balanced every year. If we add to this the wisdom of "free enterprise" interchange, markets can grow, you can enjoy a prosperous free society, with a small government and *NO DEBT*. This was the real American dream leading up to 1776, with generally bright home-schooled Citizens who were alert, paid attention and stayed awake.

Then the Rothschild minion Alexander Hamilton became U.S. Secretary of Treasury, paralleled by the first U.S. supreme Court (see Constitution) clerk named Levy, with possibly planned destruction. Privately owned "banking" was pushed by Hamilton, and due to

Levy the Court justices began calling themselves *"honorable," which is against the Law (Article 1:9:8).* How ridiculous, lawyers.

My loving wife has been a wonderful homemaker and mother, not working outside our home since the 1970s; so I leave her entirely out of this taxation study. Here are some *investigative insights on your U.S. "federal income tax"* (an excise, per the U.S. supreme Court), supposedly to supplement Constitutional excises, duties and imposts (see dictionary) intended for government income. Each private Citizen's individual payments to the IRS for income/excise taxes go to the U.S. Treasury, in harmony with Constitutional Clauses 1:2:3, 1:8:1, and 1:9:4. But then they are *endorsed to the privately owned non-federal non-government "Federal Reserve" corporation* (as exposed in chapter 6). With this, the private Citizen voluntarily contributes to the annual *INTEREST* paid on the questionable federal debt, plus *WELFARE,* gradually funding America's takeover by its Canaanite enemies.

Your U.S. federal "income tax" is, by law, just another *EXCISE tax* in exchange for government benefits, privileges, or franchises such as a driver's license, socialist social security, Medicare, and so on. This was the ruling of the U.S. supreme Court in 1921's Merchants v. Smietanka 255 US 509 and 1926's Bowers v. Kerbaugh 272 U.S. 170. Did your government schools teach you this? We will also look at the related 1916 decision in Brushaber v. Union Pacific RR Co. 240 US 1 in a bit.

BACKGROUND: A) The 1798 Congress lawfully laid a "direct tax *within the [federal] United States,* [then] apportioned to the States respectively...to provide for the valuation of lands and dwelling houses and the enumeration of slaves within the United States." That year the U.S. federal government's income was short of its expenses, so each of the 16 sovereign States was apportionately billed, based upon its population. Each State legislature in turn billed its Citizens, and each Citizen voluntarily paid his/her portion of that lawful indirect *EXCISE tax.*

B) On August 5, 1861 the Congress created the Office of the "Revenue Commissioner," to assist with taxation for April 12, 1861's Civil War. It was unsuccessful, so on June 30, 1862 it was replaced with an "indirect uniform *EXCISE tax*" that brought in $376,150,209 before it was abolished in 1872. On August 27, 1894 a *direct federal income tax was imposed, but it was declared unconstitutional on May 20, 1895* in the famous Pollock v. Farmers' Loan 158 US 601 at 624-625 and 637 ruling again. By Law, there can be no "direct" (involuntary) personal tax on America's private Citizens (capital "C" as in the original Constitution, and again with a small "s" in U.S. supreme Court). Please remember the above item A's lawful 1798 Congressional guideline.

C) The ever-busy Rockefeller (Rockenfeld) clan in 1909 pressed to change this "no direct tax" situation, spearheaded by their U.S. Senator Aldridge Rockefeller (Rockenfeld). That became *1913's* fraudulently ratified *16th Amendment*, which was passed by the Congress in the same year that the fraudulent *Federal Reserve* Act (see chapter 6), the fraudulently ratified *17th Amendment* for mob voting, the *NEA/* National Education Association for gross mis-education, and the easily manipulated *NAACP*/National Association for the Advancement of Colored People, led by the infiltrating Canaanites of Bible prophecy who headed that organization in its early years. All were then imposed while America slept. Worth repeating is socialist President Franklin Delano Roosevelt's (Rosenvelt's) confession that "Nothing in politics happens by accident; if it happens, it was planned that way." His bosses knew this.

D) However the U.S. supreme Court ruled properly in *1916's* Stanton v. Baltic Mining 240 US 103 that "the Sixteenth Amendment conferred no new power of taxation but simply prohibited the... power of income taxation...from being taken out of the category of *indirect* [voluntary Excise] taxation...the Sixteenth Amendment created no new taxing authority." But regardless, as U.S. Rep' Dr. Ron Paul warns, other countries' citizens can even enjoy debit cards that are linked to gold and silver accounts for safety, except Americans due to the criminal IRS and its state daughters. *So let's prove their fraud right now!*

In *1916* the Court also ruled in Brushaber v. Union Pacific RR 240 US 1 that its confusing propaganda, "if acceded to, would cause one provision of the Constitution to destroy another." Frank *Brushaber* was a New York State private Citizen who owned some stock in the federal U.S. corporation named Union Pacific Railroad, and thus properly he had to pay federal income/excise tax for the federal benefit of that corporation's dividends, in accordance with the 1909 Corporation Tax Act.

E) So the shrewd Canaanites were still stuck with the above 1895's Pollock decision. Such a deal! So their slippery lawyers just pretended that everyone and his uncle were strawman corporations. This is why they use names in *ALL CAPITAL LETTERS*, meaning legal U.S. admiralty maritime dictatorship of WAR, as opposed to our lower case Law of Peace. The *GOLD FRINGED FLAG* means also *admiralty of war* (you know, the admiral is dictator of the fleet), as opposed to our simply beautiful Old Glory of Peace. Another fact is that when our Old Glory flag is placed flat against our garage it means for *Peace*, while a flag hung on a pole with gold fringe again means war. Your nearest library should have all of this.

F) I used to think that the innocent tax-paying law-abiding private American Citizen might be able to find lawful relief from the IRS criminals by way of the federal U.S. district courts. But you should be aware that with a federal case one cannot start at the local level or even with a County Grand Jury. My investigations also proved all *U.S. JUDGES take a double oath* (source: Title 28 US Code section 453 at page 72 and Title 5 US Code section 3331 at page 453). To me, this means that they are *forced to rule against the private Citizen* or lose their jobs, or otherwise occasionally to make the system look good.

To support the incredible entrapment, the criminal division of the IRS maintains files on all U.S. district court judges (source: Treasury/IRS 46.002, the Privacy Act of 1974, and Resource Material Document 6372). This is a Constitutional *VIOLATION,* with the executive branch provably intimidating the judicial branch, which for starters smacks of willful treason.

G) As a law-abiding tax-paying private natural born free American National and Article 3 State Citizen, I use *"TDC" (meaning under threat, duress, or coercion)* with my signature on all government and commercial communications, since I have *NO VOLUNTARY GOVERNMENT BENEFITS*. Therefore I can respectfully but *squarely challenge* both *territorial and subject matter JURISDICTION* all the way to the U.S. supreme Court.

At the *STATE LEVEL*, when the *"CEG"/criminal element in government* is provably involved in the *Misapplication of the Law and Constructive Fraud*, as time allows I would probably share my documentation with our *COUNTY GRAND JURY*. In California the reliable Christian Common Law is alive and well, as in 1990's Rojo v. Kleiger 52 Cal. 3rd 65; and "the necessity of any Article III judge is uncontested," 1962's Gliddon v. Zdanok 370 US 530 537. Question: How can the State of California's *FRANCHISE Tax Board* impose a "franchise" income/excise tax on private State Citizens who live and work within the 50 States; have absolutely no voluntary government franchise, benefit or privilege; and do not live or work within the FTB's corporate territorial jurisdiction? It can't, although its employees try to by ignorantly using 1940's federal Buck Act's phony overlay of the 50 States to pretend that it can!

H) According to the IRS Commissioners' annual reports, following the *1909* Corporate Tax Act there were about 300,000 federal U.S. *"TAXPAYERS,"* defined in IR Code Sec. 7701.a.14 as "any person subject to any internal revenue tax." By *1914*, there were 357,515; by *1916*, there were 363,000; in *1939* there were 3,900,000 with the U.S. Public Salary Tax Act; and in *1941* there were 7,867,319. During World War II, apparently-Canaanite U.S. Treasury Secretary *Henry Morgenthau* and the movies' *Walt Disney* put together a visual promotion for the war's *"Victory Tax,"* which led millions of returning WW II Veterans to voluntarily submit their U.S. 1040 forms like ignorant, unsuspecting sheep. To this day, most of those *1945* Veterans didn't know what hit them, but this little book may help millions.

They also didn't know that their filing a U.S. income tax return switched their private natural born free American National and Article 3 State Citizen STATUS to the lower federal "U.S. citizen" level! This entrapment was later ruled so in 1974's Morse v. U.S. 494

F2d 876 at 880! Is that more U.S. government Misapplication of the Law, Constructive Fraud and Canaanite Treason or what? Talk about dumb.

While the busy/sleeping American population had grown by two and a half times from 1945 to1987, the number of federal *U.S. "TAXPAYERS"* had jumped 290 times to 104,031,000. With these proven facts, do you smell something stinking in Washington, D.C.'s IRS etc.? Seven States rejected copying the federal income-excise tax traps, while 43 agreed to follow the federal IRS Code "Rules and Regulations," designed only for federal U.S. territory, as in the Constitution for our USA at Article 4:3:2.

The *IRS word "INTERNAL"* is an important study in itself; in the dictionary meaning "inside, inner" as in item A)'s 1798 above. I honestly believe that, tricky though it is, the present U.S. Internal Revenue *Code makes plenty of good sense, if* seen when you investigate thoroughly and detect its twisted words planted by self-serving government lawyers. It is of utmost importance to determine exactly what is and what is *not applicable to you and me.* To do this you have to know that IRC §7701's federal "United States" is a *FOREIGN* corporation to our "United States of America" (source: Volume 20, Corpus Juris Secundum, §1785, and in *Black's Law Dictionary* 5th Edition, at page 1375). "Foreign" of course means foreign territorial jurisdiction.

Such *treason* again may be a good example for Luke 11:52's "Woe to you lawyers! For you have taken away the key of knowledge; you yourselves did not enter, and you hindered those who were entering." Sadly, most Americans are brainwashed into *hiring a bar association lawyer,* conditioned for a knee-jerk reaction, whenever a legal problem arises. But again, retaining one bar lawyer automatically makes the client a "ward-of-the-court," or an "imbecile," a very foolish or stupid person (source: American Corpus Juris Secundum §7 par. 2.2).

With reference to taxes, often *CHURCH people* cite Matthew 17:24–26, in which Peter was to pay the "correct customs or poll tax" with two miraculous drachmas (coins) taken from the mouth of a fish. What they often fail to include is 17:26's "the sons are *EXEMPT*;" they are not involved in the customs benefit.

The present IR Code and the U.S. supreme Court are consistent with what its Chief Justice John Marshall (1755–1835) wrote: "All subjects over which the sovereign power of a state [jurisdiction] extends, are objects of taxation [having voluntary benefits]; but those over which it does not extend [no voluntary government benefits] are upon the soundest principles *EXEMPT from taxation*... [and he added]...the power to tax is the power to destroy." As you may know, the criminal IRS has apparently destroyed millions of law-abiding tax-paying people!

Sharing some of my experiences regarding the criminal IRS may be of help to you. In the 1960s, I was *audited* by IRS and California Franchise Tax Board agents, which *resulted in refunds* to me from both agencies. In 1984, the IRS in San Diego had a revenue agent Mrs. *Maxwell* audit me. After a day, she said that my records were excellent; but added that "nobody beats the system..." I was told later that her written report to her office was packed with libelous lying, for whatever her reasons.

This *raised my investigator bristles*, with results condensed nearly 30 years later here for this chapter 20. In subsequent years I made modest investments with good potentials and some tax advantages, in solar, gold and silver mining, oil and gas, and cellular. Some were later unbelievably called *shams by the* criminal IRS, when in reality that lawless agency is the sham, as you will see here. Its arrogant changing of its rules from written guidelines has also harmed countless law-abiding tax-paying American Citizens, including me, for which the *self-serving IRS employees*, some named herein, will apparently pay dearly about 1,000 years from now in the Revelation 20:11-12's Judgment for their *self-serving "deeds."*

Another example of U.S. criminal bullies came with our cellular license experience. As mentioned earlier, in 1984 working with our team that averaged 40 financial brokers nationwide, I was asked to help market the Federal Communications Commission cellular license applications across America. We did so successfully. This resulted in our family's Article 3 Common Law Pure Trust Organization, with its form *W-8 "Certificate of Foreign Status" jurisdiction* properly filed with Payers, winning North Carolina RSA-15 Cellular License for our 126-member Bravo Cellular group. This win was then built out and operated; and after a total of 17 years of overtime efforts and great teamwork we sold to Verizon for a just return to everybody on our Bravo Cellular team. Many thanks to my superb co-manager *Phil Kosh* for his great plus-quality, and to our trustworthy Bravo attorney, (probably Hebrew-Jew) *Larry Solomon*!

Besides donating to associate ministries in 34 countries, as managing trustee I contributed large amounts to help finance Christian groups in communist China, working especially with *Every Home for Christ* and *International Students Inc.* This has proven to be so successful that I am told that an estimated 500 million Chinese citizens are now either wonderfully "into" or studying to be into (Romans 8:1-4) our real Creator Christ. My plan then had also been to provide for ongoing monthly earnings to fund our Scott Christian Ministries Pure Trust's lawful activities, working with the same associate ministries and others.

So I had the Pure Trust invest with trusted brokers, who provided me with a written money-back guarantee of performance. But when these funds went through a Cincinnati bank, the U.S. Customs temporarily and unlawfully seized these funds, blaming its post-9/11/01 terrorist and money-laundering mentality, and then it allowed the IRS to keep the whole amount.

It is going to be interesting to see what our real commander Christ does about these, His funds, with such bureau-rats reminded herein about 1 Corinthians 6:2–3 Judgment paralleling Revelation 20:11-15's for their "deeds" some 1,000 years from now. My heart forgives 'rats, but I am not expected to forget.

Constitutionally restricted to federal U.S. Article I:8:17-18 and 4:3:2 federal property/territory, earlier IRS' headquarters had provided *two letters* that clearly show our *private lawful Pure Trusts have "no tax requirements."* The reason for this is that by definition, again these trusts *are classified as "foreign [form W-8] complex irrevocable American Common Law Pure Trusts"* in status, not subject to such tax, and also because the managing trustee is not a Beneficiary, which I am not.

You may have guessed that the *IRS changed its crooked criminal mind*, and filed an unlawful federal U.S. IRS lien against me personally, although I had and have no liability to it. Am I disgusted about it? You betcha! Exposing these criminal Canaanite-type activities by the IRS people is among reasons for this chapter 20 on Lawful Taxation, supported by teachings such as Titus 2:15's "These things speak and exhort and reprove with all authority. Let no one disregard you." Meanwhile, it is a delight to be "looking for the Blessed Hope and appearing of the Glory of our Great God and Savior, Christ Jesus," as in 2:13.

So the following *two lawful Affidavits* are intended just for you readers who have *problems* with the IRS-CEG (criminal element in government), please:

One of the finest lawful ways of countering while replying to an IRS inquiry or charge is with *honest timely appropriate good faith questions*. In harmony with this, one of the best sources for what is and is not Constitutional Law is *supposed to be the U.S. supreme Court*, as will be referred to here.

Many people have been misinformed that 1913's 16th Amendment to the Constitution imposes federal U.S. income tax on most everybody. But *that lie was easy to correct* with the foregoing 1916's Stanton v. Baltic Mining and Brushaber v. Union Pacific RR cases, wasn't it? Please keep in mind that I do not tell others what they should do, except with chapter 8's "COME OUT!" But rather it is right and lawful for me to responsibly share what I might do in similar circumstances, with absolute unalienable Rights to do so, without prejudice (meaning reserving all of my Rights).

Here are my questions to consider as Administrative Procedures and *Discovery*, and documentation of *Good Faith*. Respectfully, with a reply Affidavit-letter such as these samples, I would send a copy of my Affidavit to whoever the IRS agent is. My reply letters are always notarized, via certified mail, with delivery receipt requested, and if appropriate I would also send a copy to the agent's superior.

Using ZIP CODES without surrounding brackets can grant <u>federal U.S. jurisdiction</u> – as can the use of TWO-LETTER STATE

ABBREVIATIONS (CA, AZ, NY etc.). So I place <u>brackets around the Zip Code, and spell out State names</u>, to reserve my private Natural Born free American and Article 3 Citizen status. Now to my important sample Affidavits:

(#1) *Christian <u>Affidavit of Revocation</u>*, Common Law © 2012 by Dr. Neil Alan (Doc) Scott

Dated _____

[Sample only – you take responsibility for your own, of course.]

Dear IRS Agent:

In reply to your communication dated ___/___/___, copy enclosed, because your IRS as Proponent has the legal resources for you to answer these questions timely and in writing for my *Discovery*; please do so *within 30 days* of today's date (source: 1946 *Administrative Procedure Act*, Title 5 USC 556–D, showing that *as Proponent you have the burden of proof* in this.)

I, Neil Alan Scott, being duly sworn, do affirm the following and affix my signature here this date. I have studied these laws and facts personally at our county law library and otherwise. All law cites are for reference only and all special emphasis is mine.

1. Am I right in understanding that voluntarily filing an IRS form 1040 would change my *Status*, from a natural born free *exempt* private American National and Article 3 State Citizen, to a public federal person/U.S. citizen taxpayer subject to and liable for U.S. federal individual income/excise tax (source: Morse v. U.S. 494 F2d 876 at 880)? If so, by this Affidavit *I hereby Revoke* any and all such filings done erroneously in the past due to federal U.S. *Misapplication of the Law and Constructive Fraud.*

2. Am I right in understanding that IRS personnel, including agents, have *no written "Delegation of Authority" to work for it within the 50 States*? If you do have any such, please prove it by providing a legible copy of yours to me within this same 30 days.

3. Am I right in understanding that your IRS does not have its own *"Implementing Regulations"* that are lawfully applicable to

my status as a private American National and Article 3 State Citizen *living and working within the 50 States?*

Am I right in understanding that the federal U.S. income tax is an *Excise Tax* in exchange for *government benefits, privileges, and/or franchises* (source: 1921's Merchants v. Smietanka 255 U.S. 509 and 1926's Bowers v. Kerbaugh 272 U.S. 170)? I have no such voluntary benefits.

4. Am I right in understanding that any "Waivers of Constitutional Rights not only must be voluntary but must be knowingly intelligent acts done with sufficient awareness of the relevant circumstances and consequences" (source: Brady v. U.S., 742 at 748, 1970)? By this Affidavit I reaffirm my private, unalienable Rights, and no alien can lawfully break them.

5. Am I right in understanding that the U.S. federal government *has no authority or jurisdiction* to tax the exercise of lawful Rights of us private non-volunteering Natural Born free American and Article 3 State Citizens? (Sources: U.S. supreme [see original Constitution] Court in 1819's McCulloch v. Maryland 4 Wheat 418 at 429-431, and in 1943's Murdoch v. Pennsylvania 319 U.S. 105. The Court ruled that "A state may not impose a charge for the enjoyment of a Right granted [protected] by the federal [American] Constitution." I therefore hereby object to and squarely challenge any such alleged jurisdiction (source: 1979's Burns v. Laskar 441 U.S. 471).

6. Am I right in understanding that instructions about the U.S. IRS forms 1040 do not apply to me, living and working within the 50 States, unless I voluntarily have a federal government benefit, privilege or franchise? I do not have such. These instructions were taught to me by government, teachers, media, family and others. I do not have such a voluntary status, and due to government/IRS *Misapplication of the Law and Constructive Fraud*, I properly use the term *"TDC" (under threat, duress &/or coercion)* by my signature or initials in all communications with government and commercially.

7. Am I right in understanding that "the federal government possesses no legislative jurisdiction over any area within a State?" (Source: pages 45 and 46 of the President Eisenhower administration's June 1957 *"Jurisdiction Over Federal Areas Within The [50] States."* Isn't this in accordance with the Court's Balzac v. Porto [Puerto] Rico 258 US 299 at 312 stating "The [U.S.] District Court is not a true United States [of America, Article III] Court…is a mere territorial court" regarding jurisdiction?

8. Am I right in understanding that the *U.S. individual income tax is an Excise tax in exchange for government benefits, privileges, and/or franchises* (sources: 1916's Stanton v. Baltic Mining Co. 240 U.S. 103, and the fact that 1913's 16th Amendment "conferred no new power of taxation")?

9. And am I also right in finding 1916's Brushaber v. Union Pacific RR 240 U.S.1 affirmed that private New York State Citizen *Frank Brushaber* properly owed U.S. federal income/ excise tax on his dividends-benefit, due to his voluntarily owning federal U.S. corporation Union Pacific Railroad stock?

10. Am I right in understanding that the IRS is required by the Congress to conform to the *Uniform Commercial Code* (UCC) regarding its *liens* (source: Federal Tax Lien Act of 1966 and Public Law 89–719, 80 Statutes at Large 1125 Exhibit A, with Legislative History and Senate Report No. 1798)? Isn't the IRS ignoring these mandates, reflecting more of its *Constructive Fraud?*

11. Am I right in understanding that your IRS should have provided me with a signed Uniform Commercial Code Financing Statement Security Agreement? Aren't you in *violation* of the source: UCC §§9-402, 9-403 and Code of Federal Regulations 143.a.4.d, and if so doesn't this violation now leave your so-called Notice of Lien invalid for *Malicious Fraud?*

12. Am I right in understanding that your so-called federal U.S. IRS lien against this private Citizen and my private property

is not based upon the mandatory Uniform Commercial Code procedures, court hearings, and Due Process of the Law? Isn't it rather an attempt to steal private property in *violation of the Fifth Amendment* (source: Title 26 CFR Part 600 §601.106.f.1.1)?

13. Am I right in understanding that the Congress and your IRS look upon federal U.S. "taxpayers" as their *"enemy,"* in accord with the *"Trading with the Enemy Act of 1917" (source:* Title 12 US Code Amplified §951)? I am glad that IR Code §7701.a.14 *does not apply to me,* a private Natural Born free American Citizen with no voluntary government benefits, privileges nor franchises, under TDC.

14. Am I right in understanding that U.S. federal income/excise taxes may properly be imposed on certain other government privileges measured by income, such as bar lawyers' privileged occupations as "officers of the court" (source: 1881's Springer v. U.S. 102 U.S.586), and upon criminal gains or profits? And is my understanding right that this is consistent with 1911's Flint v. Stone Tracy Co. 220 U.S. 107, which *defines federal U.S. income/excise taxes* as "taxes laid upon the manufacture, sale or consumption of commodities within the country, upon licenses to pursue certain occupations, and corporation privileges"?

15. Am I right in understanding the often-publicized statement that "The income [excise] tax system is based upon voluntary compliance with the law of self-assessment of tax"? However, isn't this also to be applied only to corporate activities (source: 1989's Doyle v. Mitchell Bros. 247 U.S. 179)? It has never been my intention or desire to self-assess myself voluntarily for non-owed U.S. income/excise tax, nor to personally accept or have the corporation status to pay for U.S. federal interest or welfare.

16. Am I right in understanding, after examining the IR Code (sources: §§ 6001, 6011, 6012, 6331, 6331.a, 7203, and 7205), that by our American Law I am not now and never

have been a knowingly voluntary federal U.S. "person" (corporation, association, partnership, individual etc.) as referred to in those sections? In fact, and in law, isn't my private Citizen status specifically *exempt* from that status (source: 1877's U.S. v. Fox 94 US 315 and 1941's U.S. v. Cooper 312 US 600)?

17. Am I right in understanding that *nothing* in the IR Code classifies me, a private Natural Born free American National and Article 3 State Citizen *living and working within the 50 States*, as a federal U.S. "person liable," "person made liable," or federal U.S. "taxpayer" as defined in IR Code §7701.a.14, meaning "...any person subject to any internal revenue tax"? And am I right in understanding that §7701.a.26's "trade or business" is limited to "the performance of the functions of a public office"? Isn't that definition's shrewd wording more federal U.S. government/IRS *Constructive Fraud*?

18. Am I right in understanding that the only possible requirement on my private status to pay federal U.S. income/excise tax is the title of Part I Subtitle A, Chapter 1 Subchapter A, *deceptively titled "Tax on Individuals"*? But this shows *no provision in the body of the statutes imposing any liability* obligation on me for payment of a federal U.S. income/excise tax, as such law is determined not by the title but by the actual wording in the body of the statute – with the title as merely a guide. Is this not true, and is this not more federal U.S. government and IRS *Misapplication of the Law and Constructive Fraud*?

19. Am I right in understanding that the Internal Revenue Code's Chapter 21, "Federal Insurance Contributions Act" (social security), and Chapter 21 Subchapter A re "Tax on Employees," involving IRC §3101 *identifying "tax on income," is not* an "insurance contribution" nor a "tax on employees" nor on "wages," nor on "earnings?" In ignorance *don't employers defraud employees about withholding* federal U.S. income/excise tax, *and break the law when used against private non-volunteering*

Natural Born free American National and Article 3 State Citizens, *living and working within the 50 States?*

There is *no provision* in the Code that imposes this tax on an employee or that requires one to pay it. However, a signed *voluntary* form W-4 employee's withholding allowance certificate authorizes the employer to withhold money from a worker's pay for social security income and income-excise tax. Isn't it correct that employers have no authority to withhold money from a worker's pay for this socialist graduated income/excise tax, nor any other IRS tax, without a voluntarily signed W-4 form?

20. Am I right that the Title 26 Code of Federal Regulations Constitutionally at Article *4:3:2's "Rules and Regulations"* are *restricted to federal U.S. property?* [Source: 26 Code of Federal Regulations at Chapter 1 §1.1–1 shows "Income tax on individuals: (a) Imposes an income tax on the income of every individual who is a citizen or resident of the [federal] United States...(c) Who is a citizen: Every person born or naturalized in the [federal] United States and *subject to ITS jurisdiction."*]

    Black's Law Dictionary, Fifth Edition, page 1375 proves that this United States is one of *three definitions for the United States*: 1) the District of Columbia municipality, 2) United States as a sovereign *among nations*, and 3) *America* the beautiful USA. Isn't this more *Constructive Fraud?*

21. Am I right in understanding that the IR Code's §61(a), listing items that are *"sources of income,"* relates to IRS' Collection Summons form 6638 confirming these items as "sources" – *not income but just sources* such as "wages, salaries, tips, fees, commissions, interest, rents, royalties, alimony, state or local tax refunds, pensions, business income, gains from dealings in property, and any other compensation for services"? However *"sources" are not income*, but rather sources of income, unless they are entered as *"income" on a signed form 1040*, with the signer agreeing *under "penalties of perjury"* that they are

"income." Doesn't this "perjury" trap put people in prison, due to more IRS *Constructive Fraud*?

22. Am I right in understanding that IR Code §61(b) shows which other sections identify items that are included as "income," in view of what is included in gross income in Part II §71 and the following? I reviewed §§71 through 87 and verified that wages, salaries, commissions, tips, interest, dividends, pensions, rents, and royalties etc. *are not included as "income,"* and they *are not in these sections*.

23. Am I right in understanding that the federal U.S. *government unconstitutionally spends 100%* of all individual income/excise taxes on its massive debt's *annual interest and welfare*? I have just summarized President Reagan's 1984 Taxpayer Survey of the *Grace Commission Report*, pages 21-22. Shouldn't we expect these taxes instead to pay for government services for our Citizens?

24. Am I right in understanding that *the only way one can qualify* to pay federal U.S. income/excise tax, as a private American and Article 3 State Citizen *living and working within our 50 States* with *no voluntary government benefits*, privileges, and/or franchise, is *if one is dumb enough* to voluntarily file a form 1040, affirming under penalties of perjury that the same one is liable for aforesaid taxes?

25. Am I right in understanding that my reliance on U.S. supreme Court rulings, and my Constitutionally-protected 5th and 9th Amendment Rights as partially enumerated therein, in my status as a private natural born free American National and Article III State Citizen, means that I am not now and *never have been* a liable U.S. "taxpayer," subject to, or required to pay federal income/excise tax?

26. Am I right in understanding that for pseudo-Christian state church corporation organizations, the *entrapping IR Code §501.c.3 to get tax deductibility* has *replaced formerly §508.c.1.B Free Church* status? This reminds me of 1st -century Christian Churches, where their leaders and members refused Rome's

corporate "licit" or license. That would have legally placed the Roman government's Caesar over our Creator Christ (John 1:3, Colossians 1:16, Hebrews 1:8–10 with Psalm 2:12)...a no-no! For this many were martyred. They knew His future Judgment for government 'rats and their deeds (Revelation 20:11-15), choosing instead His lawful freedom, yes His Way over self-serving Roman bureaucrats.

27. Am I right in understanding that the Congress, IRS et cetera *have misled* America's private Citizens with the IR Code and published articles, so that the latter have grown up *mis-taught* that they have to file a form 1040 and report their earnings, complete a W-4 employee withholding allowance certificate, keep records, provide information, and pay tax that is not owed?

Isn't an example of this the IR Code §6331 excerpt that accompany IRS levies, which *fraudulently leaves out "§6331.a"* *to whom this applies:* "...any officer, employee or elected official of the [federal] United States (see item 13), the District of Columbia or any agency or instrumentality of the [federal] United States or the District of Columbia, by serving a notice of levy on the employer [as defined in section 3401(d), government] of such officer, employee, or elected official"? *None of those are me!*

28. Am I right in understanding, by reason of the aforementioned laws and facts, that I can revoke and render null and void, retroactively and currently, based upon the Congress' and IRS' *Misapplication of the Law and Constructive Fraud*, all form 1040 returns, all W-4 certificates, and all of my signatures on these aforesaid items? I do *revoke and void those documents* herewith as stated above.

This revocation procedure was made clear in 1979's El Paso Natural Gas Co. v. Kysar Ins. Co. 605 Pacific 2d 240, which said that "Constructive Fraud as well as actual fraud may be the basis of cancellation of an instrument," and 1878's U.S. v. Throckmorton 98 US 61 at 65 that *"Fraud vitiates [invalidates] the most solemn of contracts*, documents and even judgments." Is this not so?

29. Am I right in understanding that I am not and never was a federal U.S. "taxpayer," again as defined in IR Code §7701.14; or a "person liable," or "subject to" that Code's provisions? In fact I am a loyal *law-abiding tax-paying Christian "non-tax-payer" by definition* and as recognized by the courts (examples: 1922's Long v. Rasmussen 281 F2d 236, and 1955's Gerth v. U.S. 132 F. Supp. 89, with 1901's DeLima v. Bidwell 182 US 176 at 179, and in harmony with nearly 100 other court rulings.

Therefore I hereby propose *my "Conditional Acceptance for Value"* concerning your alleged charges as Proponent. This means that I will accept your charges *if proven liable when you reply to me with full written answers* to these *Discovery* questions. These must be mailed certified to me *within 30 days* of today's date, with documented proof that your charges are correct and not fraudulent, in accordance with 1946's Administrative Procedure Act, 5 USC 556-D. If you do not reply in accord fully and timely it means you and your IRS *agree that your alleged charges are discharged, null and void.*

30. Am I right in understanding that IRS agents, officers and superiors are in violation of Title 28 U.S. Code §3002(15) about unlawfully stealing any private non-federal property, real or personal, *within the 50 States?* Do they *mistake* this for property that may be taken from federal U.S. persons?

31. Am I right in understanding that IRS agents, officers and superiors are in violation of Title 18 USC §1001 when they are filing false and fraudulent documents *with State and County Recorders?* Does this not earn criminal punishments for willful federal U.S.' and IRS' *Misapplication of the Law and (more) Constructive Fraud?*

32. Finally, am I right in understanding that the federal U.S. government and its IRS again are restricted by the Constitution's Article 4:3:2 concerning its "Rules and Regulations"

again being applicable only to federal U.S. property and territory, as stated therein? Isn't this in accord with its *"foreign"* *U.S. Article 1:17–18 TERRITORIAL JURISDICTION*, as also made clear in Volume 20 Corpus Juris Secundum Volume 20 §1785?

Please respond as above within 30 days of this date. Thank you.
Signed this date of /s/_____ at Oceanside, California, without prejudice,
/s/_____
Neil Alan (Doc) Scott, as myself, private natural born free Christian American National and Article 3 State Citizen, as Posterity of Declaration of Independence co-signatory Josiah Bartlett, New Hampshire State Governor.
Notarized: My Commission Expires: _____
Certified Mail, Delivery Receipt Requested.
–- *(or you may want to use parts of the following alternate:)* –-
(#2) Christian Affidavit of Revocation, Common Law © 2012 by Dr. Neil Alan (Doc) Scott
Dated ___/___/___ [sample, you take responsibility for yours]
Dear IRS Agent:

This is in reply to your communication dated ___/___/_____, copy enclosed. Because your IRS as Proponent has the legal resources for you to answer these questions timely and in writing for my *Discovery*, please do so *within 30 days* of today's date. This is pursuant to the 1946 Administrative Procedure Act, Title 5 USC 556-D. It shows that you as Proponent have the burden of proof in this case.

I, Neil Alan (Doc) Scott, being duly sworn, affixing my signature hereto, do hereby affirm that:

I did not know that a completed/filed IRS form "1040" federal income/excise tax return or a W-4 employee withholding allowance certificate – authorizing an employer to withhold from my pay – are voluntarily executed instruments that could be admissible as evidence against me in a civil and criminal court to show that I voluntarily waived my Constitutionally-secured Rights; and that I ignorantly made myself subject to the federal income-excise tax provisions of the Internal Revenue Code (IRC) and the Internal Revenue Service (IRS), by agreeing "under penalties of perjury" to be a public federal U.S. citizen [26 CFR Ch. 1 §1.1-(c)] and federal U/S. person subject to that tax. Note: Court cites here are for reference only, and special emphasis is mine.

1. My present understanding is that 1974's Morse v. U.S. 494 F2d 876 at 880 verifies the foregoing. To lawfully overcome such entrapment, my signature or initials for government and commercial entities will only be done with a *"TDC,"* *meaning threat, duress and/or coercion*, to lawfully retain my private Natural Born free American National and Article 3 State Citizen status. True?

2. One day I read part of a friend's IRS form letter FL 1264 that states "The fact that you sent us this 1040 shows that you recognize your obligation to file..." It has not been my intent to show that I have any obligation to it. In fact, as a law-abiding tax-paying private Constitutionally Natural Born free American National, and Article 3 State Citizen, I do not have any such duty to the IRS, or Congress' Article 1:8-17 and 4:3:2. True? Thus I am Biblically in accord with Romans 13:1-10 and I Peter 2:13-17.

3. My status is also one of *Peace, without any voluntary government benefit*, privilege or franchise (remember my above "TDC"), a freeman, endowed by our Creator Christ [John1:3, Colossians1:16, Hebrews1:8-10 with Psalm2:12) with certain unalienable Rights including my Rights to "life, liberty and the pursuit of happiness," as are partially enumerated in the Declaration of Independence and the Constitution *for* the United States of America (see its Preamble). True?

4. My Birthright to "pursuit of happiness" has been supported both by our America's Founding Fathers, including New Hampshire military officer, judge, governor and our ancestor Josiah Bartlett, and by the U.S. supreme (as in the original

Constitution) Court, including my unalienable Rights to Lawfully *contract*, to acquire, own, deal in, rent, sell and/or exchange property of various kinds, real and personal, without need of permission, benefit, privilege or franchise from government. True? I have learned that these unalienable Rights also include my *Right to contract my labor-property in exchange* for other property such as wages, salaries and other earnings, and that I *have never knowingly or intentionally waived* any unalienable Rights (doing so must be with full knowledge of contents and consequences, source: 1970's Brady v. U.S. 397 US 742 748).

5. I understand that if the exercise of Rights were subject to federal taxation, the Rights could be eliminated by increasing tax rates to unaffordable levels; so the Courts have repeatedly ruled that government has *no authority* to tax the exercise of Lawful Rights of Private Citizens (source: 1819's McCulloch v. Maryland 4 Wheat 418 429-431, and 1943's Murdock v. Pennsylvania 319 U.S. 105, which added that "A State may not impose a charge for the enjoyment of a Right granted [protected] by the federal [American] Constitution." True?

    In past years I have been influenced by repeated public statements from the IRS, radio, television, the press and stacks of forms "1040" in post offices and banks, reminding us of the *"April 15th deadline"* for filing these. In addition I have been influenced by IRS' annual brainwashing in publications, articles and such in warnings as being "punishable by fine or imprisonment." True? These produce a dangerously misinformed American public; and even worse by lawyers', CPAs' and other tax preparers' is the *"OFFER IN COMPROMISE" trap* for lifetime subjection to the IRS.

    These misled me into believing that the fraudulently-ratified 16th Amendment to the Constitution somehow authorized Congress to impose an unlawful Article 1:9:4 direct tax on me, my property and my exchanges of property as a result of exercising Constitutionally secured Rights to contract, in direct opposition to 1916's Stanton v. Baltic Mining Co 240 US 103 that the 16ᵗʰ "…*conferred no new power* of taxation."

6. I was further misled into *believing that I had a lawful duty to file* a federal form "1040," a "W-4" employee's withholding allowance certificate, other IRS and corporate state franchise tax forms, all dependent on the federal tax code. *I respectfully object to and squarely challenge all* such traps and foreign jurisdictions now (source: 1979's Burns v. Laskar 441 US 471, and Hagans v. Lavine 415 US 528 533 at Note 5). Is this proper stand not lawful?

7. In connection with the facts in my item #5, I was influenced by employers who perhaps ignorantly (see #15) mislead their employees into believing that they are all subject to withholding of income-excise tax from their earnings, with or without their voluntary permission, based upon the employers' mistaken assumption that they are required by law to withhold income-excise tax from the paychecks of their employees. Do you know any such employee with an IRS lien? Employers may be dangerously unaware of IRS, Congress and their lawyers' *Constructive Fraud* in this regard, so please read on and share with others for your own good. True?

   Said form "1040" contained no reference to any law that would explain *exactly who is and who is not liable* for or subject to the income-excise tax. Nor did it contain any notice or warning to anyone that merely filing a completed form "1040" with the IRS would waive my Right to Privacy and to not having to be a *Witness against myself, secured by the 4ᵗʰ and 5ᵗʰ Amendments to the Constitution* for the USA (see Preamble). Nor that a filed form "1040" could be IRS evidence against me in court, showing that I ignorantly agreed to be liable for income-excise tax under penalties of perjury (in Morse, above).

8. All of this is even though, as a private natural born free American National and Article 3 State Citizen, *living and working within the 50 States* – with *no voluntary government benefit,*

privilege or franchise – and being among America's *"sovereigns without subjects"* (source: 1793's Chisholm v. Georgia 2 Dall 419 @ 471), with absolute Unalienable Rights – this Citizen is by Law *not ever liable* for or subject to any federal income-excise tax, and has no obligation to complete or file any federal form "1040" whatsoever. Is this not true?

9. At no time was I ever informed by the IRS , or by any lawyer, CPA or otherwise, that the 16th Amendment to America's Constitution – as affirmed by the U.S. supreme Court in such cases as 1916's Brushaber v. Union Pacific R.R. Co. 240 U.S. 1, and 1916's Stanton v. Baltic Mining Co. 240 U.S. 103, and its income-excise tax is an indirect voluntary excise tax in accordance with the Constitution's Article 1:8:1 – and that the 16th Amendment *does not authorize an income-excise tax on private Citizens with no voluntary (TDC) government benefit*, franchise or privilege. America can enjoy helpful taxations with Articles 1:2:3, 1:8:1, 1:9:4 and 1:9:5, period. Also, Frank *Brushaber* was a private American National New York Article 3 State Citizen Constitutionally, and a *Non-Resident Alien to federal property* by Law. But he voluntarily owned stock then in a federal (domestic) corporation named *Union Pacific Railway* Co., which was created within federal property; *so he was liable* and subject to federal income-excise tax, to be withheld at its source on its interest from bonds and dividends. True?

10. At no time was I ever informed by the IRS, or by any lawyer, CPA or other tax preparer that, because of various U.S. supreme Court rulings – such as 1911's Flint v. Stone Tracy Co. 220 U.S. 107 and 1895's Pollock v. Farmer's Loan & Trust Co. 157 US 492 – the indirect income-excise tax on "income" related to the 16th Amendment tax on *corporation privileges granted by government* and measured by the amount of corporate income (see 1909's Corporations Tax Act, Statutes at Large, Volume 36, §38, page 112). This income-excise tax may also be properly imposed upon certain other privileges

from government and measured by income, such as *bar lawyers' privileged occupations as "officers of the court"* (source: 1881's Springer v. U.S. 102 US 586); and this income-excise tax may also be imposed upon criminal gains or profits. True?

Subsequently I read parts of Report No. 80-19A (source: *"Some Constitutional Questions regarding the Federal Income Tax Laws,"* published by the American Law Division of the Library of Congress, updated January17, 1980). This publication described the *tax on "income" in the 16th Amendment to the Constitution as an Indirect Excise Tax*; adding that the "The supreme Court...first noted that the 16th Amendment *did NOT authorize any new type of tax, nor did it repeal the tax clauses* of Article 1 of the United States Constitution, quoted above," and it further stated "Therefore, it can clearly be determined from the decisions of the United States supreme Court that *the income tax is an indirect tax, generally in the nature of an excise tax."*

11. This proved in my mind that the "income tax" is *not a tax on me* as an individual, but is rather a tax as described by the U.S. supreme Court again in 1911's Flint v. Stone Tracy Co. 220 U.s. 107...*defining income excise taxes* as "...taxes laid upon the manufacture, sale or consumption of commodities within the country, upon licenses to pursue certain occupations, and upon corporate privileges." *None of these apply to me* as a private Natural Born free American Citizen using "TDC." Is this not true?

12. I was unaware of the truth in one publicized IRS statement, that "The income tax system is based upon *voluntary* compliance with the law and self-assessment of tax." It has *never been my intention or desire to assess myself voluntarily with a not owed income-excise tax*; but rather I erroneously thought that it was required. Is my lawful thinking correct?

In study and with professional counsel I examined I.R. Code §§ 6001, 6011, 6012, 6331, 7203 and 7205, and am convinced that by American Law *I am not now and never have been a voluntary* federal "person" (corporation, association, partnership, individual etc.) as referred to in those sections. True?

13. Also in study and with professional counsel re the I.R. Code, I have never found or been shown any section *that imposed a requirement on me* – as a private Natural Born free American National and Article 3 State Citizen with no voluntary government benefit, franchise or privilege, *living and working within the 50 States* – to file a federal form "1040" or pay any income-excise tax, or that classified me as a "person liable" or "taxpayer" as defined in I.R. Code Section 7701:a:14, which states, "The term *'taxpayer' means* any person subject to any internal revenue tax." And 7701: a26 with its "trade or business includes [i.e. means, Montello v. Utah 221 US 452 @ 466] the performance of the functions of a *public office*" (not a café nor tips) is *more Constructive Fraud*, IRS and Congress? Is this not true?

14. Also in study and with professional counsel I found only one possible requirement upon me in the I.R. Code – as a private natural born free American National Natural and Article 3 State Citizen with no voluntary government benefit, franchise or privilege, living and working within the 50 States – to pay a federal income-excise tax. That is the *title of Part 1*, Subtitle A, Chapter 1, Subchapter A, deceptively titled "Tax on Individuals." Further study of the Code showed that no provision in the body of the statutes imposes any liability obligation on me for payment of a federal income-excise tax. Careful study and consultation showed that such law is determined not by the title but by the actual wording in the body of the statute – and that the title of a statute is merely a guide to the statute – for *the title has no authority at law*. Is this more *Constructive Fraud*, IRS, Congress and lawyers? Is this not correct?

15. Also in study and with counsel I found that I.R. Code Chapter 21, entitled "Federal Insurance Contributions Act" (prov-

ing to be socialist insecurity), Subchapter A of Chapter 21 with "Tax on Employees" – which includes §3101 identified as a tax on "income;" *not* an "insurance contribution" *nor* a "tax on employees" *nor* on "wages" *nor* on "earnings." My attention was also drawn to the following: *There is no provision* in the Code that imposes this tax on an employee, or requires one to pay it; *however a voluntarily completed* "W-4" employee's withholding allowance certificate authorizes the employer to withhold money from a worker's pay for income-excise tax. Do you agree?

Otherwise, an employer has no authority to withhold money from a worker's pay – for the Canaanite-designed income-excise tax, a shrewd socialist/communist graduated income-excise tax, designed like a cancer *to destroy* employees and America *from within*. If there is no voluntarily "W-4" form filed, America's *enemy loses!* Furthermore, using my absolute unalienable Rights to share this, such ignorant employers could lose employees' huge lawsuits in Courts or settlements for promoting IRS, Congress' and lawyers' *Constructive Fraud.* Is this not true?

You may understand why the IRS does not publicize its Title 26 Code of Federal Regulations 4/1/88 Edition Ch. 1§1.1-1: "Income tax on Individuals...(a)...Imposes an income tax on the income of every individual who is a citizen or resident of the United States [federal U.S.]... (b)...all citizens of the United States...(c)...*Who is a [U.S.] citizen*: Every person born or naturalized IN the [federal] United States and *subject to ITS jurisdiction...*"

16. *Black's Law Dictionary* 5th Edition page 1375 shows "*United States*" as having *three different definitions,* one being the *federal* D.C.'s U.S., the second one being the U.S. that is sovereign *among nations*, and the third one being *our US of A*! Why are these entirely left out of Black's 8th Edition, do you suppose? *More Constructive Fraud*, IRS, Congress and Luke 11:52's lawyers? Isn't this true?

17. After further study my attention was drawn to IRC §61(a), which lists items that are *sources of "income."* The IRS Collection Summons form 6638 of 12/82 confirms these items as "sources," NOT income but rather just "sources:" "Wages, salaries, tips, commissions, interest, rents, royalties, alimony, state or local tax refunds, pensions, business income, gains from dealings in property, and any other compensation for services [receipt of property other than money] – for sources are not income – but rather sources *become "income" if they are entered as "income"* on a form "1040" and *signed under penalties of perjury* that they are income! Isn't this *more Constructive Fraud*, IRS, Congress and their treasonous lawyers? Is this not true?

18. The same section 61(b) clearly shows which other sections identify items that are included as "income." "For items specifically included in gross income, see Part II (sec.71 and following):" I *reviewed sections 71 through 87* and verified that wages, salaries, commissions, tips, interest, dividends, pensions, rents, royalties etc. are *not included as "income,"* and in fact these items are *not mentioned* anywhere in any of these sections. Is this not true?

    Note well: TIMID American Citizens can correct their status now with the Freedom Affidavit similar to these, and with *1 Timothy 2:7 fully understood* in the Christ Jesus' Name. *It's all a matter of status!*

19. You could mistakenly believe that D.C.'s government operates on income-excise taxes, but again President Reagan's 1984 Taxpayer Survey of the *Grace Commission Report* at page 21-22 refutes that lie with "100% of what is collected [in individual income-excise taxes] is absorbed solely in *interest* on the federal debt and by federal government contributions to transfer payments [*welfare*]. In other words, all individual income tax revenues are gone before one nickel is spent on the services which taxpayers [should read Citizens] expect..." Is this not also true?

20. From further study it is now clear to me that the only way that property could have been considered federal excise "income" when received by me: a) as a private Natural Born free American National and Article 3 State Citizen, *living and working within the 50 States* – b) with *no voluntary government benefit*, franchise or privilege – whether wages, salaries, commissions, tips, interest, dividends, rents, royalties, pensions etc. –- c) is if I was *ignorant enough to file* a form "1040" income-excise tax return – d) affirming under penalties of perjury that all given information on it was true, and that any amounts listed in the "income" block was "income" – e) thus acknowledging *under oath* that I was liable and subject to the income-excise tax and had a duty to file an IRS form "1040" ad nauseam. However, again no such *waivers* of my Rights have I ever voluntarily signed as "intelligent acts done with sufficient awareness of the relevant circumstances and consequence," as would be required to fulfill American Contract Law (source: item #3's 1970 Brady v. U.S. 397 US 742 @748). Is this not true?

21. With reliance on these U.S. supreme Court rulings, and my Constitutionally-protected *5th and 9th Amendment Rights* to lawfully Contract, work, acquire and own Property, I am convinced that I *am not* and *never have been* liable for, subject to or required to pay any federal income-excise tax. I am *not now and never have been* a federal "taxpayer" as defined in the I.R. Code (§7701:a:14); and I have *never had* any lawful obligation to file a form "1040," sign any form "W-4" employee's "withholding allowance certificate" or other IRS forms, keep any records or provide any information to the IRS. Is this not true?

22. Would you agree that so-called 'Christian' *lawyers and accountants have persuaded* countless Christian churches, pastors and boards to *switch from their freedom status of IRS §508:c:1:B*, with Galatians 5:1, to a *voluntary state corporate slavery organization status of §501:c:3* – supposedly so that members could

185

have a needless "tax deduction"? What a satanic switch! How shrewd can Satan's own (Canaanites?) be. And *how sad to complain now about their 501:c:3, for which they volunteered*! True?

23. First Century Christians *refused Rome's corporate "licit"/license*, which would have placed the emperor's status over the real Creator Christ...for the refusal of which many pastors, boards and church members were *martyred...as millions more may be*, relating to Revelation 20:4. Is this not true?

24. Because of the criminal IRS,' Congress' and their slick lawyers' *Constructive Fraud*, as proven here, with misleading words and phrases in the I.R. Code and published articles, America's deceived "We the People" have been suckered in to mis-thinking that they have a liability. Many feel that they must file a form "1040" income-excise tax return, a "W-4" employee's withholding allowance certificates with employers, keep records for the IRS, provide private information, and pay income-excise tax when they have no voluntary government benefits, privileges or franchises! Do you also know why?

25. So let's expose one more huge IRS *Constructive Fraud: IRC §6331* on levy and distraint, which in part *accompanies an IRS levy*. These shrewdly *leave out [6331] "(a)* Authority of Secretary...*Levy may be made upon* the accrued salary or wages of any officer, employee or elected official of the United States [remember item #16], the District of Columbia, or any agency or instrumentality of the [federal] United States or the District of Columbia, by serving a notice of levy on the employer (as defined in §3401(d)) of such officer, employee or elected official..." None of these are me, showing more of the Congress,' IRS' and lawyers' *Constructive Fraud, right?*

Let's remember that all such self-serving *con's will be perfectly Judged for their "deeds, "* about 1,000 years from now by the proven Creator Christ, unless they COME OUT beforehand, as in this little book! Being decision time, please tell yourself which side you are on, as time is running out? Is this not true?

26. With this Affidavit, I hereby exercise my unalienable Rights as a private Natural Born free American National Article 3 State Citizen – with no voluntary government benefit, franchise or privilege (TDC) – and supported by aforesaid Court rulings such as 1981's U.S. v. Kis 658 F2d 526 @536 citing U.S. v. Powell 379 US 48 @ 57-58 – to Revoke and render Null and Void currently and retroactively any and all signatures that I have ever rendered in this regard – including *all* form "1040" federal income-excise tax returns, *all* "W-4" employee withholding allowance certificates, *all* other related documents ever submitted by me, and *all* related corporate state nexus. Can you understand this lawful procedure?

27. This Revocation is based upon my Rights relating to the U.S. government's and its IRS' *Constructive Fraud*, as encompassed in 1979's El Paso Natural Gas Co. v. Kysar Ins. Co. 605 Pacific 2d 240, with its "Constructive Fraud as well as actual Fraud may be the basis of cancellation of an instrument," and 1878's U.S. v. Throckmorton 98 US 61 @ 65, "Fraud vitiates [invalidates] the most solemn of Contracts, documents and even judgments." Can you understand these laws?

IRS' extended *Fraud against me expensively involved* at least San Diego U.S. district court judge Irma E. Gonzalez, IRS Commissioner Douglas Shulman, ex-IRS Commissioner Mark Everson, IRS General Counsel Donald L. Korb, IRS Revenue Officer #3308739 Michael Raines, and IRS Revenue Agent #33-073447 Maria Navarro. *None have any lawful written Delegation of Authority to act for the IRS against this private natural born free American National and Article 3 Citizen within the 50* States! In 1997 Houston IRS agent Jennifer Long gave congressional testimony that the IRS teaches its agents to use "tactics" to extract unfairly assessed taxes from [U.S.] taxpayers [and not-liable non-taxpayer yours truly!]...literally ruining families, lives and businesses...viewed to be vulnerable...

many agents are encouraged by management to pursue tax assessments that have no basis in tax law from individuals who simply can't fight back...if that taxpayer [or non-taxpayer] does object, every effort will be made by the IRS to run up their tax assessment and force them to capitulate to IRS demands (source: http://taxboard.net/TxprBoR/1997/Long. html). True or not?

28. I do hereby declare that I am a law-abiding tax-paying American Christian "*non-taxpayer*" by definition, as the Courts have recognized and acknowledged: "...for *with them Congress does not assume to deal, and they are neither of the subject nor the object of revenue laws...*", as my status has been ruled in 1922's Long v. Rasmussen 281 F2d 236, and 1955's Gerth v. U.S. 132 F. Supp. 894 with 1901's De Lima v. Bidwell 182 U.S. 176 @ 179! Is this not true?

I now affix my Signature to these Affirmations, without prejudice, this date of ___/___/___:

/s/_____

Neil Alan (Doc) Scott, as myself, private natural born free Christian American National and State Citizen, as Posterity of Declaration of Independence co-signatory, Josiah Bartlett, New Hampshire State Governor.

Notary _____ My commission expires:

Certified Mail, Delivery Receipt Requested

CHAPTER
21

LAWFUL GOVERNMENT

You and I live in a flash world now, where government and other emergencies can develop with lightning speed, would you agree? There are many indications that certain people in the federal U.S. government plan such a sudden national emergency, with martial law and deadly charges. Thus these last three chapters' titles include the word "Lawful..."

Some loyal Citizens will recognize that "It is not the function of our government to keep the Citizen from falling into error; *it is the function of the Citizen to keep government from falling into error*" (source: U.S. supreme Court's American Communications Association v. Douds 339 US 382 @ 442).

But too often America's government-public-schooled people have been unknowingly mistaught. Please consider also: "Because of what appears to be a Lawful command on the surface, many Citizens, because of respect for the Law, are cunningly coerced into *waiving their Rights due to ignorance*" (source: U.S. v. Minker 350 US 179 @ 187). Add to that the fact of employees in the Library of Congress working to destroy America's written history, and Citizens can feel like they are using a canoe without a paddle.

By the word "*Lawful*" let's agree that I mean "*Constitutional*," which is said to be America's "*supreme Law of the Land*" as in its Article 6:2. Opposing this, including a conned president Woodrow Wilson, and White House boss so-called 'colonel' Mandell House (Heusman), were I John 3:10 "children of the Devil" Canaanite enemies who also worked against General MacArthur to destroy America's Law and Land.

But "An unconstitutional act is not Law; it confers no rights; it imposes no duties; affords no protection; it creates no office; it is in legal contemplation as inoperative as though it had never been passed" (source: U.S. Supreme Court in Norton v. Shelby County, 118 U.S. 424 at 442).

You will probably agree that governments sometimes seem to be hilarious. One example is the present Food Stamp Program, administered by the U.S. Department of Agriculture, which is proud to be distributing free meals and food stamps to over 46 million people. At the same time the National Park Service, administered by the U.S. Department of the Interior, pleads "Please Do Not Feed the Animals." Its stated reason is because the animals will become *dependent on handouts*, and will not learn to take care of themselves (hmm, sick socialism).

Let's remember that we stand on the shoulders of the giants who formed this nation – George Washington, Thomas Jefferson, Patrick Henry, Ben Franklin, John Adams, John Jay, James Madison, James Monroe, John Quincy Adams, Daniel Webster, William McGuffey and so many more.

As mentioned in our chapter 2, in 1943 I lived with Ed and Dorothy in Arlington, Virginia, commuting daily past the majestic Jefferson and Lincoln Memorials on my way to Central High School in Washington, D.C. After school my best friend Lincoln Fenno, a descendant of Abraham Lincoln, and I would do kidlike investigations especially at the Library of Congress, National Archives and the Smithsonian Institution. One afternoon at the Library of Congress two U.S. senators helped me trace our family ancestors, including Elijah Barker and Elizabeth Bartlett, who in 1630 sailed to America from England, 10 years after the Mayflower. So we honor all of our founders' loyal efforts to live freely.

My notes from that time are as accurate as this-then 13 year-old could copy them in these D.C. institutions, beginning a life-long hobby of collecting treasured sayings by America's Founding Fathers and other greats (Obama will prove to be a fraud); not necessarily chronological. My goal was to understand what these leaders thought, said and wrote, along with their peers. You can look up their quotations in your public library. *We honor all dedicated investigators for their contributions*, with everlasting thanks. So we share these hard-to-find treasured insights for truth from our Founding Fathers and peers:

1. *George Washington* (1732-1799): 1ˢᵗ President of the USA: — he was a devout believer in Jesus Christ, as can be read in his own prayer book, and — a freeman contending for liberty is superior to any slavish mercenary — there is no greater error than to expect favors from nation to nation — the fate of our unborn millions will depend under God on the courage of this army — It is impossible to rightly govern the world without God and the Bible — [Every session of Congress begins with a prayer by a preacher, whose salary has been paid by the taxpayers since 1777] —

    One of Washington's early official acts was the first Thanksgiving Proclamation, in part: "Whereas it is the duty of all nations to acknowledge the providence of Almighty God, to obey His will, to be grateful for His benefits, and humbly implore His protection…" He added the Constitution's Article 7:2's the 12ᵗʰ, with no human being of higher standing.

2. *Thomas Jefferson* (1743-1826): 3rd President — Author of the Declaration of Independence (56 signers) — in his 2nd Inaugural address, "I am a real Christian.....a disciple of the doctrines of Jesus" — God who gave us life gave us liberty — We are all Republicans, we are all Federalists — I have sworn upon the altar of God eternal hostility against every form of tyranny over the mind of man — and he borrowed from the famous minister Roger Williams of "...*the wall of separation between the garden of the church and the wilderness of the world, God hath ever broke down the wall...*" — The Constitution is a mere thing of wax in the hands of the judiciary, which they may twist and shape into any form they please —

   He (Jefferson) placed the Bible and Isaac Watt's Book of Psalms and Hymns in the District of Columbia's public schools [so much for atheists' separation of church and state rubbish] — and he worried that the U.S. supreme [see original Constitution] Court would overstep its authority; instead of *interpreting the Law to fit the Constitution*, it would begin making law; exactly as it has done — To compel a man to furnish contributions for the opinions in which he disbelieves is sinful and tyrannical — If a nation expects to be ignorant and free...it expects what never was and never will be.

3. *Patrick Henry* (1736-1799): One of my many favorites, he taught himself law — was the only American governor elected five times (Virginia) — he turned down President Washington's offers to be Secretary of State, Chief Justice of the U.S. supreme Court, U.S. Senator etc. — as tensions mounted against British slavery, his fiery speech of March 23, 1775 to the Second Virginia Convention included: "For my own part I consider it as nothing less than a question of *freedom and slavery*...it is only in this way that we can hope to arrive at truth, and fulfill the great responsibility which we hold to God and our country...Sir, we are not weak if we make a proper use of the means which the *God of Nature* hath placed...we shall not fight the battle alone.

There is a just God who presides over the destinies of nations...the battle, sir, is not to the strong alone; it is to the vigilant, the active, the brave...Is life so dear, or peace so sweet, as to be purchased at the price of chains and slavery? Forbid it, Almighty God! I know not what course others may take; but as for me, give me liberty or give me death!" — It cannot be emphasized too strongly or too often that this great nation was founded not by religionists but by Christians, not on religions but on the Gospel of Jesus Christ.

He also drew the first <u>non-legislative American Christian Common Law Pure Trust</u>, irrevocable, complex and Constitutionally "foreign," now properly using IRS' form W-8 Certificate of Foreign Status, territorially foreign to Congress, as Article 3 is Constitutionally to 1:8:17-18 and 4:3:2.

That first American Common Law Pure Trust protected Governor Robert Morris family's property from British legislation and armies; and my latest information is that his first Pure Trust is still going strong in Chicago as the *"North American Land & Cattle Company."* We enjoy these lawful non-legislated American Common Law Pure Trust beauties, and therefore I do not have to own much in this world. Of course lawyers make more money drawing up corporation or equity trust papers, imposed on America from England shortly after the Civil War, as legislated creatures of the state.

It cannot be emphasized too strongly or too often that this great nation was founded not by religionists but by Christians, not on religions but on the Gospel of Jesus Christ. No wonder that Patrick Henry's name has been left out of modern government public schoolbooks. Take heed PTAs and NEA for allowing or promoting relatively poor U.S. educations!

4. *Ben Franklin* (1706-1790): From poor candle-maker parents of 17 children — taught himself 5 languages and had only 2 years of formal education — was a printer by trade and

publisher of his annual Poor Richard's Almanac (1732-1757) — taught to eat to live, and not live to eat (1733) — God helps them that help themselves (1735 — was Father of the Articles of Confederation — was the only man who signed all four founding documents: Declaration of Independence, Treaty of Alliance with France, Treaty of Paris on 9/3/1783 with the British that ended the Revolutionary War, and America's Constitution —

— Our Constitution is in actual operation; everything appears to promise that it will last, but in this world nothing is certain but death and taxes (1789) — We must all hang together, or assuredly we shall all hang separately — They that can give up essential liberty to obtain a little temporary safety deserve neither liberty nor safety — he was a great inventor and scientist, called "the Newton of his age" with philosophical, practical and scientific writings — From the Continental Convention, when a lady Citizen asked him what kind of country we have, he replied "You have a Republic... if you can keep it" —

European universities granted "Doctor" Franklin three honorary doctorate degrees — he was famous for inventing his Franklin stove — he discovered electricity with his famous kite experiment — he invented the lightning rod — he was a likeable and respected American, founder of Pennsylvania University, entered public service as a member of the Pennsylvania Assembly — was deputy postmaster of the Colonies, U.S. representative in England — and stated that only a virtuous people are capable of freedom; as nations become vicious and corrupt they have more need of masters. —

— Ben has been called a "deist" (in an impersonal distant god), so let's examine his letter to Yale University president Ezra Skyles — Here is my creed: I believe in one God, the Creator of the universe. That He governs it by His Providence...He ought to be worshipped...That the most acceptable service we render to Him is in doing good to His other children...That the soul of man is immortal, and we will be treated with justice in another life respecting its conduct in this —

Without believing in the now-proven real Creator Christ Jesus (please enjoy chapters 15 to 18), the above acts can be Judged to be good "deeds" of Revelation 20:11-13, John 5:29 and Matthew 25:31-46. I find no evidence that America's brilliant and beloved Dr. Ben knew or accepted the real Creator Christ, or the "first resurrection" of Revelation 20:5b-6. But for his good deeds, the real Christ's vital Blood sacrifice, and if Ben's name is in Rev. 20:12's "book of life," he should enjoy salvation about 1,000 years from now. — "Here Skugg lies, snug as a bug in a rug."

5. *John Adams* (1735-1826): 2nd President — The 10 Commandments and the Sermon on the Mount contain my religion — Our Constitution was made only for a moral and religious people; it is wholly inadequate to the government of any other.

6. *John Jay* (1745-1829): 1st Chief Justice of the U.S. supreme (see Constitution) Court — with his famous 1793 ruling in Chisholm v. Georgia 2 Dall. 419 @ 471, stating that natural born free American Citizens are among this nation's "sovereigns without subjects" [of course, as self-governing law-abiding tax-paying Christian Citizens] — Americans should select and prefer Christians as their rulers.

Now as you walk up the steps of the U.S. supreme Court building, near the top is a row of the world's law givers; each one facing the middle one who is facing forward...it is Moses, holding the 10 Commandments...as you enter the supreme Court courtroom the two huge oak doors have the 10 Commandments engraved on each door...as you sit inside the courtroom, right above where the supreme Court judges sit is a display of the 10 Commandments...and there are

Bible verses etched in stone all over the federal buildings and monuments in Washington, D.C.

7. *James Madison* (1751-1836): 4th President: — Author and Father of America's Constitution — We have staked the whole of all our political institutions upon the capacity of mankind for self-government [a Republic, not democracy], upon the capacity of each of us to govern ourselves, to control ourselves, to sustain ourselves according to the 10 Commandments of God — Religion is the basis and foundation of Government — 52 of the 55 founders of the Constitution were members of orthodox churches in the Colonies — The belief in a God All Powerful, wise and good, is so essential to the moral order of the world and to the happiness of man.

8. *James Monroe* (1758-1831): 5th President — The liberty, prosperity and happiness of our country will always be the object of my most fervent prayers to the Supreme Author of All Good [2nd Inaugural Address March 5, 1821] — home schooled by Reverend William Douglas — served as a lieutenant colonel in Washington's Revolutionary Army, then in the Virginia Assembly, the Constitutional Convention, U.S. Senate, Governor of Virginia, Minister to France, Great Britain and Spain, served as Secretary of War, negotiated the Louisiana Purchase from Napoleon, Florida from Spain, and added Maine, Illinois, Missouri, Alabama and Mississippi as new States — while his Monroe Doctrine prohibited European powers from interfering with the independent Western Hemisphere nations.

9. *John Quincy Adams* (1767-1848): 6th President — and his wife were devout Christians, recommending to their son a lifetime habit of reading five chapters of the Bible each morning, which took him about an hour.

10. *Daniel Webster* (1782-1852): — By the blessing of God, independence forever — there is nothing so powerful as truth –- God grants liberty only to those who love it, guard and

defend it — Whatever makes men good Christians makes them good Citizens —

11. *William H. McGuffey* (1800-1873): America's Schoolmaster, educator, professor — president of Ohio University — first published McGuffey's Reader in 1836, the most widely used textbook of all time, with 125 million copies sold as of 1963 — he wrote that the Christian religion is the religion of our country — included for youth are the Evening Prayer, Don't Take Strong Drink, On Speaking Truth, the Bible for English literature — he added that in making selections I have drawn from the purest fountains of English literature... for the copious extracts made from the Sacred Scriptures I make no apology — The morality taught by Jesus Christ was purer, sounder, sublime and more perfect than had ever before entered into the imagination, or proceeded from the lips of man.

12. *Alexis de Tocqueville* (1805-1859): French statesman and writer-observer of 1830s America: Upon my arrival in the United States the religious aspect struck my attention...religion and freedom were intimately united and reigned common as Americans combine Christianity and liberty — I am certain that they hold religion to be indispensible to republican institutions — there is no country in the world where the Christian religion retains a greater influence over the souls of men than in America...the most enlightened and free nation of the earth — religion in America must be regarded as the foremost of political institutions, it belongs to the whole nation — Christianity reigns without any obstacle...by universal consent...this is a Christian nation, pre-eminently the land of the Bible, the Christian church.

13. *Abraham Lincoln* (1809-1865): 16th President — With his reputation as "Honest Abe," he was of the common people, raised in a log cabin, cleared the land and split the rails, taught himself law, became an Illinois judge, State legislator, U.S. Congressman and Republican President — It is believed

that he accepted the real Christ Jesus in 1862, after their son Willie died at age 12 and Abe saw the Gettysburg battlefield in 1863 — He stated that he never had a feeling politically that did not spring from the sentiments embodied in the Declaration of Independence…which gave liberty not alone to the people of this country, but hope to all the world…I would rather be assassinated on this spot than surrender it —

No man is good enough to govern another man without the other's consent — I believe the Bible is the best gift God has given to man…all the good Savior gave to the world was communicated through this Book…but for this Book we could not know right from wrong — Common-looking people are the best in the world; that is the reason the Lord makes so many of them — A house divided against itself cannot stand [Mark 3:25] — Let us have faith that right makes might, and in that faith let us to the end dare to do our duty as we understand it — Our reliance is in the love of liberty which God has planted in us — the eternal struggle between these two principles, right and wrong — The philosophy of the school room in one generation will be the philosophy of government in the next —

Conservatism is adherence to the old and tried, against the new and untried — with a task before me greater than that which rested upon Washington — being a humble instrument in the hands of our Heavenly Father, as I am and as we all are, to work out His great purposes, I have desired that all of my works and acts may be according to His will… so I have sought His aid — Without the assistance of that Divine Being who ever attended him, I cannot succeed, with that assistance I cannot fail — Our reliance is in the love of liberty, which God has planted in us — My paramount object in this struggle is to save the Union, and is not either to save or destroy slavery —

If I could save the Union without freeing any slave, I would do it; and if I could save it by freeing all the slaves,

I would do it — Men should utter nothing for which they would not willingly be responsible through time and in eternity — Whenever I hear anyone arguing for slavery, I feel a strong impulse to see it tried on him personally — Abe knew that Southern economy was based on cheap Black labor, while poor White men's labor there had to compete against it — He would have favored Black Jamaican Garvey's advocacy to repatriate Blacks to Liberia for economic progress, blood integrity and racial nationality —

Abe issued the Emancipation Proclamation effective 1/1/1863 — And at Gettysburg Abe Lincoln added his "Fourscore and seven years ago our fathers brought forth on this continent a new nation, conceived in liberty, and dedicated to the proposition that all men [and women] are created equal...that this nation, under God, shall have a new birth of freedom; and that government of the people, by the people, for the people, shall not perish from the earth" — As with President Kennedy's assassination and the *"coincidences"* (chapter 6), President Lincoln's worst enemies apparently were also the Canaanites of Bible prophecy —

Similar to President Kennedy's anti-Canaanite Executive Order #11110, Lincoln had just acted to repeal their National Bank Act; wanting the U.S. government to finance itself, issuing full legal tender greenbacks; and for all time free America economically, as he had done for the Blacks by signing the Emancipation Proclamation — His last act with Congress was to have the motto "In God we trust" placed on our money.

Rothschild's agent Rothberg apparently used Canaanite gold to bribe and recruit former Confederate officer and plantation owner Andrews in Montreal, who in turn bribed and recruited egocentric actor John Wilkes Booth and his associates. Their first idea was to kidnap Lincoln, which failed; then to assassinate him at the Ford Theatre on April 14, 1865, Good Friday. Booth was subsequently killed as planned; and when Rothberg arranged to poison Andrews with a drink of wine in Montreal, the suspicious Andrews switched glasses, and Rothberg died in his shady prime of life.

14. The *U.S supreme Court* in 1892's Church of the Holy Trinity v. U.S. 143 US 457-465-470-471: 'This is a religious people...from Christopher Columbus...to Sir Walter Raleigh in 1584...in propagating of the Christian religion'...[and quoting the 1620 Mayflower Compact:] "Having undertaken for the glory of God and the advancement of the Christian faith..."

15. *Noah Webster* (1758-1843) condensed it well with his findings that "The religion which has introduced Civil Liberty is the religion of Christ and His apostles, to this we owe our free Constitutions of government" — Education is impossible without the Bible — He authored the famous 1828 Dictionary, which we enjoy.

16. Judge *Learned Hand* (1872-1961): Liberty lives in the hearts of men and women; when it dies there, no Constitution, no Law, no Court can save it.

17. General *Douglas MacArthur* (1880-1964): By the grace of Almighty God, our forces stand again on Philippine soil — In war there is no substitute for victory — Military alliances, balances of power, leagues of nations, all have failed, leaving the only path to be by way of the crucible of war...We have had our last chance. If we will not devise some greater...system, Armageddon will be at our door (source: the deck of the "Missouri," Tokyo Bay, September 2, 1945).

18. *William H. Rehnquist* (1924-2005): Chief Justice U.S. supreme Court: There is simply no historical foundation for the proposition that the framers intended to build a wall of separation [between church and state]...The recent court decisions are in no way based on either the language or intent of the framers — [Chief Justice John Roberts' incredible swing-vote favoring Obama's terrible health care traps is for federal U.S. property and persons, while its page **170 EXCLUDES us**

non-volunteering non-federal non-resident alien State Citizens.]

19. The *Star Spangled Banner* National Anthem sums these up: — "Blessed with victory and peace, may this Heaven-rescued Land, Praise the Power that hath made and preserved us a Nation! Then conquer we must [at times too much], when our cause is just; and this is our motto: In God [which God?, in our chapter 9] is our trust! And the Star-Spangled Banner in triumph shall wave, o'er the Land of the Free and the home of the Brave" — [This reminds me of a big convention of U.S. Veterans in Memphis, Tennessee 20 years or so ago, with most of them as loud as many of us vet's can be; until someone mentioned the law-breaking "IRS." Then from fear you could have heard a pin drop. (They should enjoy our chapter 20, with great American Law that they can use!) Of course *they were not free or brave!*

20. The song *"America"* pretty much tells it all: — "My Country 'tis of Thee, sweet Land of Liberty, of Thee I sing. Land where our fathers died, Land of the Pilgrims' pride; from every mountainside, let Freedom ring. — Our fathers' God to Thee, Author of Liberty, to Thee we sing. Long may our Land be bright, with Freedom's Holy Light [Bibles]. Protect us by Thy Might, Great God our King."

21. *Barack Hussein OBAMA* II, U.S. **president(?)** [2009-2012] — is seen by many loyal American Citizens as an ever-smiling question mark. Some have proven that he is not qualified to be America's elected president, because by Constitutional Law that position can only be filled by a **"natural born"** American Citizen (Constitution at Article 2:1:5), with the only exception being while a parent is assigned elsewhere on U.S. duty. They have proved that he was not "natural born" in America, and not an exception. **So let's see:**

   21.1) Investigative reporter, correspondent and journalist Steve Kroft for "60 Minutes," honored with nine Emmy and three Peabody awards, introduces us to OBAMA's primary sponsor, multi-billionaire apparent-*Canaanite-Jew terribly "evil man"* **George SOROS** (born August 12, 1930 as *Gyorgy Schwartz*). In World War II's 1944 when Hitler's henchman Eichmann went to Hungary, Soros loved being his Jewish property- seizer and murderer of up to a half-million fellow Jews. After WW II *Soros* attended the London School of Economics, mentored by atheist Jewish professor Karl Popper on Fallibilism, the open society, aka *social engineering*. In 1956 Soros moved to New York City, was absolutely ruthless, amoral and clever (Luke 16:8's shrewd) with Wall Street's hedge funds and currency speculations, like a butcher quickly making his first $billion. By the 1980s he was well on his way to becoming a global powerhouse.

In 1992 *Soros* shorted the British pound, leveraging $billions in aiming to break the Bank of England and millions of British citizens, who almost overnight saw their homes devalued and their life-savings cut. In 1994 *Soros* pulled off one of the greatest social robberies in human history, collapsing the former Soviet empire. Not content, in 1997 *Soros* nearly destroyed the economies of Malaysia and Thailand, while being called a "villain and a moron" by Malaysia's Prime Minister Mahathir Mohammed, and named a "Dracula" who "sucks blood from the people" by Thai's activist Weng Tojirakarn. Soros went on to cause big trouble in Yugoslavia, Georgia, Ukraine and Myanmar (Burma), calling himself a "philanthropist for globalization and the New World Order" (the Pax Judaica) – while promoting his own financial gain – without conscience – absolutely amoral. This satanic Canaanite *Soros* wants open borders, a one-world foreign policy, legalized drugs, and euthanasia. His open society is not about freedom; it is about license (source: writer Rachel Ehrenfeld). You can see much more about this rat on the *Internet* at "Discover the Networks." This *filthy (Revelation 22:11) George* **SOROS'** **GOAL** is to **destroy America from within**, *and he is on schedule while HIS MEDIA has a majority of Americans sound asleep!*

Whistleblowers David Horowitz and Richard Poe's book, *"The Shadow Party"* (as a source) details *how Soros highjacked the Democratic Party*, and now owns it by ousting the moderates and packing it with radicals, which brings us to the *Soros'* (and thus Rothschild and Canaanite tribe's) dupe *OBAMA*.

21.2) In Mombasa, *Kenya*, Africa, the Coast Province General Hospital's Registrar of Births has testified that *OBAMA's* **Kenya birth certificate** *there is genuine*. We have a copy of Obama's Kenyan *"Certificate of Birth,"* obtained by Lucas Smith, assisted by a colonel, who got the "Certificate of Birth" directly from that hospital. Are you now detecting some of what our General MacArthur called the *"insidious forces working from within?"*

21.3) **The Kenya papers show** that Obama was born there at 7:21 P.M. on August 4, 1961, with his grandmother affirming that she was in attendance. Four days later his mother flew with him to Hawaii, and unlawfully registered his birth in Honolulu with a *"Certificate of Live Birth"* **that omitted the place and hospital** of birth. In 1961 most anyone could buy one of these certificates, and Obama's grandparents in Hawaii were wealthy. Since then Obama and his sponsors reportedly have paid nearly $2,000,000 for 11 law firms to hide these facts. Why?

21.4) The woman who signed the Hawaiian certificate of live birth, *Mrs. Verna Lee*, has cooperated with high-level investigators, who devoted about 2,000 hours over more than six months to prove *probable cause of Obama's long-form certificate of live birth being a forgery*. Among other data, she has proved that *the word "African," appearing on his phony certificate, was not used until 1989* to show the race of a parent from Africa on similar Hawaiian certificates of live birth. Also Obama's certificate of live birth's *numeric codes indicate that parts of it were not originally there but* **were entered on it later**.

21.5) Obama's real *"certified copy of* **registration of birth**" in *Kenya* shows that its Colonial Registrar in 1961 was England's

Sir Edward F. Lavender, as also in its Kenya Dominion Record #4667. He was in charge of the Registrar's office from 1959 until January 1964.

21.6) Obama's recently-released Hawaiian *certificate of live birth* has been proven repeatedly to be a **forgery, a fraud and a counterfeit;** even if the reportedly-homosexual U.S. supreme Court Chief Justice John Roberts, a majority of his court justices, and the U.S. Congress refuse to rule Constitutionally on this forged crime. They should pay for their "deeds" in Revelation 20:11-15's "Judgment," do you agree?

21.7) Another high-level investigation has been headed by retired Bergen County, New Jersey police detective Mike Zullo. He was retained by the Posse of Arizona Sheriff Joe Arpaio, after some 250 of his Maricopa County's Citizens petitioned for a lawful investigation of Obama's real status. *Detective Zullo has concluded that Obama's birth certificate is a total forgery:* "...We uncovered key evidence that proved beyond a shadow of a doubt that the document presented to the American people by the White House [Obama's 'birth certificate'] is *a total forgery...*" (source: American Free Press, 7/17/12 Washington, D.C., telephone 202/544-5977).

21.8) *The 1991 Harvard Law Review's* profile on Obama reportedly *still shows him as "...**the first African-American** president of it, **born in Kenya** and raised in Indonesia and Hawaii. The son of an American anthropologist and a Kenyan finance minister, he attended Columbia University and worked as a financial journalist and editor for Business International Corporation. He served as project coordinator in Harlem for the New York Public Interest Research Group, and was Executive Director of the Developing Communities Project in Chicago's South Side. His commitment to social and racial issues will be evident in his first book...."

21.9) Columbia University's Obama classmate, Wayne Allyn Root, class of 1983, now a successful businessman in Las Vegas, shared these remembrances by e-mail on June 6,

2010, confirmed by Snopes: "Barack Hussein Obama is no fool. He is not incompetent. To the contrary, **he is brilliant**. He knows exactly what he is doing. *He is* **purposely over-whelming the U.S. economy** *to create systematic failure*, economic crisis and social chaos – thereby destroying capitalism and our country from within [remember General MacArthur's fear of the *insidious* forces working from within!].

"*He is* **a devout Muslim**, do not be fooled. Look at his czars, anti-business, anti-American. As Glenn Beck correctly predicated from day one, Barack Hussein *Obama is following the* **plan of Cloward and Piven,** *two professors at Columbia* University. They outlined a plan *to* **socialize America** *by overwhelming the system with government spending and entitlement demands*. Add up the clues below. Taken individually they're alarming. Taken as a whole, *it is* **a brilliant Machiavellian game-plan to turn the United States into a socialist communist Marxist state with a permanent majority that desperately needs government for survival.** [This is what 2012 presidential candidate Mitt Romney accurately charged.] And they can be counted on to always vote for even bigger government. Why not? They have no responsibility to pay for it.

"**Universal health care**! The *health care bill had very little to do with health care*. It had everything to do with **unionizing millions** *of hospital and health care workers, as well as adding 15,000 to 20,000 new IRS agents* (who will join government employee **unions**). Obama doesn't care that giving free health care to 30 million Americans will add trillions to the national federal debt. What he does care about is that it cements the **dependence** of those 30 million voters to Democrats and big government. Who but a **socialist revolutionary** would pass this reckless spending bill in the middle of a depression?

"*Cap and Trade!* Like health care legislation having nothing to do with health care, *cap and trade has nothing to do with global warming. It has everything to do with redistribution of*

205

income, government **control of the economy**, *and a criminal pay-off to Obama's biggest contributors* [apparent Canaanites again?]. Those powerful and wealthy unions and contributors (like GE, which owns NBC, MSNBC and CNBC and pays few taxes) can then be counted on to support everything Obama wants. They will kick-back *hundreds of millions of dollars* to the Democratic Party and Obama *to* **keep them in power.** [Bill Clinton reportedly played this treasonous game too, besides his female victims, and covering up his and Hillary's Arkansas murders of teenage drug witnesses that may cost their souls.]

"The bonus is that **all the new taxes** on Americans with bigger cars, bigger homes and businesses help Obama 'spread the wealth around.' Make Puerto Rico a State? Why? Who's asking for a 51st State? *Who's asking for millions of new welfare recipients and government entitlement addicts* in the middle of a depression? Certainly not American taxpayers! But this has been Barack Hussein Obama's plan all along. His alleged goal is to add two new Democrat senators, five Democrat Congressmen and a million loyal Democratic voters who are **dependent on big government.** *This will tip the balance of those living off the government to more than those who must pay for it,* and we Citizens are to be overwhelmed.

"*Legalize 12 million illegal Mexican etc. immigrants.* Just giving these 12 million potential new federal U.S. citizens *free health care alone could overwhelm the system* and bankrupt America. *But it adds 12 **million reliable new Democrat voters** who can be counted on to support big government.* Add another few trillion dollars in welfare, aid to dependent children, food stamps, free medical, education, tax credits for the poor, and eventually Social Security...*the end justifies the means...* Reagan wanted to dramatically cut taxes in order to starve government. Barack Obama wants to *dramatically raise taxes to starve his political opposition*...voters dependent on big government, a vast privileged class of public employees who work for big government, and a government dedicated to destroying capitalism and *installing themselves as socialist rulers by overwhelming the system.*

"Add it up and you've got the perfect Marxist scheme – all devised by my Columbia University college classmate *Barack Hussein Obama using the Cloward and Piven plan*...What will your lives be like under *socialism/communism?*..."

21.10) Other loyal investigators have produced documentation suggesting that *Obama* is more a *narcissist socialist closet-communist actor.* He was reportedly *selected years ago, groomed and financed for this presidential assignment by his apparently-Canaanite bosses –- Rothschild, Rockefeller, Soros, Bronfman, Strong, Mellon cabal* (who also pay few U.S. income-excise taxes!). These appear to be the descendant rich and filthy (Revelation 22:11) potentials of Bible prophecy, also known as Revelation 18's "merchants of the earth."

It is also interesting to observe Obama's wife *MICHELLE,* who's been *spending big-time at your expense,* and who matches him in *acting* ability. One was her huge bill for a caviar lunch at the Waldorf Astoria Hotel (ask her, under oath). A 2011 trip to South Africa saw her meeting with ANC terrorist leader Nelson Mandella in his home, who also posed with an ANC Marxist flag and Jewish communist Joe Slovo. Since their people took control of South Africa in 1994, over 70,000 Whites have been murdered, with media silence (source: American Free Press, 9/17/12, p.11). Are you aware of *Michelle's* personal assistants, all 22 ladies, taking salaries of more than $6.3 million a year?

21.11) Watch out for *Obama's* dictator-like *executive orders and directives*, which unlawfully circumvent his Constitutional requirements to get approval of the Congress! His behind-the-scenes appointed staff of 31 so-called "czars" also reportedly following orders from Soros+. For example Obama executed *warfare against Libya for the United Nations, without the U.S. Congress' authority* (against the law). And more recently Obama has decided to use *drone missiles*, some as small as a model airplane, remotely guided from U.S. laboratories, with which his czars can have anyone on earth assassinated.

21.12) Consider **Obama's teachers**, book-writers of his *Dreams of My Father* and *Audacity of Hope*, and his Marxist *political communism and economic socialism* from communist Bill Ayers (like Obama's parents). And then there are communist/socialists Saul Alinsky, Tony Rezko, Frank Marshall Davis, Dr. Zbigniew Brzezinski (who taught Obama how to swing audiences), and his former anti-American pastor Dr. Jeremiah Wright. How ridiculous – **Obama never ran a business** to get experience, and he did less than that as a U.S. Illinois senator! Yes, his first noteworthy claim to fame was when he was asked to be keynote speaker at the 2004 Democratic Convention, invited by the above George Soros.

21.13) One of Obama's first 2009 presidential acts reportedly was his executive order that U.S. reparations be paid to Black American farmers, followed by pushing the anti-American environmental Cap and Trade treason. Who else but Obama would also direct that the month of June be named special for sodomite-homosexuals, shoving aside real female June brides? Who else would demand expensive *entrapping socialist Obama-healthcare*, pushed by the bought-and-paid-for U.S. House's Speaker Nancy Pelosi and Senator Harry Reid with the Canaanite-owned major media? Have you ever investigated their **phony "41 million people without health care,"** which we thoroughly explore here? Why did Obama give aid to his fellow Muslim, the al Qaeda murderer at Fort Hood, Texas, who loudly boasted of his Muslim "Allah Akbar?" And why does Obama wear a Muslim-inscribed ring on his wedding finger?

21.14) Obama stated "You might say that America is a **Muslim nation**" (source: Egypt 2009) — that America has been arrogant — that we are no longer a Christian nation [*ask him to read this book!*] — and after 9/11 America didn't always live up to its ideals [only our Creator Christ Jesus has perfectly done so].

21.15) We will not waste much time on Obama's later childhood, such as his registration at Jakarta, Indonesia's Fransiskus Assisi School under the name Barry Soetoro, also showing his religion as "Islam."

21.16) American Citizen singer/actor *Pat Boone* in his 8/22/10 e-mail asks Obama "Just what country do you think you're president of?" Pat reminds us of the Muslims' Shari'a law, with its "break the cross, kill the infidel" hate [in return we are to Agape-love all comers in Christ Jesus' Name, to honor Him].

21.17) Investigators from Americans for Freedom of Information found Obama's Occidental College transcripts named this same Barry Soetoro, receiving Fulbright Foundation financial aid as a *foreign* undergraduate student from Indonesia. To qualify for this aid the student must claim a *foreign citizenship*, **again showing that Obama is not a "natural born"** *American Citizen*. With him signed up as foreign to America, *there is no evidence that he ever applied for an American, or federal U.S., citizenship!*

21.18) Loyal American Citizen *Dr. David Barton* acknowledges Obama's speaking ability when he uses a teleprompter, but wanted to help him be a one-term president. Dr. Barton does not share Obama's horrors on abortion, Marxist economics, adding over $5 trillion to U.S. government debts, raising taxes, horrible unemployment, shorting our military, secrecy about his life, educational, passport(s) and Social Security(ies) records, wanting to strip Citizens of their Constitutional Habeas Corpus Rights, his big-government anti-business and anti-individualism remarks, his amnesty for illegal aliens to get their votes, and promoting blatant *sodomite-homosexuality*. You may have read *Newsweek magazine's* May 13, 2012 cover story, allegedly with Obama referred to as "The *First Gay* President?" Bi-sexual may apply better.

21.19) Also Obama's pushing *same-sex marriage*, his questionable inconsistent contributions re *global warming CO_2*, to Islam over Mideast *Israel*, unprovable *Muslim beliefs* (see chapter 8), expensively demanding *Obama healthcare* to replace America's generally advanced system (which provides free health clinics for our poorest, despite Canaanite-media propaganda), Obama's coddling of *irreverent celebrities* who attack the Name of our God the Father and His Son our Creator Jesus Christ. Nor do we share Obama's and Hillary Clinton's wishes to restrict Americans Citizens' *2nd Amendment* defensive firearms, to ease *capital punishment* for proven criminals, and to restrict Americans' *unalienable Rights* to life, liberty, happiness/property and free speech under Obama's preferred United Nations (sounds like George *Soros*). As Lord Acton wrote, *"Power tends to corrupt, and absolute power corrupts absolutely."*

21.20) I am reminded too of popular radio talk show host *Michael Savage's* recent warning to his listeners, sounding a bit radical but this steel-cold reality has happened before: "If Obama is re-elected (done 11/6/12), I think we are going to be living closer to being a South American Chevez dictatorship! Obama's is the most corrupt, incompetent dangerous tyrannical administration in American history. He has a long history of being at odds with *American values*, with the government-media complex party line on a daily basis. *Pay attention, people! Your freedom is at stake."*

21.21) And some people think that our Almighty God is not going to act timely, while Obama's filthy Canaanite bosses seek to remold (**"change"**) the world closer to the desire of their infamous *"Pax Judaica!"* You may agree in finding that just beforehand, Revelation 6:8 prophesies World War III, with 1/3rd of mankind to be killed! COME OUT while you can!

21.22) U.S. Presidential candidate *Rick Santorum* told an Iowa audience that: "Obama **has divided this country** like

Franklin Roosevelt did in the Great Depression, and that Roosevelt is his hero — government takes money from somebody and gives it to somebody else — Obama controls both the Executive and Judicial branches," plus by proxy he heads the Justice and other departments including the Department of Homeland Security [designed by potential-Canaanite Michael Chertoff], now shared by Obama's two high-level Muslims. These facts should help to explain why the U.S. supreme Court recently voted unbelievably that Obama's **terrible socialist healthcare trap is [GEOGRAPHICALLY] Constitutional**, with Chief Justice John Roberts voting yes because **it is only for federal U.S.** Articles 1:8:17 and 4:3:2 people, property ***and volunteers*** (with social security, driver's license etc., without "TDC"). However please note that on Obamacare's ***page 170 my status is EXEMPT***, *as a **non-resident alien non-volunteering*** *natural born free private Article 3 State Citizen not in federal U.S. territory.* This fact is Constitutionally for us who are living and working within the 50 States, and thus *"foreign"* by law (with due respect) to federal U.S. territory, *with Volume 20 Corpus Juris Secundum §1785* in accord. That federal U.S. government has been ruled a "**foreign**" corporation [last incorporated 6/11/1878] with respect to a State.! *Biblically this reminds me of Matthew 17:26's famous customs tax, with "...the sons [male and female] are EXEMPT."*

21.23) **Another *fraud*** is the *"47 million Americans without healthcare"* U.S. government and major media propaganda this past decade. Please realize that of this 47 million, 1.8 million could afford but did not want it; 8.4 million were ages 18-25 and indestructible; *12.6 million were illegal aliens*; 9.4 million were temporarily uninsured between jobs; 8.0 million were not yet signed up under their parents' insurance; and 3.5 million were eligible but not yet signed up for government health programs (source: San Diego County's North County Times, 7/27/09, page A-7) — *And many sound-asleep Americans bought that lie!*

211

21.24) So *let's make time for* **Obama's 2700+ page House Bill 3200 "Patient Protection [HA!] and Affordable [HA!] Care Choices [HA!]** *Act of 2009,"* also known as HB-3200, aka Obamacare, aka health care bill, aka health care reform. **Watch out for** DC's Constitutional Articles 1:8:17-18 and 4:3:2's "REFORMS" that are **restricted as to U.S. "TERRITORIAL JURISDICTION"***(authority), applicable only to the U.S. Government's very own 26 federal states (alphabetically Baker Island to Wake Island) and volunteers, but* **NOT APPLICABLE WITHIN** *our unincorporated free* **NON-VOLUNTEERING** *United States of America's 50 States with their non-volunteering private Citizens!*

21.25) ***Here is that horrible enslaving Act in part,*** starting with this review from *Judge Kithil* of Marble Falls, Texas: — Its page 50 §152, provides coverage for all non-U.S. residents [with]-in the US, including illegal aliens — Page 58-59, government bureaucrats will have access to all participants' bank accounts, with authority to make bank transfers from those accounts — Page 65 §164, allows government subsidies to be given to all union members including retirees and *community organizations such as Acorn* — Page 203 lines 14-15, provides for a tax imposed that will not be treated as a tax —

21.26) — Page 241 and 253 provides that medical doctors will all be paid the same regardless of specialty or training, with *government setting all medical fees* — Page 272 §1145, *cancer hospitals will ration treatment* according to patient's age — Page 317 and 321, *government will impose* prohibitions on hospital expansion, however communities may petition for exceptions — Page 425 lines 4-12, *government will mandate* advance-care consultations, with those on Social Security required to attend "end-of-life" planning seminars every five years — Page 429 lines 13-25, government will specify which medical doctors can write an "end-of-life" order — this *HB 3200* ***will not apply to members of Congress***.

21.27) And as reported by *Dr. Stephen E. Frazer* of Indianapolis, Indiana, MD anesthesiologist, in his March 2010 letter to U.S. Senator Bayh, this Obamacare's 2,700+ page bill includes: — Page 22 requiring that government will audit books of all self-insured employers — Page 30 §123 has an appointed *government committee that will decide what treatments and benefits* each participant gets — Page 29 lines 4-16, each participant's heath care is rationed — Page 42, *the "Health Choices Commissioner" will choose what benefits you can get; participants have no choice* — Page 50 §152, *coverage is provided for all non-U.S. citizens, illegal or not* — Page 58, *government will have access to participants' finances and a "National ID Health Card,"* *to be issued* — Page 59 lines 21-24, *government will have direct access to participants' bank accounts, for elective fund transfers* —

21.28) — Page 65 §164 *provides subsidized plans for union members, retirees, families and community organizations* — Page 84 §203, *government is to mandate* all benefit packages for private health care plans in the "Exchange" — Page 85 line 7, specifies each plan's benefit levels, with rationing of their benefits — Page 91 lines 4-7, *government is to mandate* appropriate linguistic (illegal aliens') services — Page 95 lines 8-18, *government will use groups (such as Acorn etc.)* to sign up participants — Page 102 lines 12-18, Medicaid participants must be enrolled in this HR 3200 — Page 124 lines 24-25, *government cannot be sued* for price fixing, and there is no judicial review for this monopoly —

21.29) — Page 127 lines 1-16, *government will tell medical doctors and their AMA what they can be paid* — Page 145 line 15-17, *employers must enroll employees* into the "public option plan," with no choice — Page 126 lines 22-25, *employers must pay for part-time* employees and their families (increasing unemployment) — Page 149 lines 16-24, employees with payroll 401k and above, not providing a "public option plan," *will pay an 8% tax on all payroll* (and you think that Obama is pro-America!) — Page 150 lines 9-13, employers with payrolls of $251,000 to $401,000 not providing a "public option plan" *will pay a 2-6% tax on all payroll* — Page 167 lines 18-23, *all individuals who do not have acceptable health care according to government will be taxed 2.5% of income* —

21.30) — Page 195, health bill administrative officers and employees will have access to all participants' finances and individual records — Page 203 lines 14-15, "The tax imposed under this section shall not be treated as tax," but rather a fee — Page 239 line 14-24, *government will reduce physician services for Medicaid seniors,* with low-income and poor affected — Page 241 line 6-8, *medical doctors all will be paid the same,* regardless of training and specialty (Obama's socialism) — a patient during initial admission that results in re-admission will be penalized — Page 253 line 10-18, *government will set values of the medical doctor's time, profession, judgment etc.* — Page 265 §1131, *government will mandate* and control productivity for private health care industries —

21.31) — Page 268 §1141, *federal government will regulate* the rental and purchase of power-driven wheelchairs — Page 272 §1145, specifies treatment by certain cancer hospitals — Page 280 §1151, *government will penalize hospitals* for whatever government deems preventable — Page 298 lines 9-11, *government will penalize medical doctors* who treat a patient during initial admission that results in a re-admission — Page 317 lines 13-20, *government will tell medical doctors* what and how much they can own — Page 321 lines 2-13, hospitals may apply for exception, but community input [like Acorn] is required — Page 335 line 16-25 and Page 336-339, *government will mandate* outcome-based measures aka medical rationing —

21.32) — Page 341 lines 3-9, *government can disqualify* HMOs and Medicare Advance Plans (forcing members into this U.S. plan) — Page 354 §1177, *government will restrict* enrollment of "special needs people" — Page 379 §1191, *government will create more bureaucracy* with its "Tele-Health Advisory Committees" — Page 425 lines 4-12, *government will mandate* [end of life] "advance-care planning/consulting" — Page 425 lines 17-19, *government will require* that it instruct and consult on living wills, durable powers of attorney etc. — Page 425 lines 22-25 and page 426 lines 1-4, government will provide an "approved" list of end-of-life resources (assisted suicide) —

21.33) — Page 427 lines 15-24, *government mandates* orders on "end of life" (how your life ends) — Page 429 lines 1-9, *government "advanced-care planning" consultants* will be used as participant's health deteriorates — Page 429 lines 10-12, *government may order* an "advanced care consultation" for end-of-life plans, with an order to die — Page 429 lines 13-25, *government will mandate* which medical doctors can write end-of-life order — Page 430 lines 11-15, *government will decide* what treatment participants will have at end-of-life —Page 469, *government will appoint* community-based non-profit home medical services similar to Acorn — Page 489 §1308, *government will dictate* marriage and family therapy — Page 494-498, *government will dictate* mental health services, including defining, creating and rationing.

21.34) From a long list of other reasons to object to this ruinous Obamacare trap, *let's just consider the medical costs in this HB-3200*: Originally the Congressional Budget Office estimated the next 10-year costs to be $115 billion. Then this was raised to above $1 trillion. The Pacific Research Institute then raised that *estimate to $2.5 to $3 trillion*. Factu-ally, nobody knows exact expenses when bureaucrats are at the helm! And this is being pushed by Obama, who has never even run a popcorn stand!

21.35) Obama, his Treasury Secretary Timothy Geithner, with his cabal relatives who own the private Federal Reserve corporation, escalated the ongoing economic housing crisis with multi-trillion-dollar U.S. giveaways to foreign banks, governments etc., certainly plunging this country into unprecedented *debt. Obama's claim to fame is always to blame someone else, right out of communist Saul Alinsky's book Rules for Radicals!* Now watch out for his (and his bosses') *programs scheduled to go into effect January 1, 2013, with the economic burdens and increased taxes on everyone.* These could be enough to cause the economic collapse of our country. Obama then can declare Martial Law and assume total control. Can you stop this power-grab? Or will you wait for the long-prophesied "springtime" war, as in our Preface?

21.36) Publisher *Billy James Hargis II*, Christian Crusade Newspaper [P.O. Box 21228, Tulsa, Oklahoma 74121] — reminds us that the *Constitutions of all 50 States of America give honor* to our Creator, Almighty God, Author of Existence, God, Supreme Being, Supreme Ruler, Divine Guidance, Sovereign Ruler of the Universe, and the Great Legislator of the Universe.

It is hoped that *with this little book many Americans can convince people within government*, the federal courts, the Soros-backed *ACLU*, the *NEA*, those with agnostic and atheist beliefs, the Canaanite children of the Devil, and millions of others *to find a new beginning now in the real proven Creator Christ Jesus*. Please *pray for these in Jesus' Name, aware of* Matthew 7:7 and 18:3-4: "Ask and it will be *given to* you..." And let the telephone do your walking to a simple full-Bible teaching and believing church near you, with great fellowship! Please *start today*, while you are looking at this.

21.37) 2 Chronicles 7:13-14 always rings true — "If... My people who are called by My Name humble themselves and pray and seek My face and turn (repent, change path) from their wicked ways, then I will hear them from Heaven, will forgive their sin and will heal their land" — Good idea, right?

The 1929+ Great Depression left many Americans, our parents included, with a loss of understanding the Biblical battle between liberty and power, both of which the real proven Christ is winning. One reason for this brief review and reminder is that as you know *freedom is not free*, and *you are wise to be alert!* One example of enemies watering down documented truth behind the American Revolution is the half-baked charge that the Founding Fathers were generally *"deists,"* defined in Webster's Dictionary as "the existence of a god [at a distance], based upon evidence of reason and nature." Of all of America's great Founding Fathers, Dr. Ben Franklin probably came closest to this accusation, as above, but he was trying.

21.38) Living not far from us is Dr. *Irvin Forbing,* giving more insight with his e-mail of 6/24/10: "... Ben Franklin [see item #4 above] stated at the June 28, 1787 Constitutional Convention that "God Governs in the affairs of men' [question: *which God,* of three named in Bibles and in our chapter 9?]. 47 signers of the Declaration were either ministers (29) or affiliated with one of the Christian groups, while the religions of only 7 remain unknown. The first Continental Congress (9/5/1774) opened with prayer that lasted 3 hours [far too long Biblically, Matthew 5:7], and prayer has opened Congress since then, thanks to Franklin. The 10/4/1982 Congress set the *Year of the Bible* as 1983 because of Bibles' contributions to the U.S. formation [source: http://www.gemword. com/USA vsUS-BIBLE.htm]..."

Educated people would probably agree that semi-free democratic-type governments often operate on the basis of the Canaanite-controllers Soroses, "compromise" and "debt-credit." Right now many of the nations in Europe plus the United States are in turmoil over their *"debts,"* mostly incurred through careless wars and socialist giveaways that they could not afford. Meanwhile their citizens have been conditioned to crave temporary artificial affluence, with freebies, and to unwittingly support behind-the-scenes Soros warmongers who bask in bloody profits from terrible holocaust wars fought by others.

21.39) *Antichrist* "turmoil" is coming quickly, called "sea" in Bible prophecy such as Revelation 13:2. Note how quickly he eliminates governments' and his individual followers' vicious debts and interest, *probably by imposing Special Drawing Rights* for his followers, and from the beginning he makes "a firm covenant" for *seven years* with Daniel 9:27's Israel etc., only to break it half-way through (Rev. 13:5). Mark my word, he/she or it is coming; just you watch! This will be the prophesied *"Antichrist,"* as named in any Bible, Bible Concordance or Bible Dictionary." This big 'A' is called a "man" and a "he" in 2 Thessalonians 2:3-6, with his followers losing as promised in 2:11-12.

But meanwhile he will solve the world's chaos, again apparently by proclaiming impossible economic debts cancelled, and replaced by his followers' *Special Drawing Rights*. More insights are in Revelation 13:1–18, with his getting Daniel 9:24-27's one week (a week of years, or *seven years*) covenant signed with Israel, and then breaking it half way through...

21.40) *Barack Hussein Obama's* promised *"change"* was sold to youngsters, coated with trained charisma and clever words and phrases, apparently written by his "czars" and the Soros-Rothschild tribe aiming toward Canaanite world government Pax Judaica dictatorship. While partially impeded by his political opponents, as of this writing *Obama's record smells with terrible morals in Chicago and sick economics in Washington*: 46 million Americans on food stamps; one in 6 living in poverty; the U.S. misery index at a 28-year high; the worst housing crisis since the 1930s' Great Depression; the 23 million worst unemployment record of any modern president for his four years in office; the highest Black unemployment rate in 28 years; the $4,599 drop in household income, $5.5 trillion of new U.S. debt, $2.6 trillion for *socialist-Soros Obamacare*, 100% increase in gasoline prices, $1.9 trillion in new taxes in Obama's budget (source: U-T San Diego 10/27/12,

p. B-7), the lowest consumer confidence in 30 years; and the worst U.S. credit rating in American history. Now add that "anything not of faith is sin," Romans 14:23b, with all of us making mistakes and sinning (3:23); and you have a monumental mess to fix. We *pray in Jesus' Name for Obama, his family and staff that they too will choose to* "COME OUT!"

A government with huge debts tends to be vulnerable to whatever rats are in competition, including satanic Canaanites. Due to the *debts,* the borrower is beholden to the lender. The Congress has indebted its 6/11/1878 federal United States corporation with more *debts* than all other countries combined, in fact with a total debt of more than $16 trillion plus unfunded future obligations estimated to exceed at least another $40 trillion. And it has an estimated *300,000 federal regulations* (Constitution's Article 4:3:2) on which to strangle (source: Wall Street Journal 12/14/2011 p. 8).

To top it off, the *U.S. has 760 prisoners per 100,000 citizens...7 times more than any other nation*, thanks to lawyers (source: Time magazine). We can agree that this is worse than terrible planning. Is it because Congress has been kept far too busy to pay attention? This was planned and boasted about in the enemy Canaanites' *Protocols of the Learned Elders of Zion*!

You probably will remember that the Congress of that federal U.S. corporation Constitutionally has "exclusive Legislation" power *only* over federal "United States" property, *not over our USA*. Again this is clearly seen in Articles 1:8:17–18 and in 4:3:2's equally restricted *"Rules and* Regulations," as law *only for federal U.S. property and people*. DC's politicians and bureaucrats should read these, and that its property within the 50 States is restricted to that owned by the federal U.S. government (not rented or leased), with us private natural born free American National Article 3 State Citizens and our property EXEMPT! *This is why IRS employees have no written Delegation of Authority to work for it within the 50 States!*

Most people have not been taught the foregoing *three different meanings of "United States"* in their government public schools, as mentioned before. The above *1940 Buck Act unconstitutionally imposed a fictitious federal U.S. overlay* on our sovereign 50 United States of America **without the lawful Territorial Jurisdiction** *to do so*. Its self-serving claim that Article 1:8:3's "commerce" clause changed this Law is as *phony as a rubber duck*, not unlike <u>Obama's healthcare trap</u> (applicable only to federal U.S. people, property and **unaware volunteers**)!

As mentioned too, I did not expect that the post 9/11/2001-mentality's federal U.S. Customs would seize our Pure Trust's funds, which were being lawfully invested in Europe for our Scott Christian Ministries Pure Trust's affiliate ministries in 34 countries. Nor did I expect that the IRS people would unlawfully seize all of these funds, *changing its criminal mind after issuing the two letters* informing us clearly that *"A Pure Trust [like ours] has no tax requirements."* This is because its status is from *Article III Constitutionally, and is "foreign" by territorial and subject matter jurisdiction to IRS'* federal property law at Article I:8:17–18 with 4:3:2. This law and fact is why I provided payers with a *Form W-8 "Certificate of Foreign Status" every three years if necessary*. And again, the above investment in Christ Jesus' Name still has a contractual guarantee of performance from the good Broker.

You probably remember that the "Constitution *for* the United States of America" (as in its Preamble) is "the <u>s</u>upreme Law of the Land" as at its Article 6:2. *Enemies of America have been doing everything possible to skirt around it, as have Obama and Hillary Clinton, who may be tried as willful traitors* against this once-free America nation. Their signing *treaties* with foreign nations, *while circumventing the Congress* is contrary to 1957's U.S. <u>s</u>upreme Court (source: Reid v. Covert 354 US 1 @ 17), ruling that "treaties are not equal to the Constitution." No wonder thousands of well-behaved *"Tea Party" Citizens are concerned about these apparent but elusive Canaanite enemies* and their often-hidden planned destruction of America the beautiful.

After sharing this book, *would you say that we have a government with criminal usurpations*, at least in part, replacing what once was *the land of the free and the home of the brave?* That government does not seem to care that 1793's U.S. supreme Court honored America's private Citizens as *"sovereigns without subjects"* in Chisholm v. Georgia 2 Dall. 419 471. Or that its government willfully steals private Citizens' personal property within the 50 States lawlessly, for which theft I find that its personnel will pay dearly in the real Creator Christ's promised Revelation 20:11-14 Judgment for deeds in about 1,000 years.

These criminals do not seem to care that *all Citizens with* **a state driver's license** *are now automatically voluntary subjects of the United Nations' International Civil Aviation Organization* (thank you Pastor Irvin Baxter, see Index, and his guest Mark Lerner), apparently in preparation for the Revelation 13:16–18's *"mark of the beast* [Antichrist];" while **no law whatsoever has required non-volunteering private natural born free American National Article 3 State Citizens to get a state driver's license** (read the Code, and *believe it or not)!* Would you call that more gradual brainwashing, government entrapment, *Constructive Fraud and Misapplication of the Law?*

We have discussed 18th century B.C. Babylonia's Hammurabi, with his "eye for an eye" benevolent dictatorship, and the *huge problem that superior human leadership has always ended with its death.* Is this another of man's continual problems, *not being able to keep an unmatched leader alive to lead?* **This problem will end when the Christ Jesus reigns everlastingly**, thank God, as promised in Daniel 7:13–14: "To Him was given dominion, glory and a Kingdom, which all the peoples, nations and men [men and women] of every language [the real Church, plus Hebrew-Israel and the great tribulation survivors] might serve Him. *His dominion is an everlasting dominion which will not pass away*; and His

Kingdom is one which will not be destroyed." Not a bad promise, mathematically-perfect (chapter 17), which we can all honor.

22) *Antichrist* (2013? to –), the coming world-dictator, may be cruel, but he *certainly will know how* to *lead,* with his father Satan's delegated power. *He is named "Antichrist" in* I John 2:18, 2:22, 4:3, 2 John 1:7, 2:18; the "beast" in Revelation 13:2-4 *with his "fatal wound"* in 13:3 with Zechariah 11:17; the *"man of lawlessness"* in II Thessalonians 2:3; and as the *"horn"* in Daniel 7:21+23+25+8:11-14 etc. He will quickly impose a "one week" (meaning in Bible prophecy a week of years, *seven years) peace covenant* between Israel and the nations, as in Daniel 9:24–27. *He will break that covenant halfway through,* as it shows there with Revelation 13:5. And he will eventually be deserted by his followers, nearing his end as promised in Daniel 11:45 with Revelation 19:20. The *Armageddon battle locations* are shown in the book of Joel, with Armageddon, Jerusalem and Edom or Jordan. *Antichrist will be a liar, as are his father Satan and his half-breed tribe of Canaanites referred to in John 8:41–44.*

Having some fun now, you may have heard about the CNN photographer who hailed a taxi and then telephoned the airport to reserve a plane flight. Upon arrival, he paid the taxi driver, rushed to the waiting airplane, threw his gear aboard, climbed in, and said, "Let's go!" The pilot faced the plane into the wind and roared off into the wild blue yonder. Approaching mountains, the photographer said to the pilot, "Let's go over these mountains and down into the valley so that I can take pictures of the big fire."

The pilot hesitatingly said, "Do you mean you are not my flight instructor?"

23) The *near-future Millennium,* meaning the future thousand years of Revelation 20:5b–6 and 20:4. The location will be on this re-perfected earth, with "The Lord is there" promised in Ezekiel 48:35. If *"approved"* due to your dedicated "faith" in the

real Creator Christ (your choice), you will be *"perfected"* (no more human sickness, aches, pains, hunger, thirst, ignorance, doubts etc.), Word-pictured in Hebrews 11:39–40 with 1 Corinthians 15:51–58. You will be in charge of many possessions. You will *"reign with Him"* (Revelation. 5:10, again 20:5b–6, and 20:4 and 22:5). You will be *"radiant," "thrill and rejoice"* (Isaiah 60:5) and you just might want to *go fishing* as in Ezekiel 47:10!

You can then *"fly like a cloud"* (as in Isaiah 60:8,) just as the Christ can. Your society will be *"righteous,"* as promised in 60:21 (dominantly *with responsible Agape-love*; and no lies, no rapes, no women-beating, no stealing or other filthy deeds will be allowed). You will *"proclaim liberty"* and *"freedom"* to the *many **people who survive the "great tribulation."* And the Almighty Christ will indeed rule Rev.19:15's "Nations" perfectly, *"with a Rod of Iron."*

You will be "called oaks of *righteousness"* for your *faith* in our Creator Christ Jesus, Isaiah 61:3. And you can enjoy Isaiah 11:6-12's promise that the *"wolf will dwell with the lamb…the leopard will lie down with the kid…the lion will eat straw like the ox…the nursing child will play by the hole of the cobra…the Lord will again recover…the remnant of His people who will remain…from the four corners of the earth."* Here is the ***non-Church** that will populate the earth, over which you may reign* in the future Millenium.

"You will be called the *priests of the Lord,"* probably wearing *casual clothes*, but certainly not Babylonian black, and "you will be spoken of as *ministers of our God*, and eat the *wealth of nations,"* as promised in Isaiah 61:6. You will have *"everlasting joy"* (61:7). And *your "offspring…descendants"* will also be *easily recognized as you are (radiant)*, clothed within the *"garment of salvation* and the robe of *righteousness" (your faith, again)*. You and yours will be called *"the holy people* [this reminds me of 1 Peter 2:9's "holy nation"], the *"redeemed of the Lord"* ("redeemed" also being the great redemption-"escape" referred to in paragraph three of our Preface..

This leaves you and us with *exactly One proven everlasting Leader, Who has never lied*, has always *Agape-loved you and us*, and *Who has provided a road map into His and our Proven Future*. What an exciting free choice you are making. Oh yes, Isaiah 65:20b promises that the "*...one who does not reach the age of 100* will be thought accursed [could that still be the satanic Canaanite seed line?]."

Your little book here has included a reverent snapshot of my modest but delightful experiences, the *Hebrew-Jews and Canaanite-Jews*, the "*approved*" Church, the conflicting man-made religions without proofs of truth, *our Friend "God-Somebody,"* keys to *Bibles, trustworthy role models* like my 12 families, Katsuki and General MacArthur, *opportunities in my post-military life*, my wife Fran and our *children* Sally and Mike thank God, *your proven Future, Proofs to Win,* and *Lawful Government*.

Our chapter one's *Friend "God-somebody" turned out to be the Creator Christ*. My delightful walk with Military Government interpreter Inatsugu-san together *with Jesus' written Word*, as in Romans 8:1–4 with 6:4, helped us to find *proven Truth with prophecies in the Sciences, History, Mathematics and Signs* of the Times – while this world's *man-made religions fell off the map* when *fully tested with responsible Agape-love*. All signs now point toward your Future, as discussed with options in chapter 14. Now what on earth would my kid sister Miriam, you and I do without our Friend "God-Somebody?"

Thank you for coming along!

Dr. Neil Alan (Doc) Scott, without prejudice, private natural born free Christian American National, Article 3 State Citizen Constitutionally (and *NOT* a federal U.S. citizen subject serf), by great American Law, thank God!

POSTSCRIPT

The years have come and gone since 1941. My kid sister Miriam in chapter 1 and I are still good friends, now at ages 77 and 83, with both of us having lived full lives. My beautiful bride of 54 years, phenomenal Fran, has probably edited this manuscript with others and me more times than we could count.

Years earlier my two years as one of General MacArthur's economics investigators were highly fulfilling, beginning a lifelong challenge from him to "...*prove who is knifing America in the back in Washington, and why...*" The simple answer to these is in chapter 5, the opposites of the real Creator Christ's Hebrew-Jews and Satan's Canaanite-Jews. In review, these became more obvious when the latter proved themselves to be MacArthur's (and the real Christ's) dedicated enemy, as I John 3:10's "children of the Devil" and his "tares" in Matthew 13:25-40...proved only in Bibles.

I am just an American Christian investigator, with Agape-love for all concerned and a goal to help more people qualify for the "approved" status of chapter 7, with tested proofs in chapters 15 to 18.

Yes these are *dangerous times*, certainly in need of Titus 2:13's "*blessed hope*." For example, the article by former U.S. Rep. Dan Hamburg (D-Calif.) and Lewis Seller stated that "Beginning in 1999 the government has entered into a series of single-bid contracts for $385 million with Halliburton's subsidiary Kellogg, Brown & Root (KBR) *to build detention camps (concentration camps)* at undisclosed locations [mostly on off limits military bases] within the United States. The government has also contracted with several companies to build thousands of *railcars*, some reportedly equipped with shackles, ostensibly to transport detainees" (source: San Francisco Chronicle 2/4/2008).

President **Obama** is keenly aware of these, having given a speech on May 21, 2009 at the National Archives in Washington, D.C., on *"prolonged detention" (concentration camps)* for all those who supposedly pose a threat to U.S. security, giving rise to the president's advocacy of an Orwellian Big Brother nation with the use of *"preventive incarceration" to keep certain people in prison indefinitely* without charges.

Wannabe emperor Obama, an alleged front man for Canaanite-Jews George Soros ala Rothschild, has also vowed to *"reshape the standards that apply to our rule of law"* (i.e. prolonged military detention and denial of Habeas Corpus etc.).

Respected leaders *warning of these U.S. concentration camps* have been U.S. Rep. Paul Brown (R-Georgia), investigator Victor Thorn (see Index), investigator Michel Chossudovsky, U.S. Rep. Dr. Ron Paul (R-Texas), former presidential candidate, Dr. Pastor Chuck Baldwin, priest Frank Morales and MSNBC's commentator Rachel Maddow. And guess what real Almighty Power is on the latter's side.

Coming from the pro-dictatorship position, besides Obama is U.S. Rep. Alcce Hastings (D-Florida), who introduced HR 645, which would have the Department of Homeland Security (DHS) establish *national emergency centers for large-scale imprisonment of American Citizens on military installations* after martial law is declared (by Obama). All prisoners would be under military jurisdiction, finding it nearly impossible to enforce their Rights protected by the Constitution, have a fair trial or even have legal representation.

The DHS' *"Operation Endgame"* suggests the removal of "potential terrorists," while working with the Federal Emergency Management Agency (FEMA). This is reminiscent of when President Reagan signed 1984's *"Rex 84,"* with an undisclosed number of *"concentration camps throughout the United States for internment of dissidents and others potentially harmful to the state."* And add to these unconstitutional entrapments the Washington, D.C.'s *"Operation Garden Plot,"* described as *"a master plan to suppress democratic opposition in the United States."* And add to that *"Operation Cable Splicer,"* for "the orderly takeover of state and local governments by FEMA and related federal agencies.

U.S. Representative Dr. Ron Paul (MD) wrote in 9/2008 that "Even though we know that [DC's] *detention facilities are already in place*, government now wants to legalize the construction of FEMA camps *on military installations*, using the ever-popular excuse that the facilities are for the purposes of a *national emergency*."

Now that you have potentially read these important insights in your book, *An American Christian's World (with exciting <u>proven hope</u> for your future!)*, let's do a "WHAT IF:"

1) What if the above information is accurate, as documented? 2) What if the real Christ was tempted by Satan the Devil, as promised in Matthew 4:1-9? 3) What if I John 3:10's "children of the Devil" and Matthew 13:25-38-39's satanic "tares" are for real, working feverishly to enslave you, wanting to do their father's desires as in John 8:44? 4) What if many of these (notice Matthew 13:30) are his satanic "Canaanites," working for him in Washington, D.C. et al. and carrying out his *(insidious)* plan to ensnare your USA and then the world?

5) What if occupants for their U.S. concentration camps include you and your friends, among America's loyal law-abiding tax-paying Citizens who refuse to join the New World Order, choosing instead Constitutional freedom and real life as *"approved" Christians* – praying *for this world's corrupted* anti-constitutional fascist government bureaucrats and politicians or otherwise – and falsely accused of being an "enemy" of the failing Canaanite socialist and communist losers?

6) What if you were arrested for being one of these targets? 7) Would there be enough evidence for you as a real "approved" Christian of chapter 7 to be in Luke 21:35's "escape," Revelation 3:10's "keep you from," 20:5b-6's "first resurrection," and excluding you from being among 20:4's beheaded martyrs?

8) Let's please remember, as in chapter 7 of our book, *in order to return* with the real Almighty Creator Christ (Colossians 3:4, I Thessalonians 3:13, Jude 14 and Zechariah 14:5), after earth's coming "great tribulation," *you have to be gone first, right?*

Based upon these 70+ years of thorough investigations, I find that *World War III will explode in the late "springtime," killing 1/4ᵗʰ of mankind, driven by Revelation 6:7's "ashen [pale **green**] horse"* =**Islam**. 3½ years later will bring the deaths of 1/3rd of mankind, Revelation 9:18, knowing that our Creator Christ is patient and many of those will be judged for their "deeds" about 1,000 years later. **What do you find?** We love you in Christ Jesus' Name. Thank you for choosing to "COME OUT" (chapter 8), and to come on along now "**approved**," with plenty of proofs as to why in chapters 15 through 18!

INDEX

www.ingramcontent.com/pod-product-compliance
Lightning Source LLC
Chambersburg PA
CBHW060240290526
45789CB00001B/131